WINGS BUT NO ANGEL

WINGS BUT NO ANGEL

KEN SMITH:
HIS LIFE AND STORIES

C. K. SMITH

Copyright © 2024 C. K. Smith

The moral right of the author has been asserted.

Apart from any fair dealing for the purposes of research or private study, or criticism or review, as permitted under the Copyright, Designs and Patents Act 1988, this publication may only be reproduced, stored or transmitted, in any form or by any means, with the prior permission in writing of the publishers, or in the case of reprographic reproduction in accordance with the terms of licences issued by the Copyright Licensing Agency. Enquiries concerning reproduction outside those terms should be sent to the publishers.

Troubador Publishing Ltd
Unit E2 Airfield Business Park,
Harrison Road, Market Harborough,
Leicestershire. LE16 7UL
Tel: 0116 2792299
Email: books@troubador.co.uk
Web: www.troubador.co.uk

ISBN 978 1805144 656

British Library Cataloguing in Publication Data.
A catalogue record for this book is available from the British Library.

Printed and bound in Great Britain by 4edge Limited
Typeset in 12.5pt Minion Pro by Troubador Publishing Ltd, Leicester, UK

Dedicated to Mya and Logan Witt.

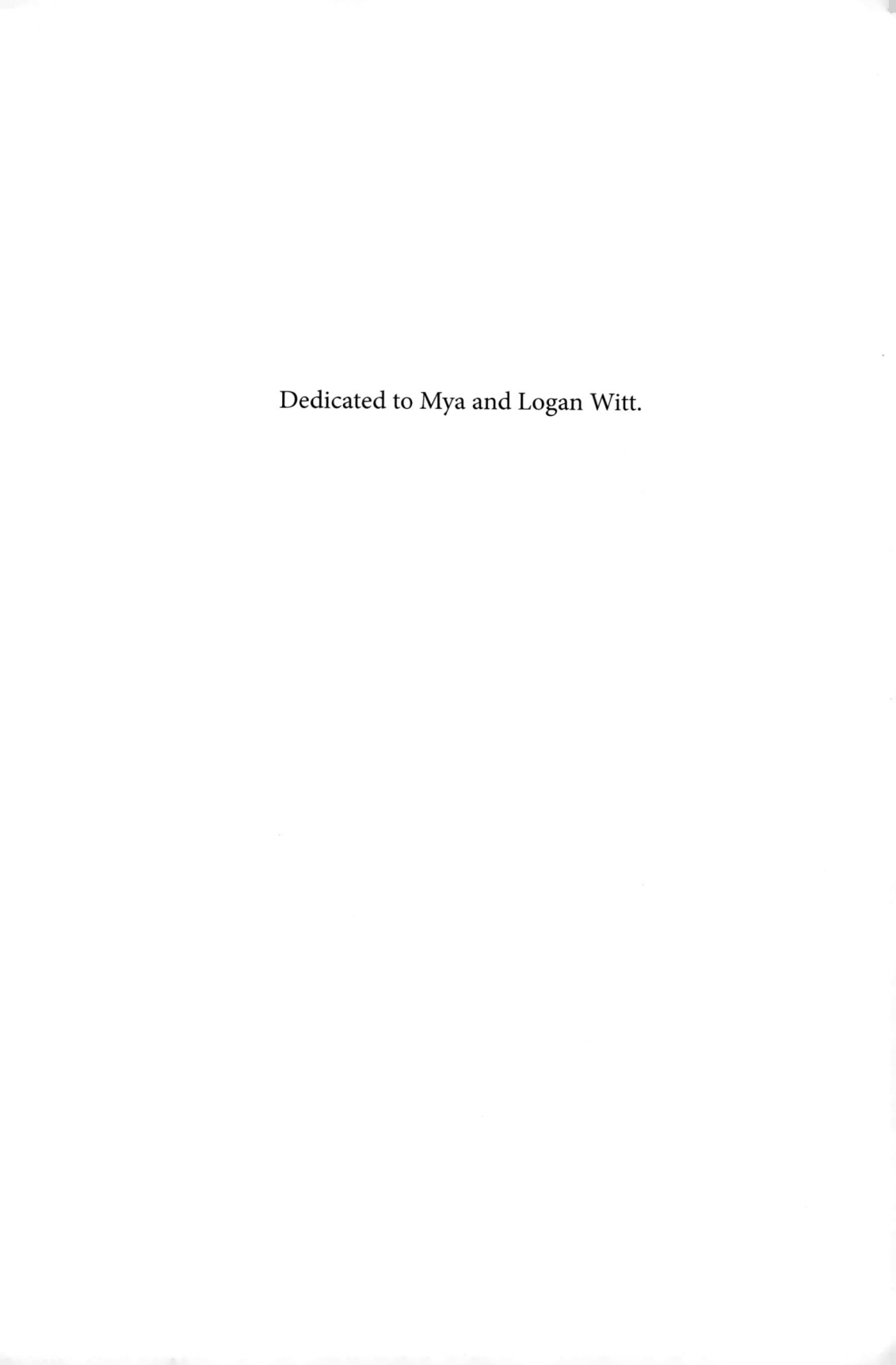

Cover design by Mya Witt, aged eleven (Ken's great-granddaughter).

ACKNOWLEDGEMENTS

Wesley Richards, QGM. A most sincere thank-you for the research, expert guidance and inestimable input to the draft manuscript. You were fortunate enough to have known both Ken and Ralph, and they you.

Rhona McPherson, daughter to Sergeant John McPherson from the 'Jock Patrol'. She was privileged to have attended many of the post-war reunions as her father's escort and as such heard the stories first-hand. Her corroboration and input were invaluable.

Graham Quick for your expert knowledge, friendship, and much help with the photos and illustrations. Also, credit must go to you for the book's title.

Ellen Cook, journalist, for the initial scrutiny and proofread.

Diane Jeffries, author/friend for guidance.

Carolina Santos/Jessica Woodward and all at Troubador for 'holding my hand' through the publishing process.

Princess Lauren and Justin, both with the patience of a saints in guiding their analogue father in the digital age, and to all family and friends who endured my long preoccupation with the project; especially my wife Lyn, whose magnanimity knows no bounds.

CONTENTS

1	Introduction	1
2	Recruitment	16
3	HMS *Manchester*	21
4	HMS *Penelope*	35
5	A Brief History of the SAS/SBS	43
6	Folbot	58
7	Selection and Training	61
8	Further Training	71
9	The Greek Islands	78
10	Simi	94
11	North Africa	123
12	Italy	130
13	Albania	136
14	Lussin Map	149
15	Yugoslavia	150
16	Tansy and Tommy	164
17	Comacchio	170
18	Wars End	198
19	After the War: Civilian Life	209
20	George Smith	230
21	Ralph Bridger	235
	Appendix 1	247
	Appendix 2 Ralph Bridger's Lussin Story	251
	Appendix 3 Lady Madeline Lees' Letter	257
	Postscript	261
	Appendix 4 2004 Lussin Trip	263

1

INTRODUCTION

From a choirboy on the *Victory* to an early recruit of the Special Boat Service and Special Air Service (SBS/SAS) and witness to many traumatic events of World War II, Ken Smith was often heard to say, "I never expected to see the end of the war." He did survive and credited the SAS with saving his life but carried a permanent reminder for over seventy years: a bullet embedded in his arm.

As a Royal Marine he survived the North Atlantic, Arctic and Mediterranean, with his two ships eventually both being sunk. His poignant vow, "I'll do any bloody thing to get off the ships", was acted upon. What followed is the stuff of legend: being part of one of the unit's largest ever missions; cradling his mortally wounded officer in his arms; sitting alongside an officer, in the same canoe, when he earned his Military Cross. Ken was also there, as part of a specially selected force, when the legendary Dane Anders Lassen earned his posthumous Victoria Cross. These were just some of the multifarious missions he was involved in.

After the war his longed-for 'peace and quiet' saw him go on to raise ten children: one girl and nine boys, including one with Down's syndrome.

Truly, a life worthy of recording.

As we go through life, we all have numerous significant experiences, gather tales, store memories. These are later recalled and retold, maybe added to and expanded; years may fade and blur the stories, sometimes mixing or exaggerating, but mostly forgetting. How many great tales have been lost to time?

This is not a story about the SAS, but the story of a man who happened to have served in the SAS. Anyone expecting this volume to be a 'blood-and-guts' depiction of warfare will be disappointed. Ken's tales were never told that way. His renditions of events were more about trying one's hardest, perseverance, comradeship, humour, and not wanting to be the one who lets the side down. However, it is dressed up, however distasteful it may be, one of the primary objectives of warfare is to kill one's fellow man – but at what cost to one's own humanity? The more intense and prolonged the conflict, the more profound the effect upon the individual.

What follows is a truthful attempt to tell the 'life story' of Ken Smith – his biography, if you like, but maybe a little more. How his life affected others', and others' his; his legacy; his influences and how they shaped the man. This book was first envisaged as a record of one man's extraordinary war stories. He was ageing and his enthralling tales were about to be lost; a collection of vivid memories that had become folklore amongst family and friends. He would often talk of those pivotal years, 1939 to 1945, not in a glorifying way, but as a factual account of what had transpired, often interspersed with humour. As he told these tales his eyes would take on a distant focus as he drifted off to relive the moment in his mind.

What started as scribbled attempts, a disjointed collection of notes, gradually evolved. Photos were collected; dates verified; supporting information amassed. The stories started to link together. As other accounts were studied, occasional differences arose. Some of this book's content may be at variance with

Introduction

well-established versions of events; this could be down to differing perspectives, viewpoints or memory. A decision was made to tell Ken's version despite any contradictions. There are some stories that have never been recorded, the odd answer or explanation to a long-standing question, and some small details that may shed new light on previous accounts. Ralph Bridger, a close friend and fellow member of Ken's patrol, was able to verify most of the documentation and add to the stories concerning the SBS.

These pages are not intended to be a work of historical fact or reference, although much effort has been made to verify this version. Time has elapsed and to any differences from established versions Ken would candidly say, "They got it wrong." But let us just say that there are a few differing opinions. In this account, no offence is meant. Hopefully it will in some instances fill in a few pieces of the jigsaw puzzle, giving a more complete picture of events.

The core of Ken's story occurred during a few short, tumultuous years of warfare: World War II. It was a time that had a profound influence on the world and its history. Many millions of people were affected and anticipated destinies altered. Ken only played a very small part in the proceedings, but his minor role is considered by some to be worthy of documentation. Here there is an insight into his early formative years, childhood, upbringing, family, friends, education, sporting activities, work, etc. All that helped to shape the man and enable him to become part of what is considered a legendary fighting force. Why him? What made this man special? Circumstances definitely played a part, as did luck. Being in the right place at the right time. But then he went on and seemingly excelled; thrived, having found a vocation, so to speak.

His story did not stop in 1945. There was far more to the man than those six years. How did he cope with the sudden end to hostilities? What effect did it have on him and his subsequent family, and is there any legacy? Many of his former comrades had sad returns to normality, finding it difficult to integrate back into society. Heavy drinking and aggressive behaviour were common. Some even resorted to taking their own lives. Shell shock, now known as post-traumatic stress disorder (PTSD,) were often dealt with by being told to 'be a man' and 'get on with it', or simply by being ignored, but at what cost? Those years of warfare were so traumatic and etched into the minds of a generation; Ken's maybe more so than most. Increasingly, as he grew older, he withdrew into his memories.

Much effort has been used to put into context Ken's tales with reference to dates and events, sometimes quoting from published works, most notably *The Filibusters: The Story of the Special Boat Service* by John Lodwick, an ex-SBS officer (published 1947), and *The SAS and LRDG Roll of Honour, 1941–47* by Soldier X, QGM.

Ken's life story

We all have a tale to tell, a life story. Whether anyone would be willing to sacrifice the time to read or listen to it is the question. A life story is affected by so many variables: people, era, status, opportunities, physique, etc. The adage of nature versus nurture; DNA versus circumstances. There are many extraordinary people with fascinating experiences that go amongst us unnoticed. It could be said that as individuals we are all special and worthy of note, but surely some have a more interesting history than others? Imagine if all lives – highs, lows, funny incidents, moving moments, etc. – could be condensed and sympathetically penned. How many epics, moving bestsellers have we missed?

The reality is that one's life is usually reduced to a couple of paragraphs as an obituary, or tributes spoken at a funeral service. An A4 sheet of paper folded in half, containing a few photos, an

Introduction

order of service, and a few lines. That sheet of paper is then filed away in a drawer, cupboard, or box in the attic, or (as is more often the case) discarded after a few days. True, the memories of that person will live on for a generation or two with loved ones, friends, colleagues and associates, and even with enemies and adversaries. But most life stories will be lost to time.

Sometimes snippets of a person's life are recorded for posterity. The rich and famous may leave an enduring record, but rarely will 'ordinary' individuals leave a lasting historical footprint. In truth, the most we can hope for is a few lines in the local newspaper's obituary column. In Britain it is considered an honour of the highest magnitude to make it onto *The Times* newspaper's obituary page, especially if the notice is accompanied by a photograph. Such a distinction is reserved for the great, the good and the powerful. Imagine how stunned the family of Ken Smith were when he was included. The man himself would have said that he knew of many far more deserving than himself. He was no saint, far from it; his family would bear testament to that. With a short fuse and at times an explosive, aggressive temperament he might now be diagnosed with PTSD, or at the very least as needing some counselling. Some of his behaviour in the post-war years would seem to indicate this.

Ken Smith's is one life truly worthy of recording. The ripples from his life have affected many; some profoundly. In later years he could be found quietly tending his allotment or garden, producing vegetables to feed his large family of ten children. It is generally agreed that those hours were not primarily concerned with the production of food but with giving him the peace and quiet he craved. He was certainly afforded little if any recognition by those who passed him by. How many would have been intrigued by his tales, if only they had taken the time to listen? It's true that countless unrecorded stories are lost to the grave. These pages will try to ensure that for Ken this is not the case, by telling his story.

There were numerous times when fate smiled upon him. Why did an American newspaper record him as being an Oxford University sports star? Just how did he get that bullet, still embedded in his arm when he died some seventy-two years after the event? Three ships sinking with large loss of life – he could so easily have been on any one of them. Active service with the SBS/SAS and being present when a posthumous Victoria Cross was won. He was part of one of the 'Regiments' largest ever raids and another that has been recorded as being amongst its worst. Should he also have been awarded a Gallantry Medal? He was alongside Captain Bimrose, in the very same canoe, when he deservedly received the Military Cross, Britain's third highest award for gallantry; this being less than five weeks after Ken had been wounded and with the bullet still in embedded in his arm. This is his story.

Early Days

"It was my brother's turn to wear the shoes today, sir."

The British children born in the years following the Great War of 1914–1918 have been labelled by some as the country's Greatest Generation. Born into the aftermath of the War to End All Wars and a severely traumatised society, by the time they reached old age they had witnessed, through their efforts, a huge rise in living standards, the death of an empire, the formation of a commonwealth, and the birth of the welfare state and National Health Service. One Prime Minister, Harold Macmillan in July 1957, even went as far as to say that the country had "never had it so good". Those children were raised by parents mentally and sometimes physically scarred by the carnage of the trenches. With so many men of that generation lost

Introduction

to the conflict, the survivors and the women (especially the women) had to pick up the pieces, carry on, and strive to make things better. Then society endured the Great Depression of the late 1920s and well into the 1930s. It must have been thought that it could not get any worse when in 1939 along came Adolf Hitler and the Second World War. This time the battlefields would not be largely restricted to Central Europe; the war would become a truly global affair that would embroil large civilian populations in the conflict.

Kenneth Herbert Smith was born on 12th April 1922 on Portsea Island, Portsmouth, and was the eldest of three brothers. His mother, Ellen Gertrude Tait, was a local girl. His father, Harry Herbert Smith, originally from Stepney, London, and a keen Arsenal supporter, served in the Royal Navy and saw service on HMS *St Vincent, (The Vinny)*, HMS *Velux* and the battleship HMS *Barham*. There is dramatic archive film footage of the *Barham* being sunk during the Second World War: she slowly 'turns turtle' (rolls over), as hundreds of ant-like figures scurry across the turning hull before a massive explosion tears the ship to oblivion. Harry was an extremely fit sailor and could reputedly walk up the ship's metal staircases on his hands. He was also excellent at calligraphy, and when he home on leave neighbours would seek him out to neatly write letters on their behalf. Initially, the family lived close to the dockyard before moving to the other end of the island at Hilsea Crescent. According to Ken, they were the third house in at the posh end of the street. The Galloways lived at the other end. One of their children, Joyce, was later to become Ken's wife.

The city of Portsmouth is located on an island – Portsea – and is approximately 120 miles south-west of the capital, London. The island was joined to the mainland by several short bridges spanning a narrow channel and a causeway. Life in the city in those years was dominated by the Royal Navy; its dockyard always congested with a vast array of warships in harbour for rest, repair, refit and maintenance. When the dockyard hooter sounded at the end of the working day, its gates would be swung open to unleash a tidal wave of bicycles, twenty or more abreast, that would surge out into the city. This peloton would rapidly disperse as riders peeled off into the red-brick terraces that housed the main workforce. Any child growing up in this environment could not help but be affected by the navy. Many had fathers who would be absent for much of their young lives, 'away at sea'.

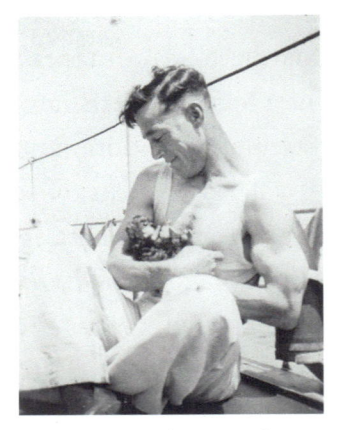

2. Harry Herbert Smith, on board ship cuddling present of a toy cat.

3. Harry Herbert Smith, 1915, aged 16.

4. Ellen Gertrude Tait, Kenneth Herbert Smith and Harry Herbert Smith circa 1924.

Introduction

The Royal Navy was the visible symbol of the British Empire parading its power and strength around the globe. Gunboat diplomacy was still very much alive. There were regular fleet reviews at Spithead in the Solent. On the 16th of July 1935 King George V reviewed 157 warships which covered the range of the Royal Navy. The fleet contained battleships, aircraft carriers, and the largest warship afloat at that time: HMS *Hood*, a battle cruiser. It was a display of Britain's naval might, lined up off Portsmouth for all the world to see and take note of.

Hilsea is the suburb located nearest to the mainland facing Cosham. Behind Cosham the ground rises sharply to a prominent chalk ridge, 130 metres above sea level, which overlooks Portsmouth. This offers spectacular views out across the city to the Isle of Wight. Along this ridge is a series of large brick forts, built by Napoleonic prisoners of war.

Ken's first school was situated a stone's throw from the main dockyard gate, and it was the same school that a young Charles Dickens had attended. One of Ken's earliest memories was of a young boy being brought in by the beagle; a truancy officer who would roam the streets looking for children skipping school. Ken could not understand why the lad would "miss off school" as he was one of its brightest pupils. When questioned about the reason for his absence, the boy replied, "It was my brother's turn to wear the shoes today, sir."

With his father away at sea, sometimes for over two years, a lot of responsibility rested on Ken's young shoulders. Life was hard, and to supplement the family's meagre income he and his brother George sang in the dockyard choir, this being quite a prestigious and rewarding commitment. Choir practice was every Tuesday and Thursday, plus two services every Sunday at St Anne's dockyard church. Every three months, providing not one service or practice was missed, they received the princely sum of seven shillings and sixpence each (the equivalent of thirty-seven and a half pence today). The wage was given in its entirety to their mother, who would give them a couple of coins for a toffee apple or similar: "Three half-crowns in a little bag; it was like gold dust to Mum." Another method of earning money was to collect empty jam jars: clean ones could be exchanged for a farthing (a quarter of a penny). When a few coppers (pennies) had been saved they would treat themselves to the Saturday-morning matinee at the picture house (cinema).

On occasions the choir would perform on the deck of HMS *Victory*, Admiral Nelson's flagship at the Battle of Trafalgar, 21st October 1805. This wooden ship is still preserved in dry dock and is the world's oldest commissioned naval vessel. Every so often there would be a Sunday service for the Royal Navy at St Thomas Cathedral in Old Portsmouth. The choir would lead the church parade from the dockyard to the cathedral, and then take their place close to the altar. From this raised vantage point, they could look at the massed ranks of naval personnel crammed into the spectacular building. The front rows would be filled with the admirals and high-ranking officers. Such was the throng that whole ships' companies would have to stand outside, listening to the service through speakers. The parade itself was quite something to behold; most large ships had a full marine band. The dockyard would resound to the call of bugles summoning the crews to parade. The ships' companies would form up on the quayside in front of their respective vessels for inspection, from small ships to aircraft carriers and mighty battleships. At this time the Royal Navy was one of the largest and most powerful navies in the world, and Portsmouth was its home port. The bands would start up and lead the crews out of the yard and through the streets of the city, each playing differing tunes, seeming to compete in volume and performance. Crowds would line the streets, and at the very head of the procession was the dockyard choir. What an impression for a young lad to be at the front of such pageantry!

Halfway up Portsdown Hill (the chalk ridge) is Queen Alexandra, now the city's main hospital. In the aftermath of World War I, it was a military convalescent hospital. Ken had vivid memories of lines of young, blind ex-soldiers; one hand outstretched and on the shoulder of the man in front. At the head of the line was the sole sighted man, often himself carrying a visible sign of war. His task was to lead the shuffling column through the streets of Cosham. These poor souls had been the victims of the horrific gas attacks that epitomised the very worst of trench warfare. No one wanted another war.

The local youth would learn to swim in the warm water created by the outflow from the city's coal-fired power station, located close to the harbour entrance and notorious for strong currents. On one occasion Ken's youngest brother Henry got into difficulty and by all accounts was going under for the third time! Ken made it to him with moments to spare. He was credited with saving his life. When Ken was about eleven or twelve years old, he was selected to represent his school at cross-country running. This caused him a problem as it clashed with his evening newspaper delivery round. Despite his protestations, he was obliged to compete. All schools in the area would be taking part. The course involved a leg across Portsdown Hill, down into Cosham, and finishing at Hilsea. Keen not to be too late for his paper round, Ken set off at a frantic pace and soon left the other competitors behind. He arrived at Hilsea before the course markers and so took a route he believed to be correct. As he neared the finishing field, he was surprised to see a runner emerge from a side path, then another followed by several more. He managed to catch and overtake all but two, which was quite remarkable considering that he had run a mile or so further than they had. There was no time to hang around and he quickly jumped on his bike to get to his job, only to receive a reprimand for being late. The following day at school assembly the headmaster made a special announcement of Ken's run.

Ken left school at thirteen years of age, finding work as a butcher's and fishmonger's delivery boy alongside his paper round, with all monies being given straight to his mother. At the time his father was away at sea. When he returned Ken proudly announced his new status as a 'breadwinner', only to be harshly reprimanded: "You can pack that in! Go get yourself an apprenticeship." Not knowing what an apprenticeship was, Ken spoke to a friend, Jack Smith, another paperboy who lived in the same street. Jack said that his round in the Hilsea/Cosham area passed a small building site, and they had apprentices. Following his directions, Ken cycled to where the development was under construction. At the entrance a shiny new car was parked, and two men were engaged in earnest conversation: one, dressed in overalls, the foreman, and the other, in a smart suit and spats (shoe covers), the boss. Patiently Ken waited at a respectful distance until the gentleman turned to him and said, "Yes, what can I do for you?"

"Excuse me, sir, do you need any apprentices?" Ken shyly asked.

After a brief moment's thought, the man replied, "Yes – start on Monday and see the carpenter." He then immediately returned to his conversation.

"Thank you, sir," replied Ken, feeling extremely proud of himself and amazed at how easy it had been. He turned and started to walk away, but only took a few paces before pulling up: there was a problem. He returned to his former position and again waited.

The men were surprised to see that the young lad had returned, and the boss curtly asked, "What now?"

Introduction

Ken started to explain his dilemma: "I'm very sorry, sir, but I have a delivery round and I need to give a week's notice. It's Thursday and if I hand in my notice now, I won't be able to start until—"

Before he could finish his explanation, the boss cut in, "Yes, yes, report when you can", clearly more interested in talking to the foreman than in the details of inducting a new apprentice.

Ken served his notice and started his new career. The first day was spent sawing staircase wedges; every riser and every tread requiring two. The vast majority the houses' wooden fixtures and fittings were being hand-made in the carpenter's workshop: windows, skirting, doors, staircases, etc. Because of the cost of timber, very little went to waste. The workshop was an old corrugated-iron Nissen hut with an earthen floor covered in duckboards. Situated on low-lying ground, water would frequently ooze up through the decking, it was bitterly cold in winter and permanently draughty, the only heating being an old pot stove fed with scraps and offcuts. During working hours this would always have a pot of animal-bone glue on the boil, giving off a pungent smell. Ken recalled spending days on end using a hand rip saw to cut stringers, the long staircase sides. His tutor was a dour old-timer who had survived the Battle of the Somme and was not noted for his banter and humour. Those early teenage years of hard graft instilled in Ken a steely determination and a strong right arm. Many people who crossed him would learn just how powerful it was. When he was about fifteen or sixteen, he and another apprentice decided to cycle to London. The pair wanted to see examples of building techniques they were learning about. It was a round trip of over 240 miles, on rough roads, pedalling heavy iron bikes. They set off at first light, making the journey there with enough time to tour the centre of the city, marvelling at the sights. On the return trip the pair made it as far as a building site on the city's outskirts. It had been spotted earlier and selected as somewhere to camp out for the night. They were woken in the morning by a policeman who, as luck would have it, originated from Portsmouth. He questioned them about their trespass and, believing the lads' story, sent them on their way, pointing out the best route home. Trips like that were not uncommon. Sometimes a small group of friends would cycle up onto the South Downs, set a fire, and burn some sausages on a stick before cramming into a small tent. Ken remembered waking early, throwing open the tent flaps, and for a split second seeing the landscape blanketed with rabbits, then a sudden flurry of activity as the disturbed mammals vanished. These were the days before myxomatosis. All these experiences helped to instil a sense of resilience, independence, determination and toughness in Ken which he would later come to rely on.

Ken, like most of his generation, was brought up religious, and he attended church every Sunday until the outbreak of war. On Sunday 3rd September 1939 he attended his normal morning church service, then raced home, switched on the radio and listened to Prime Minister Neville Chamberlain's speech.

> *"This morning, the British ambassador in Berlin handed the German Government a final note stating that unless we heard from them by 11 o'clock that they were prepared at once to withdraw their troops from Poland, a state of war would exist between us. I have to tell you that no such undertaking has been received, and that consequently this country is at war with Germany."*

Ken spent the rest of the day out in the garden, digging a trench for all the family in case of an air raid. It then rained heavily overnight. The following morning, the hole was full to overflowing with water.

Introduction

What has been called the 'Phoney War' now took place. It could be said that it was not until some eight months later, on the 10th of May 1940, that the harsh reality of the situation really struck home. This was when the German Army crossed the Dutch frontier, leading to the surrender of Holland and Belgium. Between the 26th of May and the 4th of June, Operation Dynamo managed to rescue almost four hundred thousand British and French troops from the besieged port of Dunkirk, although virtually all equipment was lost. Then on the 22nd of June, France was forced to sign an armistice. Britain and the Commonwealth now stood alone against the might of Nazi Germany and its Axis allies.

5. Ken, 14th February 1937, aged 14.

6. Ken, 2nd December 1939, aged 17.

2

RECRUITMENT

"Tonight's the night."

We shall fight on the beaches, we shall fight on the landing grounds, we shall fight in the fields and in the streets, we shall fight in the hills; we shall never surrender.

Winston Churchill

Ken enlisted into the Royal Marines at Eastney Barracks, Portsmouth, on 8th April 1940. He had to defer four days as his eighteenth birthday was not until the 12th. Initial basic training was at Deal, Kent, followed by Plymouth, Devon. This included small arms and Bren machine-gun courses. He was in 395 Squad, an entry with over 160 young recruits. It was here that he first met Albert 'Sticks' May, the man who was to become his best friend and someone who on many an occasion he was able to trust with his life. Sticks was also a Portsmouth lad, from Eastney, and had been a Marine Cadet drummer boy, hence the nickname.

At this moment in time the British forces had no commandos and marines fulfilled their traditional role in the navy: manning the guns, conducting shore patrols and boarding parties, etc. In fact, the first commandos were an all-army affair, with the Royal Navy blocking their valued marines from joining.

At Deal the young marines had the surreal experience of being drilled on the parade ground whilst overhead raged the Battle of Britain. The bright blue sky was filled with white vapour trails as aircraft duelled and occasionally plummeted to the ground. Ken often wondered why one of the German planes hadn't bothered to drop a few bombs or even strafe the parade ground; it would surely have resulted in several hundred casualties.

Some mornings the recruits would be loaded onto lorries and taken down to the shore to collect up German torpedoes. These had missed their targets after being fired at boats trying to steam through the narrow part of the English Channel under cover of darkness. Many torpedoes had run right up the beach beyond the high-tide mark, straight through the massed rows of barbed wire, and were lying on the road. After they were made safe the recruits' job was to gingerly pick up the projectiles and carefully load them onto trucks. They were then taken to HMS *Vernon* at Gosport, Portsmouth the Royal Naval torpedo school. Here they could be studied, as German torpedo technology was at that time far superior to the British. Not all ships safely made the treacherous journey, and the beaches would be covered in wreckage, spent cargo and bodies. On one occasion the shoreline was covered in bananas, but usually it was coal from South Wales. Ken would think of the high cost in lives to keep homes warm and industry going.

Some evenings recruits would be issued with a rifle and five rounds of ammunition and then taken out into the surrounding area to be dropped off at strategic locations on guard duty. The threat of invasion was very real: enemy paratroopers were expected at any moment and a few times the recruits were told, "Tonight's the night." The young, inexperienced marines would be tasked with securing vital locations ahead of the German invasion fleet, which was known to be gathering in the vicinity of Calais. The whole country was on edge, awaiting the inevitable onslaught. In this moment of crisis Britain came up with the master strategy of placing a couple of recruits, each armed with a rifle and five rounds of ammunition, in the Kent countryside at vital crossroads, bridges, etc. To supplement this meagre force a few members of the Home Guard Local Defence Volunteers (LDV) would be detailed to back them up. They would turn up when they could, armed at best with a shotgun and sometimes with only a pitchfork. Ken would tell the tale of when a couple of old-timers turned up. After a few boring hours one turned to the other and said, "It's a bit cloudy; I don't think they'll come tonight."

His pal agreed with this pearl of wisdom, saying, "I hear they have some bitter [beer] at the pub tonight, and there's a game of darts on." It must be remembered that rationing was in effect, which included beer. It did not take too long for the pair to convince themselves that the enemy wouldn't be stupid enough to invade on a night like tonight, and that the nation would be safe in the hands of a couple of marine recruits.

One night Ken did believe that the prelude to the invasion was happening. He spotted a suspicious movement and, alerting his comrade, cocked and loaded his rifle. In the dim light, with all his nerves straining, he took aim but was unable to get a good sighting. As the first light of dawn began to show he was able to make out a faint figure which slowly revealed itself to be… a cow. The lucky beast very nearly fell victim to Ken's first shot in anger.

From Deal the squad transferred to Plymouth for naval gunnery. Unusually, 395 Squad had no King's Badge cadet (top recruit). Unable to select one clearly superior candidate, it was decided to award five 'Diamonds' to very good cadets. Both Sticks and Ken were Diamonds, although Ken always maintained that Sticks

Recruitment

should have been awarded the King's Badge. After basic training Sticks was posted to HMS *Vanguard*, a battleship. For Ken, a ship's gunnery course (starting the 4th of September at Plymouth) was followed by a detachment to Eastney on the 20th of November to await his first posting. For him this was ideal as he was able to visit friends and family. One night, following a heavy air raid, he was returning to barracks. Running late, he took a shortcut through a bomb site (an area of the city that had received several direct hits). To prevent looting the streets were cordoned off but, seeing no one, he took the chance and hurried on. From nowhere an air-raid warden appeared and promptly saluted Ken, who returned the gesture of respect. Ken was in his number-one uniform and quickly reasoned that he had been mistaken for an officer.

This was to be his last Christmas at home for many years. The young and naive teenager would soon be thrust into combat and the harsh reality of warfare.

7. Deal, Kent, Basic Training 1st July 1940, 395 Kings Squad. 'Battle of Britain', Ken front row far right.

8. Eastney Naval Gunnery QR3 Class, February 1941.
Rear L to R: Ken Smith; Levac; Godby.
Front L to R: Moore; not known; Clr. Sgt. Pinnegar: not known; Sommes.

3

HMS *MANCHESTER*

"We had a field day."

9. HMS Manchester.

In February 1941 Ken was posted to HMS *Manchester*, a town-class light cruiser. Her sister ship HMS *Belfast*, now tied up in Central London, serves as a permanent reminder of Britain's maritime heritage. Ken did visit the *Belfast* on one of his London reunions. He was bitterly disappointed as there was rust everywhere: "In our day all the brass was polished, it was spotless. I once asked a sergeant, 'Why are we doing this again, when we only did it yesterday?'

"He said, 'You will do it today and again tomorrow, and the day after. If you weren't doing that, what would you be up to? Playing cards, gambling, fighting and arguing. Up to mischief. An idle mind is a dangerous mind.'"

The *Manchester* was part of the Home Fleet based at Scapa Flow, Orkney Islands, off northern Scotland. Ken joined the ship at Hepburn, Newcastle, where she was undergoing maintenance and modification work. It was late in the day when he arrived, a strict blackout was in force. He could just make out the faint silhouettes of warships, and approached a guard with his papers who, after inspecting them, pointed him in the direction of a gangway. Stepping onto the deck of a ship he asked, "Is this the *Manchester*?"

The reply was, "No, this is the *Penelope*; she's tied up alongside."

Ken had to make his way across the *Penelope* to get to his new posting but, as fate would have it, HMS *Penelope* would later become his second ship.

The work on HMS *Manchester* was nearing completion. She was being fitted out with 'degaussing gear'. This top-secret addition was an attempt to thwart magnetic mines, these having already caused the loss of much shipping. In essence, it was a large electric cable hung around the ship's hull which, in theory, when charged would repel magnetic mines.

Ken enjoyed HMS *Manchester*, saying that "it was a happy ship with a good atmosphere on the mess deck." The following months were spent on escort duty with North Atlantic and Russian convoys. There was also a spell hunting for German weather ships hiding amongst the Arctic ice floes and in Hval Fjord, Iceland. They were on patrol for some time, having to refuel at sea. The daily tasks were monotonous but essential. The sea spray would freeze upon the deck guns and superstructure, and if left in place the ship would become top-heavy and capsize. Hour after hour would be spent chipping the ice off the ship. Another equally onerous task was spent sitting at the ship's guns, rotating the elevation and direction wheels; two small steering wheels with a handgrip projection that constantly had to be turned back and forth, otherwise the ship's guns would freeze in position. And then there was submarine watch: hours spent intently peering through binoculars, attempting to spot a subs telltale periscope.

The ship's bridge would regularly request updates to keep the watch alert. On one occasion Ken and a young naval rating were on watch together when the ship's intercom called, "Senior hand starboard forward watch, how many ships of the fleet can you see?"

With bad weather and reduced visibility, Ken would give a report. Shortly after, another update was requested. Before Ken could move, the young seaman picked up the mouthpiece and said, "Same as last time: f**k all!"

The next message was a curt, "Captain of the watch, report to the bridge immediately."

As he was that man, Ken had to make his way in total darkness, feeling his way down metal ladders and around the superstructure, eventually locating the bridge door and negotiating his way past heavy blackout curtains to enter the eerie phosphorescent glow of the ship's bridge. Having never ventured to this centre of power before he was in awe, and stood to attention facing the captain, who paced about looking industrious and ignoring the young marine.

Eventually the captain turned to face Ken. Speaking in the very poshest of Queen's English he said, "For all you know a f**king U-boat could have come alongside and had a f**king tea party on the quarterdeck."

The rollicking carried on for some time. Ken was completely stunned; he had never heard an officer swear like that. After the severe reprimand he retraced his steps back to the watch location and in no uncertain terms let his assistant know his feelings. Those that have witnessed an upset Ken will be aware of just how unpleasant an experience that is.

HMS *Manchester* was lying at anchor in Scapa Flow when Ken received a telegram, from his mother, informing him that his father, who was in Haslar Royal Navy Hospital, Gosport, was dying from tuberculosis and, if possible, he was to come home quickly. He duly showed his officer the telegram but was refused leave as he was a loader on a four-inch gun, which they were short of, and "There is a war on; we need every man."

An 'old stager' who considered himself somewhat of a 'barrack-room lawyer' said, "You don't have to accept that; you have the right to take it to the very top."

So, Ken pressed on, going first to the ship's duty officer and then to the captain, being turned down on both occasions. Not being put off, and being aware of his rights, he put in a highly unusual request to see the admiral. All were stunned by this perseverance, and the request, as was his right, was granted.

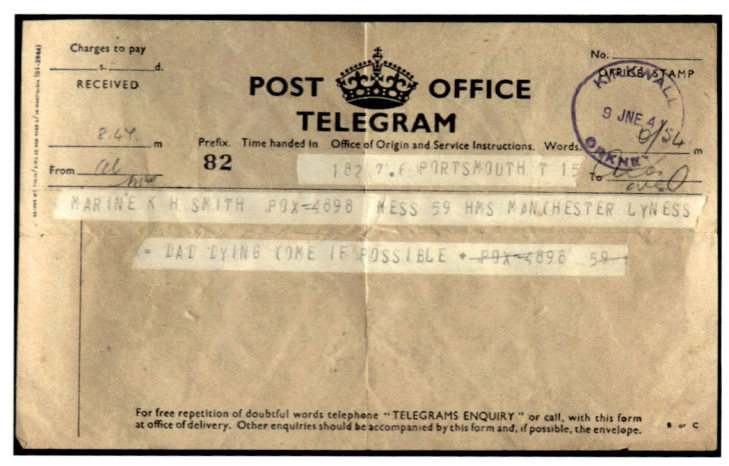

Telegram concerning Ken's father's illness.

Telegram concerning Ken's father's death.

Dressed in his spotless number-one uniform, Ken waited on deck for the small launch that would transfer him to the battleship HMS *Hood* and his appointment with the admiral. The *Hood* was the pride of the British Navy and Ken had, on the previous day, been on board as part of a 'meat party' transferring rations. Suddenly the sirens on all ships sounded as the entire fleet was called to action stations. Scapa Flow became a scene of frantic action as ships of every conceivable size brought their engines up to full power. The *Manchester* literally shuddered with the sudden burst of power: "We were doing thirty knots below and nothing above," said Ken. The fleet raced out to sea. On board the *Manchester* it was a well-rehearsed drill. Ken's position was at the forward anchor, and soon his spotless uniform was covered in seaweed and slime as they weighed anchor. Had the call come through a little while later he would undoubtedly have been aboard the *Hood* and put to sea with her. As it was, he never had the opportunity to say farewell to his father. It was the 18th of May 1941.

The cause of the furore was that the German battleship the *Bismarck*, accompanied by the *Prinz Eugen*, had left Norwegian waters and was breaking out to sea to threaten the North Atlantic Sea routes. The British fleet was split in its search for the German boats. HMS *Manchester*, together with HMS *Birmingham*, was directed to patrol the Iceland-Faroes Channel on the opposite side of Iceland from the enemy's chosen route. However, the battleships HMS *Hood* and HMS *King George V* were on a course that would intercept the German ships. On the 24th of May 1941 the Battle of the Denmark Strait took place. HMS *Hood* was blown to oblivion when a shell from the *Bismarck* detonated in her magazine. She sank within three minutes. There were only three survivors from a ship's complement of 1,418. It could so easily have been nineteen. HMS *King George V* also suffered damage in the engagement. The loss of the *Hood* stunned the British nation, and the destruction of the *Bismarck* became a top priority. HMS *Manchester* was part of the British fleet that chased, caught and sank the *Bismarck*. It must, however, be said that this was only possible after some old, almost obsolete vintage biplanes paid a vital part by crippling the *Bismarck*'s rudder, leaving her a sitting duck. The planes were so slow that the German anti-aircraft gunners found it difficult to zero in on them.

In July 1941 the *Manchester* was dispatched to Gibraltar to escort an important convoy to Malta: Force H. Ken had vivid memories of his time on 'the Rock'. A blackout in the dockyard and on ships at anchor was vigorously enforced. Finding your way back to the *Manchester* after a drunken night out was straightforward as the ship's Tannoy would blare out music, in particular 'Il Silenzio' by Eddie Calvert. This haunting piece of trumpet music would in later years bring a smile to Ken's face as memories came flooding back. It was played at his funeral service.

Another of his memories from Gibraltar was when he was on duty with the shore patrol. In the bar area a landlady rushed up, pleading for assistance at her bar. The patrol hurried to the bar to be greeted by someone flying out of the cowboy-style double swing doors. Inside the establishment a scene reminiscent of a Wild West movie: a bar brawl was in full swing. As Ken entered, he pulled up in amazement. Three stokers were stood on the bar, doing the Egyptian sand dance. They were stark naked apart from their boots. Moments later, a chair was smashed over Ken's head. As he was staggering out of the bar with blood pouring from his head, another bar owner appeared, demanding help in quelling a disturbance at their establishment. The whole district seemed to be a drunken riot. Force H personnel were aware of the risky venture they were about to undertake, and that many of their number would not be returning.

Gibraltar was the staging post and assembly point for the Malta convoys; Malta being reputedly the most bombed place in World War II. Vital stores and equipment would run the gauntlet of enemy aircraft, fast torpedo boats and submarines. Shipping losses were extremely high, and thousands lost their lives in the attempt to keep Malta supplied. At this stage of the war the island was in a desperate state, so a special convoy of fast merchant ships with a heavy Royal Navy escort was assembled. The *Manchester* carried a load of seven hundred troops that were considered vital in the island's defence against its anticipated invasion.

On the 21st of July 1941, Force H departed Gibraltar bound for Malta and Operation Substance had begun. On the 23rd the convoy was located by enemy aircraft in the Bone area: "I saw the *Fearless* go up!" said Ken. In subsequent attacks the *Manchester* was crippled when struck by an aerial torpedo on the port side in the boiler room and the rudder was jammed. Ken said, "The ship sailed in a circle for half a day on a forty-degree list, constantly under attack." After two days a temporary fix was made to the rudder by divers, and the ship was forced to turn back and head for Gibraltar. The cruiser was a prime target: aircraft would circle the stricken ship, eager to claim the prize of sinking the *Manchester*. Ken said that "During lulls in the fighting, the dead, mostly saturated in oil, were brought up from below. They were stacked behind our gun, which was already congested with spent shell casings. We could hardly move." The dead were then sewn into new blankets with a shell casing between their legs to be buried at sea. This was often interrupted by a call back to action stations. The situation was perilous. The order to don life jackets was issued and the troops aboard were moved to one side in an effort to keep the ship on an even keel. Below decks, the four-inch magazine was flooded. Six-inch shells were being fired to keep the aircraft at bay. "We fired all our ammunition, and I was left cradling one of only three four-inch shells remaining. We were being circled by an Italian bomber. The guns tracked the aircraft, and I would stagger and slide across the sloping deck, which was covered in blood and oil. It was slippery, stepping over debris and bodies, clutching the shell, ready to load. Sliding from one gun and climbing the deck again to whichever gun best came to bear!" The crippled ship limped back to the safety of Gibraltar on the 26th, remaining there until mid-September whilst temporary repairs were carried out. The surviving troops were put aboard the *Manxman* and sped through on a night passage. Most of the ship's crew were discharged. A skeleton crew, which included the football team, remained aboard. By all accounts they had an excellent soccer team, which the captain was keen to hold on to.

The *Manchester* sailed from Gibraltar on the 17th of September 1941 for a destination unknown. Speculation was rife as to where they were bound with varied locations being bandied around, but most believed they were headed for a northern British port. After several days at sea on a zigzag course, Ken said, "I think we're going to somewhere in America." By observing the sun and stars he had worked out their direction.

On the 23rd of September 1941 the ship, now renamed *S163*, sailed up the Delaware River headed to the Philadelphia Naval Shipyard for 'permanent repairs'. All signage of and reference to HMS *Manchester* had been removed and the crew were under strict orders to only refer to the ship as *S163*. As soon as they had entered the Delaware Estuary the pilot came aboard, followed by teams of dockyard workers. Pumps were put into action, compressors fired up and repairs started. This was even before the yard had been sighted. The whole crew were mightily impressed with American efficiency. The dockyard, in comparison to British yards, was clean and orderly. Lights burned brightly and the mood was upbeat, far less oppressive than the austerity back home.

When the formalities of docking were complete and some resemblance of normality had settled in, crew members not detailed for duties were allowed ashore to stretch their legs. Although supposedly confined to the immediate vicinity, Ken decided to venture forth. As he approached a guard post he saw the sentry hurry inside to reappear moments later with what must have been the entire guard detail. They formed a line, springing smartly to attention as Ken approached, they then saluted him. Feeling he should reciprocate Ken returned the compliment and brazenly strode out through the dockyard's main gate. In his blue dress uniform he had once again been mistaken for an officer.

Although late in the evening, the place was alive. No blackout or rationing here. He wandered on and came upon a news stand, and there on the front page, in big bold letters, was the headline 'HMS *MANCHESTER* in port for major repairs'. So much for secrecy. Venturing into a cafe, he noticed a small picture screen behind the counter showing newsreels. Confusion set in as he was unable to locate the projector and associated beam. It was his first view of a television and he marvelled at it, thinking, *what will they come up with next?* The dockyard was full of British naval vessels undergoing urgent and extensive repairs. The Yankee workers were constantly giving the British sailors stick, "Gee, don't you guys ever shoot back?" being a particular favourite.

Ken loved his football; or to be more precise, he loved his version of the beautiful game. To him it was a contact sport. He was captain of the ship's team and its centre forward. Several matches were arranged during their time in America. One was against HMS *Furious*, an aircraft carrier. It was a bitterly cold day with sleet and hail blowing across the pitch. American spectators drove their cars up to the touchline to watch the game in comfort. Not too long into the match, the ball was crossed into the *Furious*'s penalty area. The goalkeeper rose to collect it. Moments later, wondering what had happened, he found himself in the back of the net, still clutching the ball. Ken had put the ball (along with the goalie) over the line to score the opening goal. Immediately the cars sounded their horns in a chorus of disapproval. From then on, whenever Ken had a ball, the cars would honk their displeasure. This only served to inspire him.

Several exhibition matches were arranged against the 'cities league' and all-star teams. In one match Ken scored five times in a six-three defeat of a top local team. The local newspaper carried a report and came up with a story that Ken was an Oxford University sports star with 'letters' at rowing, soccer, and track and field. The DuPont's, an extremely wealthy and influential family, invited the HMS *Manchester* team to play an exhibition match against a DuPont team. On match day the weather was atrocious with the game easily being won by the navy. It was sportingly agreed to abandon the proceedings and call it a draw. The match had taken place in the grounds of the DuPont mansion and an after-event banquet had been laid on. Ken was under orders to attend the meal, not to upset their host, and to keep up the pretence of the newspaper article. He found himself in a privileged position, seated on a table next to the DuPont's' daughter, who had studied at Oxford University. She engaged Ken in polite conversation, asking him what college he had studied at. He had never even been to Oxford, let alone studied there, but he had taken some night classes at the Portsmouth Municipal College. So, to keep up the charade he said, "The Municipal."

She said, "Gee, I've never heard of that one, but there's so many of them."

"It's a small one," replied Ken.

Opposite them was seated his good friend Eric Hills. He delighted in Ken's predicament and took full advantage, asking questions about Oxford and university life. At the first opportunity Ken excused himself to the toilet, where he spent the rest of the party in hiding.

On another occasion, having played a Sunday match against HMS *Furious*, Ken decided to walk back through the city. A large crowd had gathered and were looking up at the neon billboard. They were shocked, confused and stunned as they stared in disbelief. It was the 7th of December 1941. Japan had attacked Pearl Harbor in Hawaii!

In the following days the newspapers were full of graphic photos of the devastation wrought upon the American Pacific Fleet. On board the British ships where the Americans were working, these pictures were plastered with the words scrawled across them, 'Don't you guys shoot back?' Ken would chuckle as he told the story, adding, "We had a field day." At a subsequent reunion dinner held at the SAS Hereford base, Ken found himself seated on a large table with an honoured guest: the head of American special forces. Ken, now in his eighties, was escorted by his eldest son Alan, who encouraged his father to tell the Pearl Harbor story. When he came to the tale's end the American sat stony-faced and some at the table were a little discomfited, but Ken didn't miss a beat. He had taken himself back to those times with a distant look and a wry smile upon his face.

Having completed repairs, HMS *Manchester* sailed from Philadelphia on the 8th of March 1942. Calling at Bermuda, on route, they encountered a severe storm with "waves as big as skyscrapers. We were rolling and pitching, and when the ship crashed down, I thought it must surely break in two," said Ken. The ship docked at Portsmouth on the 18th of March 1942. Ken was discharged from the crew to attend a gunnery and explosives course at Eastney Barracks. HMS *Manchester* carried on. Five months later, on the 13th of August 1942, she was sunk in controversial circumstances whilst taking part in Operation Pedestal; a convoy to relieve Malta which has been described as 'just about the most important convoy operation of the war'. The ship was some 4 miles off the Tunisian coast when she was hit, on the starboard side, by two torpedoes fired from Italian fast motorboats. The engine room, the after-boiler room and the 4inch magazine were flooded, the ship had no power and took on a 12-degree list. She was a 'sitting duck'. After unsuccessful attempts to save the ship, she was abandoned and scuttled. The captain was later court martial for this.

'Stormy Seas'.

HMS Manchester, 1941. Liles; Clark; Ken.

'At Reading, USA, December 1941'
Eric Hills; Harold Lipscombe; Andy Craig "Myself".

4

HMS PENELOPE

"The ship was in a bad way."

Records show that Ken Smith was discharged from HMS *Manchester* on the 5th of April 1942. From the 6th of April 1942 until the 8th of January 1943, he was based at Eastney Barracks in Portsmouth for gunnery and explosives courses, passing out QR3 qualified. Whilst there he was part of a contingent of marines – "two lorries loads" – that were dispatched to RN Haslar, Gosport. On arrival he fell behind when pausing to tie up his shoelaces. Hurrying to catch up, he ran into the mortuary to be hit with an awful sight and smell. Bloated dead bodies were stacked up. These were fatalities from the disastrous Dieppe Raid of the 19th of August 1942 (Operation Jubilee). Ken never expanded on what he witnessed.

His next ship was the famed HMS *Penelope*, a light cruiser listed in *Janes Fighting Ships* as having a normal complement of 450 men. The ship was affectionately known as 'the pepper pot' due to receiving over two thousand shell fragments in the Battle for Malta. On the way to Gibraltar from Malta she underwent three more days of attack, during which fourteen torpedoes and three thousand tons of bombs were aimed at her by German and Italian planes. In a twenty-four-day period her own guns fired thirty-five thousand five-inch shells, 6,500 rounds of four-inch shells, twenty thousand two-inch rounds and eight thousand Oerlikon shells.

Ken arrived at Scapa Flow on the 2nd of December 1942 and officially joined the ship on the 9th of January 1943. She is recorded as being on home waters duty until the 17th of January, when she left the Clyde in Scotland to join the 12th Cruiser Squadron, West Mediterranean Fleet in Gibraltar, arriving on the 22nd of January. When Ken joined the ship's complement, he was twenty years old and made captain of X Turret on the port side. This is a rare distinction for one so young and is normally reserved for QR2 and above qualified. On arrival at the ship Albert 'Sticks' May, his great friend from basic training, was leaning over the side to welcome him on board. They were able to rekindle their friendship and exchange stories.

Ken celebrated his twenty-first birthday in Algiers, North Africa. Around this time, he fractured his wrist when playing in a friendly game of deck soccer, and was assigned to guard duties at Algiers headquarters, a large building/hotel on a hillside overlooking the harbour. A senior officer, believed to be Admiral Cunningham? spotted Ken's bandaged wrist and asked why he had been allocated an injured marine as his guard. He insisted they "Get me a fit marine."

Ken was relieved of his guard duties and sent back to HMS *Hannibal*, the shore base. A colour sergeant asked if he knew anything about rum. "I know how to drink it," he replied, which was enough to make him officer of the keys, sentry to the ship's keyboard. A highly responsible task, for there can be over two hundred keys on board a ship (including those of various magazines). The sentry must ensure that no unauthorised person obtains a key, and that they are signed in and out. He also had charge of the keys for the ship's rum ration! Since the times of Nelson, the Royal Navy had issued a daily 'tot of rum' to all seamen. This practice only ceased in 1970.

Algiers was the assembly point for the coming invasion of Sicily. Troops were undergoing vigorous training in preparation. Sporting competitions, including athletics events, were organised to show off fitness levels and as a boost to the troops' morale. The culmination of track and field competition was the Mediterranean Championships, its Blue-Ribbon event being 'The Mediterranean Mile'. Ken had qualified to represent HMS *Penelope*, the Royal Navy and the Royal Marines. Quite a feat considering, "I'd been at sea for the last three months," and he didn't fancy his chances, especially when seeing that Roper was entered. Roper had been an athlete of Portsmouth Atalanta Athletic Club prior to the war. As a youth Ken would attend weekend cricket practice in the nets at the Alexandra Sports Fields, Hilsea, Portsmouth. This would often coincide with an athletic meet in the nearby stadium. Following practice, Ken would 'skip the fence' to watch the racing. Roper was a star middle-distance runner and Ken had never seen him lose. He mentioned this to his sergeant. The NCO was having no excuses and ordered him to beat Roper. Ken won the race in a little over four minutes; reputedly four minutes seventeen seconds. He was surprised and a slightly embarrassed when the admiral came over to congratulate him, commenting on how close he was to the four-minute barrier.

Being rostered for duty, Ken was forced to leave before any presentations. A corporal physical training instructor (PTI) who had come second in the one-hundred-yard sprint offered to pick up Ken's trophy. Later, back on board the ship, the corporal presented Ken with a cup, congratulating him on his achievement. When he returned to the galley and proudly showed off the trophy his crewmates were surprised as the cup was only a small one, whereas it should have been a large, prestigious cup, just like the one the corporal was now showing off! All believed a swap had taken place. Ken stormed off to the corporals' mess and confronted the PTI, who denied that any exchange had taken place. But Ken wouldn't have it ("I could tell from his face that he was lying"), saying, "If it means that much to you, you can keep it." He then turned and threw the small cup down the waste chute. It's probably still lying on the bottom of Algiers Harbour.

From the 1st of June 1943 HMS *Penelope* was part of Operation Corkscrew; initially with the bombardment of the Italian island of Pantelleria (here the ship was hit by shellfire), and then during the island's invasion. Pantelleria surrendered on the 11th of June. From then on, the *Penelope* was in almost constant action as the islands of Lampedusa and Taormina were assaulted and forced to surrender. From the 12th of July 1943, as part of Force H, HMS *Penelope* took part in the invasion of Sicily. For the remainder of July and August the ship was involved in bombardments and sweeps during the Sicily campaign.

The Italians surrendered on the 3rd of September 1943. Following this, on the 9th of September 1943 the *Penelope*, together with the USS *Boise*, as part of Operation Slapstick steamed into Taranto Harbour, southern Italy at action stations. The crew were unsure of what reception awaited them and if any resistance would be offered. The horizon was filled with "big ships; it was quite a sight" – they were waiting for the Italian fleet to sail out and be escorted to Malta. Germans were suspected of still occupying parts of the city. The *Penelope* tied up alongside the American ship and hurriedly unloaded a contingent of Paratroops. Ken was part of the detail to transfer stores and ammunition to the quayside. They raced back and forth across the *Boise*, taking a shortcut through its superstructure. The British seamen could not believe the luxury the US sailors enjoyed, saying, "We got back to our ship with almost as much stores as we dropped off. We stripped the ship of sugar and soap!"

From the 9th until the 18th of September, as part of Force Q (Operation Avalanche), HMS *Penelope* took part in the landings at Salerno on the Italian mainland. Ken recalled "seeing spitfires landing on the beach and a flying bomb hit a Yankee cruiser". We "fired every shell on board", then rearmed in Malta before being transferred to the Levant at the beginning of October to counter the threat of a German invasion of Cos. Ken now found himself transferred to the shell locker, below decks, to replace a marine with breathing problems, who needed to be in fresh air and not locked in when at action stations. Following the Italian surrender British forces had occupied most of the Greek Dodecanese Islands, which were largely garrisoned by Italian troops. However, there was still a strong German presence on the Greek mainland and the larger islands (i.e. Rhodes and Crete).

On the 7th of October, with HMS *Sirius* and other ships, the *Penelope* intercepted and sank a German invasion fleet (consisting of six landing craft, one ammunition ship and an armed trawler) off the island of Stampalia. The invasion force is recorded as being 'Completely Annihilated with the exception of one ferry barge.' While retiring through the Scarpanto Straits south of Rhodes, the British flotilla was attacked by eighteen Junkers Ju 87 Stukas and Junkers Ju 88s bombers. HMS *Penelope* received bomb damage and was forced to put into Alexandria, Egypt for repairs. Ken had vivid memories of that engagement in the Greek islands and catching up with the German invasion fleet. He said, "We sunk every boat in that force, but they caught up with us and we were badly bombed." Being locked below decks and listening to the sounds of explosions was an unnerving experience: not knowing what was going on and feeling totally helpless and unable to affect his fate. It was a relief when it was announced, "Anyone with four-inch gun experience to report topside." Hurriedly, Ken made his way up, but on emerging into the bright sunlight he was immediately forced to dive for cover as enemy aircraft machine-gun fire strafed the deck. When his eyes adjusted to the bright glare he witnessed a sight of twisted metal, shell casings and dead bodies. "The ship was in a bad way. We had to put into Alex for urgent repairs," said Ken. Whilst docked in Alexandria Ken was discharged from HMS *Penelope*.

HMS Penelope, *'The Pepper-pot', showing extensive damage.*

After repairs, the light cruiser was soon back in action. From the 22nd–29th January 1944 as part of Operation Shingle, the amphibious assault on Anzio, Italy, the ship is reported again as having fired every shell on board. On the 18th of February 1944, HMS *Penelope* was torpedoed by a T5 torpedo fired from the

German submarine *U-410*. She was struck in the aft engine room. Sixteen minutes later another torpedo hit the aft boiler room, causing the ship to immediately sink. There were 206 survivors but 415 crew went down with her, including the captain. A while later the U-boat was sunk. HMS *Aurora* picked up survivors from the German submarine including its captain, who was boasting, "I have sunk the *Penelope*!"

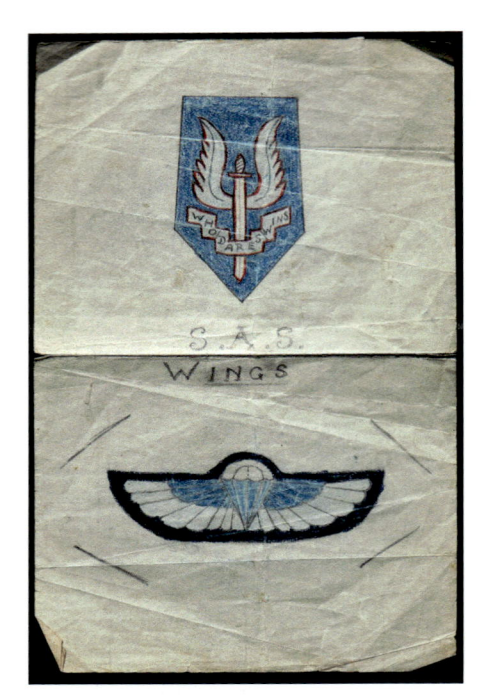

Sketch drawings by Ken of SAS insignia, sent to his mother.

Written on the reverse, "This is our badges I wear since I left the Marines, I drew these months ago and kept them meaning to send them. I don't think you have seen them, however I'll still be able to wear the wings when I return to the Marines, if I will jump when required and still get 6d a day extra."

5

A BRIEF HISTORY OF THE SAS/SBS

"These men are dangerous."

We sleep safely in our beds because rough men stand ready in the night to visit violence on those who would do us harm.

(A paraphrased Winston Churchill/George Orwell quote)

I'm sure there are some who may have issues with this attempt to put into words how the unit that Ken Smith and his comrades served in originated and grew.

From ancient times there have always existed superior warriors; soldiers who were above and beyond the norm. These troops have often been amalgamated to form elite units. Nowadays special forces are commonplace throughout the world. The SAS has been credited with being instrumental in the formation of many of the world's present-day special forces.

British 'special forces', in the modern concept, were a result of the disastrous military start to World War II. Following the British Expeditionary Force's chaotic and heroic evacuation from Dunkirk (26th May – 4th June 1940), Britain and its Commonwealth forces found themselves alone in the fight against the might of Nazi Germany and its Axis partners. On the 3rd of June 1940 Prime Minister Winston Churchill instructed his military chiefs to raise 'Special trained forces of the hunter class'. This would allow Britain to strike back, gain time to gather strength, and give a much-needed boost to morale. The sheer size, scope and range of potential missions required men out of the ordinary. The success and very survival of these soldiers would often depend upon their fitness and initiative, coupled with an ability to adapt. It is often said that real warfare rarely goes according to plan.

Roger Courtney was one of the volunteers, having already, by the age of thirty-six, lived a full and spectacular life. Amongst his many life experiences, he had been a 'white hunter', canoed the length of the White Nile (reputedly with only a sack of potatoes and an elephant spear on board), and lived with African Bushmen. As part of Layforce Commando, he formed, in response to Churchill's order, the 'Folbot Troop', (canoeist). On the 31st of January 1941 Layforce (comprising three commando brigades) were dispatched to the Mediterranean via the Cape.

Courtney trained up the Folbot Troop to be used in small-scale sabotage, beach recce, and discreet landings on enemy coastline. During 1941 the Folbot Troop morphed into the Folbot Section and then into the Special Boat Section. By August of 1941 they became an independent unit attached to the Royal Navy and expanded. As Courtney went about his work other units were also being created, most notably by David Stirling. Courtney was looking for particular types of men for his unit, as illustrated by a sign on his desk that read 'ARE YOU TOUGH? IF SO GET OUT. I NEED BUGGERS WITH INTELLIGENCE.' He also wrote a paper on the ideal recruit:

The Complete Folbotist

Are you a professional 'tough guy'? i.e. Do you imitate the film stars, wear funny hats, or walk around carrying more weapons than a Mexican bandit, get truculent after a few drinks and proceed to beat up the town?

Or have you got the true conception of 'tough guy'? Are you the quiet type of man who would not be picked out in a crowd, the unassuming type who would be expected to be employed in professional business and never in the 'thugeree' you might be engaged in?

Layforce was disbanded in the summer of 1941 and by the 11th of October 1941 all special service troops were grouped into the Middle East Commando. After December 1941 a depleted 1SB Section was lost by the navy to be absorbed into the 1st Special Air Service, there new role being small-scale raiding; more aggressive! Roger Courtney returned to the UK to set up 2SB Section, with a completely different command, structure and aims.

SAS origins

Much has been written about the SAS, but if the truth be known, until the Iranian Embassy Siege of 1980 this small unit of the British armed forces was largely unknown. When live pictures of that event were beamed around the world Ken Smith was heard to say, "I bet that's the SAS. It will be the end of them." It certainly was an end to any anonymity. Ken always maintained that "Secrecy had been drummed into the unit", and he believed this to be one of their greatest assets.

Stirling

Initially with the Scots Guards, Lieutenant David Stirling served with the Guards Commandos and then with the Layforce Commandos. It was here that he formulated the idea and principle of the SAS: a deep penetration raiding force. 'The use of minimum manpower to produce maximum effect. Performed not by force but by skill, daring and initiative; sometimes with an element of "bravado".'

With his friend Lieutenant John Steel 'Jock' Lewes, he started to experiment with parachuting as a method of troop insertion. This resulted in spending some time in a Cairo hospital following a heavy landing. It was here that Stirling wrote down his ideas. While convalescing, and on crutches, he delivered it personally and without appointment, deliberately bypassing the official channels, to General Claude Auchinleck ('Auk'), commander-in-chief of the Middle East forces. Stirling believed his plan would be snubbed if he were to go through the official bureaucratic process. The modest proposal – to recruit six or seven officers and about sixty other ranks – was endorsed by Auk. Promoted to captain and reporting directly to Auk, Stirling initially began recruiting from the now-disbanded Layforce. Much hostility and difficulty were encountered from elements of the Middle East headquarters, who treated the new formation like a renegade pariah.

In January of 1941, operating from the basement of a Cairo brothel, a Colonel Dudley Wrangel Clarke had created a fake parachute brigade. Clarke was responsible for strategic deception. Code-named 'Abeam', the fake unit was to be called the 1st Special Air Service Brigade. So, when a young officer was given permission to recruit men to parachute behind enemy lines, the connection was made to put substance into the subterfuge. David Stirling was the young officer, and readily agreed to name his new force L Detachment, Special Air Service Brigade. The new unit first emerged in July 1941 and a training camp was established at Kabrit in the Egyptian desert. The unit remained L Detachment, SAS Brigade until the 21st of September 1942, when it was granted regimental status as the 1st SAS Regiment. The 'L' was to indicate that there were other detachments. When later M and S Detachments were created, many believed that the three were named after Lewes, Mayne and Stirling. Jock Lewes and Robert Blair 'Paddy' Mayne were credited by Stirling as the unit's co-founders.

Mayne

The uncooperative officers at Middle East HQ were extremely glad of the opportunity to see the back of Paddy Mayne. This legendary man was reputedly almost court-martialled for striking a senior officer. The six-foot-four-inch former Irish international rugby player was only too willing to join 'Stirling's mob' and get into action. He went on to become one of the most decorated officers of the Second World War, DSO and three bars. Fearless and calm under fire, he demanded supreme fitness from his troops. Following Stirling's capture on the 24th of January 1943, Paddy took over command of the SAS. It was once said of him, "When sober, a gentler, more mild-mannered man you could not wish to meet; but when drunk, or in battle, he was frightening!"

An extremely strong case can be made that Paddy Mayne should have been awarded the country's highest award, the Victoria Cross. He was nominated for it on at least two occasions, and many believe that he did not receive his due recognition because of his belligerent attitude to senior officers.

Lewes

Jock Lewes, a seeming opposite of Stirling, was at first extremely reluctant to be recruited, but proved to be an inspirational choice as the new unit's second in command. It was he who devised and instigated the training regime that was so crucial in ensuring that only the right men with the correct skills made it through to operations. Stirling wanted training 'designed to foster discipline, skill, intelligence, courage, fitness, determination'. Lewes earned the men's respect because he never asked them to do something that he was not prepared to do himself.

Jock Lewes lasting contribution to explosives was the invention of the 'sticky' or 'Lewes bomb'. It was a compact, light field incendiary device responsible for the destruction of countless enemy aircraft, fuel dumps, etc.

In a letter home just prior to their first ill-fated mission, he wrote, 'We wait to prove ourselves', and that 'this unit cannot now die, as Layforce died, it is alive and will live gloriously'.

Jock Lewes was killed on operation in the North African desert on the 30th of December 1941. His vehicle was strafed by a Messerschmitt 110, and he was buried in the sand with a soldier's gravestone: a rifle stuck in the sand, with his name scratched on a steel helmet and placed atop.

On the 17th of November 1941, L Detachment's first parachute operation was described by Stirling as 'a complete failure'. However, after that inauspicious debut (which exposed the shortcomings of airborne operations), a fuller collaboration with the Long-Range Desert Group (LRDG) was born; the LRDG being a reconnaissance unit. From then on, vehicles (especially jeeps fitted out with aircraft machine guns) met the unit's transport requirements. Eventually the SAS acquired the necessary desert navigational skills and, together with its own specially modified jeeps, was able to conduct deep-penetration operations. In 1941–1942 the small unit was able to conduct a series of destructive raids against enemy airfields and important logistic points throughout North Africa. There is no denying the data: approximately four hundred Axis planes were put out of action, which was more than the RAF achieved. Paddy Mayne accomplished more enemy aircraft 'kills' than any fighter pilot in the Desert War.

The exploits of the new unit quickly gained notoriety and Adolf Hitler issued his infamous Commando Order of the 18th of October 1942, the *Kommandobefehl*:

> *From now on all men operating against German troops in so-called Commando raids in Europe or in Africa, are to be annihilated to the last man. This is to be carried out whether they be soldiers in uniform, or saboteurs, with or without arms; and whether fighting or seeking to escape; and it is equally immaterial whether they come into action from Ships and Aircraft, or whether they land by parachute. Even if these individuals on discovery make obvious their intention of giving themselves up as prisoners, no pardon is on any account to be given*

This ordered the immediate summary execution, without trial, of any captured enemy soldier found operating in Nazi-occupied territory. A captured SAS officer, Lieutenant John Tonkin, was being transported to the Campobasso headquarters in Italy to be handed over for interrogation when, realising what his destiny was to be, he managed to escape. Later he wrote, 'When a man knows he is going to be shot, it sharpens the mind wonderfully.'

Ken Smith's personal interpretation of Hitler's order was, "These men are dangerous and should be dealt with ruthlessly. If captured, they are to be handed over to the nearest Gestapo unit."

Jellicoe

With the success in the desert, the unit was expanded, allowing it to operate in the Greek islands. This task was led by the 2nd Earl Captain George Jellicoe. Having a father, John Jellicoe, who was the Admiral of the Fleet in the First World War Naval Battle of Jutland and his grave in St Pauls Cathedral; and King George V as his godfather: – this all made young George an extremely influential man. [His fathers bust was unveiled in Trafalgar Square in 1948;]

Captain George Jellicoe was clearly a man of position and authority. Also brave, dashing, intelligent, and somewhat of a ladies' man. He seemed tailor-made for Stirling's unit.

In a memorandum by George of the 1st of January 1941 he stated, 'I consider the Mediterranean basin offers the fullest scope for small scale raiding that has existed in any theatre of war since September 1939. This applies particularly to the Eastern Mediterranean.' He then went on to point out, 'For example, in Yugoslavia and Greece alone forty-eight full Axis divisions are fully occupied by fierce partisan activities. The Axis is forced to deploy at least three times as many divisions in the Balkans as in the whole of North Africa.'

On his first raid on the 13th of June 1942, to the Greek island of Crete, Jellicoe and five others destroyed at least twenty-one planes, two trucks, twelve aircraft engines, several fuel dumps, and a bomb store. In the panic following the explosions, the SAS team simply fell in behind a German patrol and, marching, exited through the camp's main gate, only to slip off and disappear into the night. In another of Jellicoe's famous exploits, on the night of the 9th of

September 1943 he parachuted onto the island of Rhodes to try and negotiate the Italian garrison's peaceful compliance with their country's armistice. Unfortunately, the five thousand Germans on the island had a different idea and took control before any peaceful handover could take place. Jellicoe was forced to hide, under the protection of the Italian Commander, in the Rhodes town citadel.

When in the early 1960s the Profumo Affair hit the headlines, with tales of prostitutes and prominent politicians, Ken Smith said, "I bet George is involved in that." There is no record of this being the case. In 1973 George did admit to having 'some casual affairs with call girls'. He then promptly resigned from the government. It would appear he did have a weakness: it was for the ladies. Ken always thought of George as "a bit of a ladies' man". A quote from one of Jellicoe's good friends said, 'He spent some time as a small boy in New Zealand where his father was Governor General. George wanted to become a wolf cub, but no pack was available, so instead he joined the Brownies. He got on very well with them.'

George Jellicoe had an extremely illustrious career, being:

The last First Lord of the Admiralty.
Made a knight of the British Empire in 1986.
Leader of the House of Lords, becoming a life peer in 1999.
For some time, the longest-serving member of the House of Lords.
Arguably the longest-serving parliamentarian in the world.
Lord Keeper of the Privy Seal.
Chairman, president, chancellor and/or fellow of numerous institutions and charities.

It was Jellicoe who conducted Ken's final interview for his SBS selection. It turned out that George was well acquainted with Portsmouth and even knew Ken's old headmaster. In later years, as the number of World War II veterans decreased, at the annual reunions Ken would find himself seated on a top table alongside George, where the pair would engage in deep conversation, often accompanied by loud outbursts of raucous laughter. Ken's family were largely unaware that he was a personal acquaintance of one so distinguished, and how he must have been held in high regard to be afforded such a privilege.

As a footnote, Ken and his friend Ralph Bridger always maintained, "We had the best officers in the world."

One of the incidents that played a crucial part in the expansion – indeed, very survival – of the unit was the second raid into Benghazi, Libya on the 21st–22nd May 1942. Military-wise the incursion into Rommel's Afrika Korps' most important supply port was a failure. There were, however, very important side effects. The lessons learnt from a succession of encounters with enemy guards and the ability to brazenly bluff your way through checkpoints became often-used tactics. But perhaps most importantly, the SBS gained a very important admirer whilst adding to their growing reputation.

David Stirling, either by design or by good fortune, had the ability to attract some powerful and influential people. One in particular, Randolph Churchill, the son of Britain's wartime leader, the Prime Minister Winston Churchill. Randolph ended up tagging along on the SAS operation. On the 24th of July 1942 a ten-page private letter was sent to Winston Churchill from his son. The existence of L Detachment had now been thrust into the Prime Minister's consciousness. The letter was exaggerated and boastful in parts, but largely accurate. Winston would often tell the tale after dinner of how a unit of the British Army had brazenly gained entry to and egress from Benghazi, hundreds of miles behind enemy lines;

spent two nights touring the port and a full day in a bombed-out abandoned building next door to a German HQ; had numerous encounters with enemy guards (which were successfully bluffed); and their leader (David Stirling) had taken the time for a cooling daylight swim in the harbour. Oh yes – and they even had the gall to fix their broken-down car on a busy road in the middle of town. It was only by a series of chances and accidents that young Randolph was there, and then promoted from observer to participant as part of the six-man squad. Shortly after returning to Cairo, Randolph was injured in a car accident and returned home to the UK. But his sole escapade with the SAS and subsequent letter home had gained the unit a very important admirer.

On the 8th of August 1942 David Stirling was invited to a private dinner with the Prime Minister at the British Embassy in Cairo, almost certainly as a direct result of Randolph's exuberant letter. Stirling borrowed his brother's dinner jacket and prepared to dine with not only the Prime Minister, but General Alexander (commander-in-chief Middle Eastern forces) and the South African Prime Minister, Field Marshal Jan Smuts. Also present at the table was another SAS officer, Fitzroy Maclean, of whom Churchill is reputed to have said, "Is this the young man who used the mother of parliaments as a public convenience?"!

Fitzroy Hew Royle Maclean was a career diplomat before the war, and therefore classed as being in a 'reserved occupation'. He was forbidden to leave his official post and therefore unable to enlist. His solution was to stand for Parliament and win a by-election in Lancaster, necessitating his resignation from the Foreign Office. He then promptly joined the Cameron Highlanders as a private and was deployed to North Africa, by which time he had been promoted from the ranks and was serving as a commissioned officer. There he met Stirling, who suggested he join the SAS.

"What is it?" Maclean enquired.

Stirling answered, "A good thing to be in."

Maclean thought for a moment, then said, "It sounds promising. I should be delighted to join."

After dinner, despite instructions not to do so, Stirling briefed and outlined his plans for the SAS. Then before leaving he asked for, and was granted, the autographs of Churchill, Smuts and Alexander on a folded napkin. He later unfolded the napkin and typed the words, 'Please give the bearer of this note every possible assistance.' The following day he was summoned back to the embassy for further discussions with Sir Leslie Rowan, Churchill's private secretary. Stirling had hurriedly knocked out a two-page memo, headed 'Top Secret', outlining what should be done to concentrate and coordinate the work he was doing:

> *All existing Special Service units in the Middle East to be disbanded and selected personnel absorbed as required, by 'L' detachment; Control to rest with the officer commanding 'L' detachment and not with any outside body; The planning of operations to remain as hitherto the prerogative of 'L' detachment.*

Basically, Stirling proposed to take over all special forces and the running of operations. It worked! Stirling had somehow managed to circumvent the establishment and fulfil his ambition, now largely free from interference and in possession of the 'signed note' which afforded them the stores and equipment needed to carry out his grand plan.

On the 21st of September 1942, Order 14521 was issued, expanding the SAS. L Detachment 'has had conspicuous success and morale is high,' read the official citation. The first new regiment in the British Army since the Boer War came into being, split into four parts: A and B Squadrons under Mayne and Stirling respectively; C, the French squadron; and D, the Special Boat Section under Jellicoe, which included Layforce's surviving Folbot Troop. On the 13th of May 1943 there was further expansion as the 2nd SAS Regiment was formed in Algeria under the command of David Stirling's elder brother Bill. A unit of Greek soldiers named after the Sacred Band of Thebes, the Greek Sacred Squadron, was also under Stirling's command. They were regarded as tough fighters and would prove invaluable in the liberation of Greece.

The initials 'SBS' can be misleading, for the last 'S' represents either 'Section', 'Squadron' or 'Service'. There were, it seems, two separate units operating in the British armed forces with the same initials at the same time: Roger Courtney's Section (beach recce and sabotage), and Jellicoe's Squadron/Service (small-scale assault raiding).

Following David Stirling's capture, in January 1943, the regiment was again restructured.

19th March 1943, D Squadron 1st SAS becoming the Special Boat Squadron under Jellicoe.

The Special Raiding Squadron (SRS) operated under Mayne. The SBS, approximately 250 strong, relocated to near Haifa, Palestine. The SRS (three hundred to 350) followed them to a separate camp nearby. In November 1943 the Special Boat Squadron were rechristened the Special Boat Service. When the SBS was reformed sometime after the end of the Second World War, it became a wholly Royal Marine venture, whereas the wartime unit was an army unit and open to volunteers from all branches of the British armed forces. In the early 2000s it again became open to all service personnel.

The first time the SAS and SBS were combined was for a raid on the port of Bouerat, North Africa in early 1942. Two members of the RN Folbot Section accompanied the SAS with the intent of sabotaging shipping in the harbour. Folbots (collapsible canoes made of canvas with bamboo poles) were included for this purpose. Unfortunately, the craft were wrecked when the vehicle struck a pothole only a few miles from the target, the port being some five hundred miles behind enemy lines. By the time the raiding party arrived the war had moved on: Rommel had retaken Benghazi, and this was now his principal port, making Bouerat redundant, and it was therefore empty of shipping.

The following dates are taken from the user guide for the official roll of honour compiled by Soldier X, QGM, 22 SAS:

6th January 1943: D Squadron, 1st SAS forms from No. 1 Special Boat Section which has already been attached to 1st SAS in its entirety and is augmented by reinforcements from Cyprus. Many continue to refer to this larger formation as No. 1 Special Boat Section. Captain Tommy Langton assumes command until the 12th, when Captain Earl George Jellicoe, DSO, returns from the UK and takes over (WO 218/97, National Archives).

19th March 1943: Special Boat Squadron forms from D Squadron as part of raiding forces (1st SAS Regiment). It comprises of L, M and S Detachments based at Atlit on the Palestinian coast (WO 218/97, WO 218/98 and WO 218/99).

12th September 1943: SBS deploys to the Aegean (WO 201/818). End of June to the beginning of July 1944: Unit expands into the Special Boat Service (1st SAS), comprising of squadrons in place of detachments (WO 204/8473).

August 1944: SBS begins to deploy to Italy for operations in the Adriatic and on the Greek mainland. It is based at Monte Sant'Angelo on the Gargano Peninsula, not far from the LRDG (WO 201/802).

30th July 1945: M, L and S Squadrons cease to exist (WO 170/7529).

15th August 1945: SBS (1st SAS) officially disbands (WO 170/7529).

The Special Boat Section was an army formation, not a Royal Marine one.

6

FOLBOT

Nothing like it; That's like the Queen Mary compared to the things we used to have.

Anyone who has raced canoes in the UK will have undoubtedly heard the name Hasler. With categories for all ages and levels of ability, British Canoeing's annual marathon series is named after him.

Lieutenant Colonel Herbert George 'Blondie' Hasler was, like Ken Smith, raised in Southsea, Portsmouth. As a Royal Marine officer, he founded the Royal Marine Boom Patrol Detachment (RMBPD); named to disguise the unit's true purpose and famed for Operation Frankton. On the 7th of December 1942, six canoes (Folbots) were dropped by the submarine HMS *Tuna* off the Gironde Estuary in France. Their task was to paddle up the river to Bordeaux (a distance of seventy miles) and mine enemy shipping anchored there. Fast ships operating out of the harbour were 'blockade running' to Japan. By the night of the 12th of December only two canoes had made it. They successfully mined six ships, sinking one and disabling the others. Blondie Hasler and a marine named Bill Sparks were the sole survivors. The 1955 feature film

The Cockleshell Heroes celebrates this legendary feat, which has been described as 'possibly the toughest special forces mission of the war'.

Blondie Hasler, together with a Captain Montanaro and Major Roger 'Jumbo' Courtney, played a crucial role in the development of the Folbot (folding boat). These three men came up with the following criteria for their invention: it was to take a maximum load of two thirteen-stone men and one hundredweight of cargo (total 476 pounds); to weigh between seventy and a hundred pounds; to travel at speeds of three to five knots, depending on load and weather; to be able to withstand a wind of force four in the open sea and being beached through surf; to have a skin that could withstand constant grounding on shingle and working alongside other vessels; to measure around sixteen feet; and to have a width that could satisfy both stability and the ability to get out of a submarine's forward torpedo hatch. They also agreed that the boat needed to be 'partially collapsible', but with no 'loose parts' and 'capable of complete assembly in thirty seconds in the dark'. Its draught was to be not less than four inches or more than six inches when loaded.

In 2011 about forty SAS World War II veterans were guests at the Hereford SAS base for the unveiling of a memorial to honour the fallen. As part of the event there was an exhibition of present-day equipment. Ken and Ralph spent some time at the display dedicated to water capability. A proud sergeant was only too pleased to interact with the two old stagers, commenting on how the Folbot had "not changed" since their day. Politely, the pair nodded in agreement, but once out of earshot they turned to each other and said, "Nothing like it" and "That's like the *Queen Mary* compared to the things we used to have!"

Believed to be Port Deremen, Turkey.

Folbot.

Ken; Sticks; Bill paddling a three-man Folbot.

About to start a race during training. Ken in black swimmers slightly leaning forward.

Training with a Carley Float.

7

SELECTION AND TRAINING

"Anything to get off the bloody boats."

The crowded harbour at Alexandria was overflowing with moored ships displaying visible signs of fierce conflict. Many were in urgent need of repair. It was all too obvious how fierce the war at sea had become. In Alex the *Penelope*'s senior Royal Marine NCO, Sergeant Major Robinson, called Ken over and said, "You're keen to get off the ships. They're after volunteers for this mob, but I don't think you'll get in; they're supposed to be something special!"

"Put me down for it," replied Ken. "Anything to get off the bloody boats."

He was shown a notice attached to the bulkhead. It read, 'Volunteers required for hazardous duties with small boat skills… Special service of a hazardous nature.'

The ship's captain was reluctant to lose any of his crew, especially a QR3 qualified gun captain, but Ken was desperate to leave. He had volunteered on several occasions for postings that would get him off the ships; even as an air gunner, widely considered one of the most dangerous jobs in the military. Every marine on board the *Penelope* volunteered for the SAS but only four made it through the interviews: Bill Mayall, Tommy Tucker, Albert 'Sticks' May and Ken Smith. Sticks was on fatigues, (military punishment), at the time for being 'bolshie' and by all accounts the captain was only too glad to see the back of him.

Ken always maintained that SAS selection saved his life. "The ships were going down all the time" with massive loss of life. His date of discharge from HMS *Penelope* is recorded as the 31st of October 1943. He and the others set off for training/selection not knowing what they had volunteered for, but thankful to be off the ships and on dry land.

> *People would rather die than think. Many of them do.*
> (Philosopher Bertrand Russell.
> A paraphrased quote used to start lectures to new SBS recruits, 1943.)

Following the Italian surrender on the 3rd of September 1943, the Greek Dodecanese Islands had briefly been occupied by a mixed collection of British forces which included the SBS. However, a strong German garrison remained on Rhodes and Crete, and together with (largely coerced) Italian troops they dominated the Aegean theatre. A German offensive, Operation Eisbär (Polar Bear), was launched on the 3rd of October to retake the Greek islands. By late November, after some fierce resistance and with no aircraft cover, the British were driven out. Survivors made their way back to Allied lines through neutral Turkey and Syria.

In April 1943 the SAS had left their base at Kabrit, Egypt for a new base south of Haifa, Palestine. The SBS were upgraded from a section to a squadron, under Major George Jellicoe, and relocated to Atlit, approximately eight miles south of the city. It was by all accounts a pleasant bay, approximately one mile wide, with a ruined crusader castle at one end. The Special Raiding Squadron

Selection and Training

(SRS) under Paddy Mayne were based a few miles north of Atlit at Azzib. Inter-unit rivalry was fostered with football, boxing, etc., adding some relief to the tough training regime. Anyone failing to make the grade was RTU'ed (returned to unit).

The SBS was formed into three squadrons, L, M and S, the initials standing for the surnames of the three commanders: Tommy Langton, Fitzroy Maclean and David Sutherland. Each squadron was then divided into four patrols (later increased to five) of ten men. Each of the twelve patrols was allocated at least one signaller. Sutherland's second in command, Milner Barry, was responsible for new recruit training. 'Volunteers For Hazardous Duties' had netted an initial batch of thirty-seven Royal Marines from hundreds of applicants. Milner Barry, upon finding that they were not infantry men, commented in his diary, 'They seem to be a cheerful lot of chaps and goodish specimens physically. They also appear too well disciplined, at the moment, for SBS troopers.' These initial thirty-seven marine recruits included Ken Smith, Tommy Tucker, Bill Mayall and Albert 'Sticks' May, all from HMS *Penelope*. Ken 'Scouse' Joynson (from Liverpool) and Jim Horsefield also joined from HMS *Dido*. Jim was a marine King's Badge Man, and both Ken and Sticks were marine Diamonds. The navy were reluctant to release marines, but an order had been issued overriding their opposition. At about the same time a new officer, Lieutenant James 'Jimmy' or 'Tansy' Lees, also arrived at the unit. By the 13th of November all were undergoing intense training at Atlit.

The request for volunteers had stipulated that 'small boat skills' were required. This well suited the marines. At his initial interview Ken remembered being asked if he could "swim two miles and speak a foreign language. I could swim long distances and I'd picked up a little bit of French in Algiers." Those that knew Ken will testify to his ability to destroy the French language, and in fact any foreign language he attempted! But he also credited "winning the Mediterranean Mile (at the athletics championships in Tunis) and my knowledge of explosives" with helping to get him through.

Following a successful interview, the new recruits caught a train from Cairo bound for Haifa. Ken believed that he was one of twenty that made it through the interview stage and on to selection out of a few hundred. A Sergeant Pat Scully escorted them on board the train and, as it slowly pulled out of the city, he gave the marines a knowing look, saying, "we had too much kit and we wouldn't need it where we were going". He then proceeded to "toss a few items out of the window. We followed suit: we threw most of our kit out of the train windows. It was funny to see Arab children running alongside the train with (far too big) pith helmets on. By the time we got to Haifa we had our toothbrushes, underwear and a rifle," said Ken.

The new recruits were picked up from the station by the unit's solitary truck for transportation to Atlit Camp; this being somewhat of a grand description of a few tents and a small concrete drill area. Ken recalled, "We were told they weren't quite ready for us, given a few quid [pounds], and told to lose ourselves for a few days. So, a lot of us went off to Jerusalem."

At camp they initially, "slept under the stars until a few more tents arrived," said Ken. Milner Barry noted in his diary, 'Rather a busy morning. Marines on map reading and shooting again, in the afternoon, basketball.' The training became ever more intense. "Every morning, we were swimming." Also, "forced marches with heavy loads, shooting, map-reading, languages – very concentrated and everything you could think of," recalled Ken. The training culminated in the infamous forty-five-mile heavy-load march from Atlit to the shores of Lake Tiberias. "I was on my hands and knees at the end, crawling to Tiberias in the dark," said Ken "I was

Selection and Training

so determined to make the unit, and I did. We also did a lot of canoeing on the Sea of Galilee, getting dropped off a couple of miles out to sea and told to swim back, small arms, parachuting, explosives, etc." All the time the recruits' fitness and endurance levels were being increased. Ken was "loving it, as most days we got to play football".

After a few weeks the truck pulled in with more new marine recruits. Ken was first to the vehicle and as the rear tarpaulin was drawn back, he called out, "Any of you play football?"

Ralph Bridger was one of the recruits. Pointing to another, Ray Iggleden, he said, "He played for Leeds United, and I was in Shoreham's side as goalkeeper."

"Quick, grab your kit and put it in that tent. You're in the Marine Patrol," said Ken. He was starting to form a useful team. H Patrol, as the Marine Patrol was officially known, was by now under the command of Lieutenant 'Tansy' Lees.

On the 26th of November Jellicoe arrived at Atlit, followed over the next few days by the SBS survivors from the initial Dodecanese campaign. He was heartened to see how well the expanding unit had developed and determined to start concerted operations in the New Year.

One of Ken's fondest memories, that he would often recall, occurred whilst at Atlit. He was rostered for camp guard. "We weren't big on drill and bull," reflected Ken. "Tansy called me over and said we had some bigwigs coming over to see what's going on. He asked me to muster up a squad and put on a guard for their arrival. So, I went around the tents and managed to get together a guard squad. I explained to them what was to happen." They were to form a line on the edge of the parade ground (the basketball court) and, on the given order, come to attention, march forward a dozen or so paces, halt, dress to the right (i.e. turn the head right, raise a straight right arm to touch the shoulder of the next man, and if necessary shuffle into a straight line), smartly come back to the attention, and then stand at ease. All extremely straightforward for seasoned soldiers. At the due time they formed a line at the edge of the small concrete parade ground. "It was a mishmash of troops. Jocks, Durham Light Infantry, Guards, London Rifles, Marines, East Kent. At the appropriate time I gave the order: 'On your right marker, fall in.' I couldn't believe what I saw."

The guardsman gave a display worthy of being on duty at the gates of Buckingham Palace, smartly coming to attention by bringing his knee up almost to his chest before slamming his foot into the ground and then striding out in the very best guards regimental style across the concrete pad to halt, right-dress, and stand at ease. The problem was that by the time he set off the man from the Durham Light Infantry, who march at twice the pace of the guards, had already arrived and was stood at ease. The squad had all undertaken the order in the manner instilled in them during their different regiments' basic training. Unfortunately, the British Army does not have a common uniform drill code amongst its many regiments, and as a direct consequence of this the result was a scattering of squaddies all arriving at separate times and by different methods. Finally, the drawn-out spectacle came to an end, by which time, Ken said, "I was bursting to laugh out loud and had tears running down my face. Desperately I tried to compose myself, and after taking a few moments I turned to face Tansy and reported, 'Guard ready for duty, sir.' Tansy was if anything in a worse state, shaking and hopelessly trying to suppress his laughter, with tears pouring down his face. There was never any mention of how impressed the bigwigs were."

Whilst on about drilling, Ralph remembered when a Sergeant Major Reilly of the Irish Guards decided to instigate some parade-

Selection and Training

ground discipline. He formed the men up (who had only recently returned from operations; they were unshaven and sporting long hair) for inspection. In best drill instructor tradition, he stood in front of one trooper, his face barely inches from that of the poor soldier about to be the recipient of a severe dressing-down. "Am I hurting you?" he snarled. "I should be, I'm standing on your hair."

Jellicoe called the sergeant major up and told him in no uncertain terms, "Don't you ever parade those men again." The military training was to be to the very highest of standards, but drill was the exception.

One training exercise undertaken was set in the nearby salt pans. Seawater is allowed to flood a large, flat area, several football pitches in size, and then evaporate. When dried out by the heat of the sun the resulting salt residue is collected in large mounds. The process is repeated, eventually resulting in a prominent feature on the landscape. One exceptionally large salt pile, resembling a small hill, had been selected. On a bright moonlit night this became the target for the troops to try and make it too unobserved. After dark, the trainees set off. Ken thought he knew a good route, and for several hours on his belly he inched his way forward. Often, he heard the challenge as one by one his comrades were discovered. Eventually, seeing no way through, he reversed his route and when out of sight sought another approach. Throughout the night he stealthily repeated the procedure several times from differing angles, always with the same result. On a couple of occasions, he came unbearably close, only to spot an alert sentry, sometimes witnessing the discovery of a colleague. Finally, just as dawn was about to break, he made it and triumphantly stood up, only to discover that he was alone. It was believed that everyone had been 'captured', the exercise had ended, and all had returned to base. By the time he made it back to camp they were finishing off breakfast. He was treated to a chorus of comments such as "What have you been up to all night?", and "Did you fall asleep?"

Official records show that Royal Marine POX 4898, Kenneth Herbert Smith, was recruited into the 1st SBS/1st SAS on the 1st of November 1943. He served with this unit until the 12th of June 1945, when he was discharged back into the marines and took passage back to the UK from Italy. During his time with the SBS he successfully completed the following courses in Palestine in October, November and December 1943:

Schmeisser and Luger, Nahariya.	Palestine
Folbot (collapsible canoe), Atlit.	:
Parachute, Ramat David.	:
Pistol and close combat, Jerusalem.	:
Saboteuring and explosives, Nahariy.	:
Winter camp and revision, Tiberias.	:

Also:
Sniping and camouflage, Cairo, Egypt, 12th January 1944.
Skiing, LaCeres, Lebanon/Syria, 27th February – 31st March.

Ken came top of the class in the small weapons course (Schmeisser and Luger), and this was the reason why he made selection for the New Zealand-run sniping school near Cairo.

At the start of 1944 the Germans were in a strong position in the Aegean. They had been reinforced, received a small fleet of vessels for transport/resupply, and had complete air superiority. Maintaining a division on Rhodes, they deployed four thousand troops to Leros, two thousand to Samos, eight hundred to Scarpanto, two hundred to Stampalia, and 150 apiece to both

Simi and Piscopi. They also deployed a force to randomly garrison islands for limited periods of time. The British soon learned of the enemy's strategy and 'it was decided upon that the SBS, working in constant rotation, would restart operations, with the intention of making the German occupation as disagreeable and painful as possible'. Or, as Ken put it, "They thought they were going on holiday. We gave them some bloody holiday!"

On the 15th of January 1944 the *Tewfik*, a 180-ton schooner best described, by many of the troops, as an 'ugly old tub', sailed for the forward operating base, Degirmen Buku, in Turkish waters at the head of Bodrum Bay; known to the SBS as Port Deremen and today as English Harbour. Nowadays it even has a German bar in which most drinkers are unaware of its wartime history. On the 1st of February 1944 the SBS again started raiding the Greek islands, transported by the Levant Schooner Flotilla (LSF). This Royal Navy unit consisted of motorboats, Greek caiques and fishing boats. The neutral Turks turned a blind eye to the British presence on the understanding that they choose a 'really deserted spot'. Port Deremen fitted that description and benefited from a small freshwater stream. Occasionally a Turkish border guard would approach and receive some cigarettes or the like. On the 10th of March 1944 'Jimmy' Lees and twenty-four other ranks arrived for their turn at harassing the enemy. The SBS had departed from Beirut, Lebanon, then transited via an isolated base on the only Allied-held Greek Dodecanese Island, Castlerosso/ Kastellorizo, before covertly transferring to Port Deremen. H Patrol were about to embark upon active duties.

The campaign in Italy, fought by British and American forces, was to become a long, drawn-out affair. During this time the Greeks, the Albanians and the Yugoslavs (under Tito) were fighting what has been described as one of the bloodiest series of guerrilla campaigns of the Second World War. The SBS were added to this theatre with the intent of causing as much mayhem as possible.

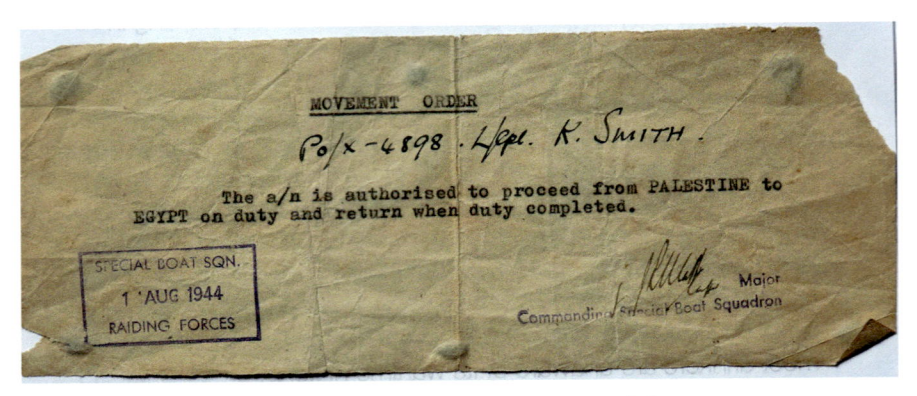

SBS pass to go on snipping course in Cairo.

8

FURTHER TRAINING

"Three matelots hitching a lift in the middle of the bleeding desert."

Ken must have been an exceptional shot as he was selected to attend a sniper school run by New Zealanders just outside Cairo. This was situated close to the Great Pyramids, with the range butts being the Sphinx! Upon successful completion of the course he was issued with a specialist rifle, zeroed in to his eyesight. It came in its own protective case. There were very few of these weapons in the British forces. Its value and importance were stressed upon him, and he was required to sign a lengthy document before being entrusted with its care. All understood snipers were particularly loathed by front-line troops and no mercy could be expected if captured in possession of such a weapon.

Prior to leaving for the sniping course, he was approached by a group of SAS recruits who had just passed the parachute course and asked if he would pick up eight embroidered parachute wings badges. These cost a tanner (sixpence) each. The recruits would now be entitled to wear their 'SAS wings' on their upper right arm. The embroidered badges had reputedly been designed by Jock Lewes and company whilst sipping cocktails in the bar of the King David Hotel, Cairo, a much-favoured officers' hang-out. Their initial sketch, on a napkin, had been taken across the road to an Arab tailor's shop. The tailor's version of a bird wing had a distinctly Egyptian look. Upon Ken's return to base all those that had placed an order had moved on and he now found himself out of pocket to the tune of four shillings, which he was none too pleased about. Much later in life he would bring out a small packet of pristine badges, unique to that period of the war, still bemoaning his financial loss.

> *The present wings have upturned ends, but wartime was flat, even the very early ones. There is a whole myth about locally produced odd, shaped wings, mainly to prop up the fake market (collectors have an agenda). The tailor shop in Cairo was a sub-office of a respected London tailor who produced very high-quality items, so much so that they are better quality than the 1944 versions made in the UK.*
>
> Author of *The SAS and LRDG Roll of Honour, 1941–47*

Ken was in the rear truck of three travelling through the Palestine desert. They were on their way to the Syrian mountains for ski and mountain warfare training. For some reason the small convoy stopped, and he stuck his head out to see why. "Here, you'll never believe this," he said. "There are three matelots [sailors] hitching a lift in the middle of the bleeding desert!"

Jellicoe, who was in the passenger seat of the front truck, told the sailors to jump up in the last vehicle. Next thing Ken was aware of was a pair of hands appearing on his tailgate. Leaning over to give a hand, he pulled back in shock.

"What are you doing here?" both men said in unison, as Eric Hills' head came into view.

Eric was on the *Manchester* with Ken and on the ship's football team, playing on the left wing with instructions from the sergeant major to "Put it on Smithy's head and he will frighten anybody." (Eric said, "And I did, and he did.") The pair had not seen each other since being discharged at Portsmouth. Soon they were locked in avid conversation. Eric explained that following a spot of leave in Jerusalem they had made their way to Bethlehem and were now trying to make it back to base in Beirut. He was now crewing small boats as part of the Levant Squadron, the SBS 'taxi service'.

H Patrol undertook ski training at 'Cedars' in Lebanon for what most considered a suicide mission; fortunately, it was cancelled at the last minute. They were intended to form part of a small task force assembled to parachute onto the Brenner Pass in northern Italy. All were volunteers; their mission: to kill or capture Otto Skorzeny, the legendary leader of the elite German Brandenburg troops. These fanatical soldiers were considered an equal of the SAS. Otto was billeted in a *Schloss* (castle), surrounded by about two hundred of his troops. He had been responsible for the daring rescue of Benito Mussolini, the Italian Fascist dictator. Rumour had it that the mission was dreamt up as a form of one-upmanship.

To prepare for the operation the volunteers were taken high up into the mountains above Damascus, Syria, and taught to ski. "On a clear day you could see people swimming in the Sea of Galilee." Their instructor was an Austrian Jew who had represented his country at the Olympic Games. He had different-coloured eyepieces in his snow goggles which enabled him to pick out any changes in snow conditions. Most of the troops hated skiing but Ken "loved it".

As there were no ski lifts on these hills, many hours of uphill effort were required before the exhilaration of flying down the slopes could be experienced. Even at the end of a gruelling day's training

Ken would go out on his own onto the "crisp snow glistening in the moonlight" to have another run down the slopes. Towards the end of the training camp a downhill race was organised which was seeded allowing the slowest to set off first. The course was well known to the participants, who had all skied it many times. Halfway down there was a pinch point: a narrow gap with a small drop. It was anticipated that some of the weaker competitors would fall and create a 'logjam', making it essential to arrive early. Ken was the last to set off and threw himself down the slope at a frantic pace in a desperate attempt to arrive before any snarl-up. Despite his best endeavours he arrived at the choke point too late. A couple of men, having crashed, were in the process of picking themselves up and trying to extricate themselves from the tangle. Ken did not let up and flew over them. According to Sticks he "almost took the head off" one of his rising comrades. In Ken's words, "I won by miles."

Ken eventually did pay for his recklessness, having gone out for one of his solo skis. Racing down the hill at breakneck speed, he lost control, crashing and "tumbling over and over" for what seemed an eternity. "I thought it would never end," said Ken. Eventually he came to rest and was relieved to find himself still alive. *Good*, he thought, first managing to move one arm, then the other. Next one leg… but just as he was thinking, *I've got away with it*, upon trying to move his left leg he cried out in pain. His ankle had been damaged – luckily it was not broken, but badly sprained. Months later, on the long trek through Albania it was to cause him much aggravation.

The instructor skied up to him, coming to an abrupt halt, and shouted at Ken in broken, guttural English, "You silly bloody fool – you could have killed your bloody self!"

Further Training

*Parachute Jump School, Egypt.
Back row: Capt. James Lees; 3rd left, Clr. Sgt. Horsefield; 2nd from right, Marine Smith, no hat.*

SBS training, Palestine. Formation of 'M' Squadron showing some of 'H' Patrol: Marine Smith, Kneeling in centre; Marine Tucker, right foreground; Marine Joynson above Smith's left shoulder.

On board base ship Levant Schooner 'Tewfik' moored in neutral Turkish waters. Part of 'M' Squadron showing some of its members resting after a raid on the island of Cos in the Aegean, pictured L to R:
Army Sgt. Not known; Marine Tucker; Marine May; Marine Mayall; Marine Hughes; Full face centre, Marine Smith; Sitting in front, Clr. Sgt. Horsefield; above army private, not known; top right, Marine Joynson.

The 'Tewfik', Port Deremen, Turkey; now known as English Harbour.

Eric Hills and Ken Smith, Beirut.

9

THE GREEK ISLANDS

"Should've let go."

From early March 1944 H Patrol started operating in the Dodecanese Islands. A system of rotation was employed so that patrols were almost constantly being deployed. Initially the raids were restricted to specific Dodecanese Islands before being allowed to expand out into the Cyclades and Northern Sporades, and eventually all islands were considered legitimate targets. Many tributes have been paid to the Allies operating in the Greek islands, whether they be raiding forces, agents or Greek partisans, and one in particular is gratifying to those concerned. Captured German orders from Mykonos include the sentence '*Wir benfinden nuns in feindesland*' written across the middle page of security instructions. A rough translation is 'We are living in an enemy country.' In May 1944 the Germans posted an additional four thousand soldiers to the Aegean Islands, at a time when they were desperately needed elsewhere. This, just prior to the Normandy landings, helps to demonstrate how effective the Allied strategy in the area was.

By this time the squadron was operating as far as the Northern Sporades. The *Tewfik* served as HQ. Another schooner, the

Takiarkis, was tied up alongside and used as troop accommodation. Below decks the boat was fitted out with a tight series of sleeping racks. It was an airless place with a pervasive sweaty odour, so the men usually preferred to sleep out on the open deck. The days were spent cooking, eating, reading, taking a cooling swim and generally resting up. However, those days were infrequent as most of the time, when based at Port Deremen, the raiders were either being briefed, gearing up, away on recce, raiding, debriefing, cleaning gear or checking weapons.

Ken was once asked by a present-day serving SAS operative, "How many raids did you do?"

"Hundreds," came the swift reply. "We were always on raids."

Ralph Bridger was once told by Sticks that they "did at least thirty-six on the Greek islands". Records have the unit as having undertaken 381 raids on some seventy islands in the Aegean from October 1943 to mid-December 1944.

Ken would often tell (and repeat) short stories about his time raiding in the Greek islands. Some of his tales were short; no more than a few sentences as specific memories came to mind. What follows is at times a disjointed collection of his reminiscences, much as he would have told them. Also included are a couple of Ralph's tales, and one about Lieutenant Bob Bury and John McPherson (a sergeant from the Jock Patrol and a good friend of Ken's). Their story is one that helps to illustrate the ambiguity of war, how cruel fate can be, and how special the men were who volunteered for SAS duty.

One sortie Ken would often recall was a ten-man mission to the island of Kalymnos/Calino. It was meant to be a reconnaissance patrol. They had only just returned from Calchie and were immediately turned around.

The assignment had an ominous start when the radio battery was lost. The landing took place, as usual, in darkness onto a rocky shoreline and in rough conditions. "We always chose to land at the most impossible places where we would be least expected and there were likely to be no guards," said Ken. Another Smith, 'Smudger', was passing the battery to Ken. It was windy and the sea was rough. Believing that Ken had hold, he let go, and it disappeared into the depths. With no radio communications the backup plan would be instigated: a prearranged pickup schedule would be activated for some days later.

From the rocky shoreline they had to negotiate a sheer cliff. Halfway up, the stitching went on one of Ken's boots. He had on a brand-new pair of parachute boots. The sharp rocks appeared to have severed the stitching and the sole was flapping around. With a heavily loaded pack on his back, it was impossible to climb any further and he was in danger of falling off the cliff face. Somehow, he managed to get the pack off, take the lace out of the damaged boot and use it to tie the boot on. He said, "I don't know how I got up."

At the top of the cliff the patrol found an old shepherds' cave in which they could base themselves. Each day, in small groups of two or three, they would be dispatched to various locations. The groups would be rotated each day to have fresh eyes and it was unlikely that the same observation post (OP) would be reused. This minimised the chances of missing anything. The procedure was to note down every detail, no matter how trivial, so that a clear picture of what was taking place on the island could be formulated. The teams would depart in darkness to be in position at sunrise.

Ken had been teamed up with his good friends Sticks May and Bill Mayall. On the first day their group was dispatched to observe Varty, a small harbour with a known German garrison. They managed to get an excellent position extremely close to the harbour, and from there they were able to note down much: queuing for breakfast, comings and goings, gun positions, changing of guards, dispatch riders, transport movements, and even the swimming in the bay. They watched and noted down everything until dark, then stealthily withdrew, making their way back to the cave. The various reports were collated and OPs for the following day allocated.

Early the next day, Ken's party departed for a different location. Just before dawn, and only a short distance from the objective (overlooking the little village of Correo), gunfire was heard coming from the direction of the previous day's OP. Quickly all relevant details were noted: the number and type of shots, direction, estimated distance, time, etc. Ken remembered writing down, 'Seventeen shots, easterly direction.' At that time the group were crossing a small, flat area with a road bisecting it; the chosen location for their OP being on the far side of the road amongst a group of large boulders. They were forced to wait for a shepherd girl to move on. This prevented the party from gaining the sanctuary of the lookout. Following the shots, the road "came alive with traffic". To remain unobserved the trio were forced to take cover behind a large rock. Although hidden from the road they were in open ground and exposed to the sun, it rose and began to beat down mercilessly on the now-trapped marines. There was no opportunity to seek a more sheltered location as the traffic stayed busy all day. Sticks, with his fair complexion, suffered badly.

Finally, the sun set and with the cover of darkness they were able to retrace their steps back up the steep slope to collapse, exhausted, on a narrow track near the top. Sticks could go no further; the precious water supply had long ago been consumed. So, leaving Sticks, Ken and Bill set off to replenish the team's three Italian water bottles. The group had passed a well not too distant from their location that morning. Making their way to the well, the pair discovered that there was no rope or bucket. A couple of small pebbles were dropped down the well to confirm the presence of water. Hearing the faint sound of splashes far below lifted their mood. Suspending a bottle from the end of their joined lanyards proved way too short. The line was gradually extended by adding items of clothing – shirt to shirt to trouser leg, etc. – until the pair were stripped naked. Even this proved to be insufficient. Eventually Bill himself was added to the length, and by suspending him by his ankles and bobbing him up and down, far below the faint, distant *gurgle-gurgle* of water entering the bottle could be heard. Quickly the flask was retrieved and immediately poured over their heads, only then did they take a drink. "We were so thirsty it felt like energy surging back into the body," said Ken. Ever since then he would often remark on how precious water was, "to sip and savour the taste". When the pair met up after the war and they relived the experience, Ken would always finish off with the remark, "Should 'ave let go!" The procedure was quickly mastered and repeated several times until they were sated and the containers full. On returning to Sticks, he did likewise, pouring the water first over his head before gulping down a drink and ravenously taking his fill. This brought on an almost miraculous recovery, and soon the group were able to set off for the sanctuary of the cave.

They had only made it a short way before exhaustion swept over them, forcing a temporary rest stop. The trio instantly fell asleep on the pathway. Anyone taking that track would have fallen over them in the dark. The cold eventually woke the group up and still shattered, they set off. Normally villages and habitation were skirted but they were far too drained for the lengthy route, instead opting to make a beeline for the refuge, "straight back through a village". Luckily, they were not spotted, although a couple of dogs did start barking. Upon arrival back at where the cave was thought to be, there was no sign of it. They proceeded past the spot only to retrace their route back to the believed whereabouts of the hiding place. Confused and disorientated, with hushed whistles and whispers they called out.

Suddenly a bush was drawn back, and a voice urgently whispered, "Quick, in here." The cave entrance had been expertly camouflaged. From the hidden grotto the rest of the patrol had watched the Germans searching the surrounding mountains all day. It transpired that a group led by Sergeant Jim Horsefield, which included Ralph Bridger and Ray Iggleden, had just arrived at their OP: coincidentally, the location watched on the previous day by Ken's group. A young girl tending some goats had spotted them and reported the sighting to a nearby sentry post. Two Germans, with their rifles still slung over their shoulders, approached the hidden group. With a cliff behind them and nowhere to go, Jim had jumped out and, with a short burst from his automatic weapon, shot the sentries. The three men quickly made their way back to the cave. The alarm had been raised, saboteurs were now known to be on the island, and its entire garrison was turned out to search for the assailants. The other patrol members had long since arrived back at the cave and it was assumed that Ken's group had been captured. Tansy and the rest of the patrol were mightily pleased to see them. Not just because they were a close-knit group, but because the very real danger existed that the cave's location could be revealed, perhaps under torture. It had been an anxious day for all. The route taken back to the hideout, through the village, was probably the safest. All were amazed that they had made it back as "the island was crawling with Jerries".

The patrol stayed concealed for several days until a lack of water forced their hand. Tansy set off to replenish the water bottles, taking with him some food to bribe or barter with the locals should he be spotted. To everyone's consternation he returned with an old shepherd – usually a strict rule was observed that no one was to be trusted. In broken English and accompanied by much arm-waving, the old man excitedly gave them news of a great landing: "*Multi Anglaises, multi-Americanos.*" The patrol interpreted this as a landing in Greece or somewhere close. It was the 6th of June 1944, D-Day; the assault on the beaches of Normandy, France, and the opening of the Second Front. The shepherd was starving, so they gave him some biscuits, promising to leave behind the rations when they departed. He explained that the Germans were still in the hills, searching for them.

It was an anxious few days until the scheduled rendezvous and pickup. On the prearranged night the patrol made their way down to the shore and flashed a signal out to sea, but with no response they were forced to make their way back to the cave. However, on the second night the signal was answered, and a small dinghy came in to take them off the island. Luckily the conditions were calm and all managed to clamber aboard the small craft as "the water was up to the gunnels".

On a separate occasion a patrol led by the Dane Anders 'Andy' Lassen raided the island of Santorini (Thira). There, Marine Sammy Trafford was badly wounded in both the arm and the leg. Ralph replaced him for one raid and was offered the chance to become a regular member of that patrol. He turned down the offer, saying that he would rather stay with Tansy and his mates. Secretly he thought that Lassen pushed his chances to the limit, even being "reckless".

Another mission that Ralphs remembered was led by an officer, Captain Macbeth, to an island with "five-hundred-foot cliffs". The target was a lighthouse situated at one end of the island. A sergeant went in through the front door whilst Ralph covered the building's rear. The lighthouse was manned by three men: two Greeks, and an Italian who was married to a local Greek lady. The trio proved to be extremely cooperative, supplying important information about shipping movements and troop transportation. The SBS team withdrew, leaving all in place. Over time the unit was able to garner much useful intelligence from this well-positioned intelligence outpost.

"We were looking for somewhere to lay up," said Ken. "There was a rock – it was too small to call it an island – with a big hole in it. Big enough to conceal a boat in. It was known that E-boats would sometimes use this place."

Dawn was approaching and the boat the patrol was travelling in needed somewhere to hide for the day. The S-100 class E-boats were the German fast attack craft, heavily armed and capable of over forty-three knots. They were faster, better armed, and at thirty-three metres long far bigger than the British motorboat/launches (MTBs). The MTBs had a top speed of up to thirty-nine knots.

A decision was made to send a canoe to investigate the hiding place. The craft was dropped over the side and Ken seated himself in the front. As a sergeant attempted to get into the rear he stood on the side, capsizing the boat. "It was a near one," said Ken. "I was upside down with a Schmeisser wrapped around my neck, but they managed to fish me back on board. Anyway, there wasn't an E-boat there." This is how a near-drowning experience was casually described.

One of the last acts to take place before landing on an enemy shoreline (always at night) was to have a last hot meal. Or rather, a can of stew, soup or the like. These were special cans, like a thermos flask but with the vacuum filled with a chemical mix. When the seal was broken a reaction took place, causing the can to heat up and warm the inner flask's contents. Being in close proximity to hostile territory, all actions were undertaken with extreme caution and great stealth. On one such occasion Ken activated his can only for it to cause a minor explosion, like a firework. Immediately he threw the offending can overboard. The resulting tension was palpable and anxious whispers – "Who was that?", "Bloody fool" and other unprintable comments – were heard. All were now on edge; more so than normal. Had they been spotted? Would there be a hostile reception awaiting them? Unfriendly glances were cast in Kens direction. He appeared to be more concerned about the loss of his hot meal and was quietly complaining but received no sympathy.

Whilst on about food, another tale concerned a cage of liberated chickens. Their short spell of freedom was about to come to an end. It was dinner time, and they were destined to take centre stage, but first came the simple task of preparation. Ken's brief time spent as a butcher's boy would now prove useful. He had on many occasions witnessed how, with a swift twist of the wrist, a chicken's neck could be wrung. Although he had never tried this himself it did not deter him. Having witnessed this technique many times he felt sure he would be more than up to the task – after all, how difficult could it be? Reaching into the cage he grabbed a hen and violently twisted the neck, throwing it aside before repeating the process several times. Initially he was not concerned about the supposedly dead chickens running around the boat's deck, loudly squawking their disapproval. On many occasions he had seen this reflex action before suddenly the birds would keel over, dead. But much to his embarrassment and everyone else's delight, the very annoyed birds continued to run around, violently complaining about their treatment and sporting bright red necks.

Ken had recently returned from reconnoitring one of the smaller Dodecanese Islands (he believed it to be Calchi) and was expected to be part of the upcoming raid. Circumstances dictated otherwise. He was approached by a Trooper Jackson, who asked what the island was like as he had been rostered for the mission. "All quiet. Nothing to worry about," Ken answered.

Unbeknown to the raiders, the island's garrison had been reinforced and 'they took on a hornets' nest.' In the ensuing battle Jackson stuck his head out around a corner only to have his ear shot off! On his return from the mission, he complained to Ken about his judgement, but no sympathy was shown instead, he suffered a barrage of comments including "You now have a nice hole for an earring" and "You will only have to pay half price to have your ears pierced. What are you complaining about?"

Bury and McPherson

Lieutenant Bob Bury was leading a patrol on board a caique off the island of Volos. 'We approached a large bay which was known to be held by Royalist Guerrillas,' wrote his sergeant, John McPherson. 'From what we learnt later, these partisans were expecting an attack by their rivals and deadly enemies, ELAS (Greek communist partisans.) At any rate, they opened fire on us.' The caique's helmsman and McPherson were both hit. Bob Bury steered a course towards the shore and closer to the point of fire, hoping to alert their assailants as to their identity. With no means of communication other than shouting he tried to make them aware of who they were.

It was as he tried to attend to his wounded sergeant that Bury was shot and killed. Bob Bury was an extremely well-liked and respected officer and had spent most of his adult life at war. He was once described as "one of the most able, most devoted and most unselfish officers who ever served in the SBS". He was only twenty-four years old when he died and was buried the next day by the men who had mistakenly shot him.

Sergeant McPherson, a Scotsman from the islands, loved the sea. He was in Africa with an anti-aircraft regiment when he heard that they were looking for recruits for the 1st SAS. After selection and qualification, he did a parachute course and then went on to earn his 'wings'. He saw action in Sicily and Italy before transferring over to the SBS. There he took part in multiple raids in Greece and the Aegean Islands.

McPherson was taken to a farmhouse where he was treated, having been shot three times in the leg. His family still have one of the bullets as a macabre souvenir. He was there for five weeks; in which time his leg was amputated on a kitchen table due to the onset of gangrene. With no anaesthetic available, hard liquor (ouzo) was poured down his throat in an attempt to deaden him to the pain.

 Eventually a fishing boat (skippered by a Royal Navy lieutenant, Alex McLeod) came and picked McPherson up, taking him to neutral Turkey. From there it was a painful and exhausting journey back, overland, to a force's hospital in Cairo, Egypt. There, to save his life, a further section of his leg was amputated.

He was eventually repatriated back to Erskine Hospital in Scotland for the long and arduous road to recovery. Despite all he had been through he settled and went on to raise a family. One of his daughters, Rhona, was a frequent guest at the post-war SAS/SBS reunions, acting as chaperone to her father. She felt both proud and privileged to be amongst such men and to listen, enthralled, to their gripping stories.

On one of the Greek islands, H Patrol were on board a motorboat, under camouflage on a remote piece of shoreline. Ken and the coxswain, a naval petty officer, were sent off over a mountain to the nearest habitation. "It was a pretty little village with a few houses sat close to the water's edge in a picturesque bay," said Ken. No one could be seen, and the pair approached a house and knocked on the door. A young couple, who were obviously scared, opened the door and quickly ushered them inside. Ken and the petty officer asked if there were any *Tedeschi* (Germans) around. Immediately the young couple rushed around the house, closing any curtains and doing their utmost to make the visitors welcome. The guests were offered some dry biscuits and a drop of wine, and the host even started up an old wind-up gramophone. The man went to a back window and pointed to a monastery on the summit of a nearby hill. Ken fished about for a pencil but could find no paper; all he had was a matchbox to record any information on. A couple of gun emplacements on the hillside were pointed out. Ken took a bearing from the bay, noting this down with approximate distances and any details. He then noticed, through a gap in the front curtains, some movement outside. Further investigation revealed that it seemed everyone in the neighbourhood was aware of the visitors and had turned out to see them. An old lady at the rear of the crowd caught Ken's eye. She was trying to attract their attention and was pointing up the hill to where a figure could be seen making their way towards the monastery. "Straight away we got out and scarpered," said Ken. The figure was obviously on their way to inform the enemy of the pair's presence.

With desperate haste Ken and the petty officer rushed back over the mountain and down to the boat to reveal that they had been reported. Immediately there was frantic activity: the camouflage was checked and improved upon. Everyone took up arms, finding defensive positions not only on the boat, but concealed within the rocky coastline. Armed with grenades, automatic weapons and other munitions, the defenders awaited their fate.

When the pair had arrived back it was quickly decided that there was no point in trying to make a run for it as their motor launch would be easily outmatched by an E-boat or aircraft sent out after them. A glass-bottomed sponge-fishing boat had laid at anchor close to the launch. It was almost comical to witness the two Greek crew members in their haste to vacate the vicinity, attempting to speed off with the anchor paid out and one of the crew still clambering aboard.

Shortly an E-boat appeared, slowly cruising close to shore at action stations. That day the boat made several circuits of the island. "How it didn't spot us I don't know. It was on top of us," said Ken. "We waited for dark and slipped away." He had no recollection of what island it was. "There were so many of them. We would go on scouting missions to see if we could find someone to annoy, but eventually it got too hot. We were withdrawn back to Palestine, then on to North Africa," he added.

During a sharp exchange in the House of Commons of the British Parliament in 1944, the Conservative Member of Parliament for West Dorset stood up and asked, "Is it true, Mr Prime Minister, that there is a body of men out in the Aegean Islands, fighting under the Union flag, that are nothing short of being a band of murderous, renegade cut-throats?"

Churchill's magnificent put-down reply was, "If you do not take your seat and keep quiet, I will send you out to join them."

The Prime Minister later wrote about the SBS that it was 'composed of soldiers of the very highest quality', as a fighting force that had been 'Transformed to an amphibious unit resolved to recreate at sea the fame which it had won in the sands of the desert' (Winston S. Churchill).

The Greek Islands

Saturday 1st April, on leave, Allen; Bill Mayall; Sticks May; Ken Smith; Tommy Tucker; Beirut.

Waiting for truck to return from leave, all looking as if they have had a good time! Sticks, centre, with bunch of flowers. Ken over his right shoulder.

Written on the rear: 'January 23rd, 1944, North Barrage, near Cairo. Rear L to R: Hyde; Sudanese Police Sgt.; Ken smith: Gartland. Front L to R: Ken Joynson; Sgt. John McPherson; Ginger Williams'.

Written on rear: 'Alexandria, Saturday 27th May, on leave. Sticks beside me also lives in Pompey, he was also in my squad and joined the Penelope when I joined the Manchester. He has made himself look a bit sloppy here but he is far from it and a great pal of mine.'

On leave in Alexandria, Egypt. L to R: Fred Moore, Gravesend, Kent; Ralph Bridger, Brighton; Bill Williamson, Sussex; Ginger Williams, London.

10

SIMI

"The thick Jocks had forgotten the bloody flag!"

Operation Tenement on Simi, (Symi), remains one of the largest and most successful raids the SAS has ever undertaken. On the 13th–15th July 1944 a combined force of SBS and Greek Sacred Squadron conducted an operation against the Greek Dodecanese Island of Simi. The island had been raided several times before, as had most of the Aegean Islands, but this was to be different. Rather than a small-scale incursion it was to be a raid-in-force and had the tactical aim of convincing the Germans and Italian Fascists on Rhodes that a British and Greek force had captured and was occupying Simi; the idea being to tempt a rescue force out of Rhodes.

The official records dated the 7th of June 1944 state:

Simi, situated as it is, covers the shipping route between Leros and Rhodes. All raids on the island and our previous occupation have caused the enemy to react every time. If the enemy can be induced to think that Simi has been occupied by us, it is probable that he will send an expedition in force to recapture the island. Should this operation be launched by the enemy it should prove an excellent target for the Royal Navy and Royal Air Force.

Strength of enemy on the island; 70–100 Germans and 130 Italian Fascists.

Intention: -
To land and liquidate the Simi garrison.
To destroy all installations in the harbour.
To capture, or destroy if the former impracticable, all shipping at Simi.
To evacuate within 24 hours of landing, leaving behind a small force to simulate the occupation of Simi.

As well as considerable naval support the Rhodes garrison, some six thousand German and three thousand Italian troops, enjoyed air supremacy in the region. Rhodes is situated less than fifteen miles (just over twenty-four kilometres) from Simi, which is barely five miles from the Turkish mainland. The island of Simi is about eight miles long by five miles wide. In past times the Simiaki residents had their olive groves situated on the Turkish mainland.

Before the raid, in mid-June, Royal Marine canoeists of the SB Section (Royal Navy SBS) had limpet-mined two German destroyers anchored in Portolago Harbour, Leros, to prevent them interfering in the operation. To achieve this the canoeists had paddled into the harbour, crossing two booms, placed their charges and emerged without loss. Badly damaged, the destroyers were towed to Piraeus, where they were subsequently sunk by Allied bombers. A daylight attack was decided upon as intelligence had revealed that the enemy was now 'standing to' during the night and 'standing down' by day.

The Axis forces had become accustomed to being attacked during the hours of darkness and would therefore not be expecting this change in tactics. On the 20th of November 1943 Lieutenant Bob Bury and Sergeant 'Tanky' Geary had conducted a raid on Simi under the cover of darkness, in which an enemy patrol of eight were killed.

The landing points were chosen so that if the enemy became alerted to the attack, it would not be possible to send forces to oppose the landings in under two hours. The time for the attack was initially scheduled for 0700, which might appear to be late, but the enemy time was one hour behind the British. Numbers vary slightly in differing accounts but according to John Lodwick, an SBS officer, a force of ten motor launches, two schooners, eighty-one SBS and 139 Greek Sacred Squadron were concentrated inside Penzik Bay, Turkey, under camouflage, on the 8th of July 1944. The final briefings were carried out multiple times as the fleet was scattered throughout the bay. The official report on Operation Tenement states, 'The use of camouflage was outstanding when lying up on the Turkish coast opposite Simi, as the area was recced by German reconnaissance aircraft twice daily.' Turkey, being a neutral country throughout the Second World War, turned a blind eye to the SAS incursions into its territory.

One of the difficulties encountered in the build-up to the operation was that the troops required were widely dispersed and had to be gathered from Palestine, Cairo and Alexandria and a large part of the force were already operating and spread across the Aegean. The latest intelligence information prior to the raid said that the garrison 'appear to be in a state of nervous tension, a maximum number are on duty at night, with a full dawn stand-to'. It also revealed that Molo Point had fifteen Germans and Fascists manning a seventy-five-millimetre gun position, possibly an eighty-eight millimetre, and two light machine-gun posts. Also, the position was surrounded by wire and anti-personnel mines. This was to be the initial target of G Patrol, comprising one officer and nine other ranks with two Royal Engineers.

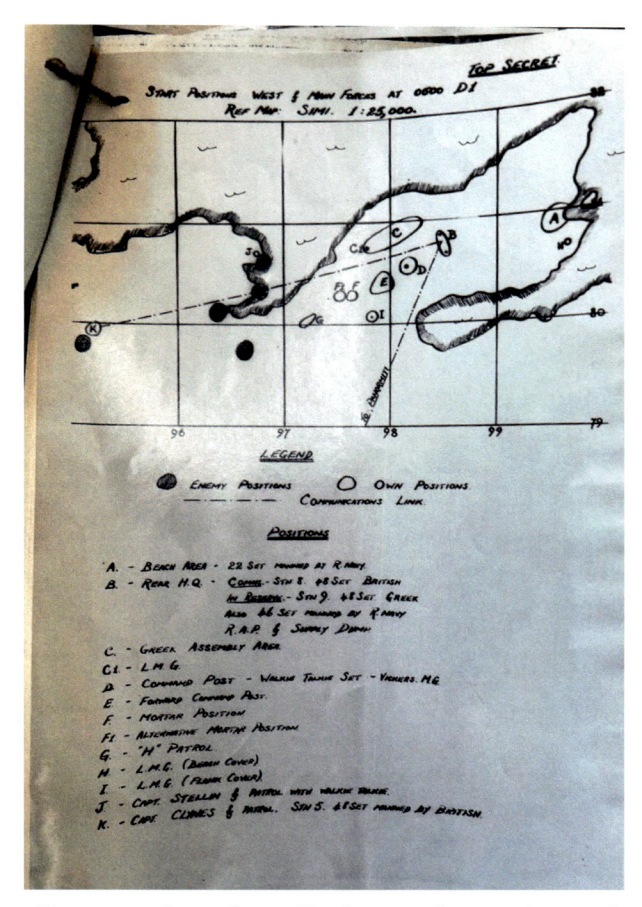

Photocopy of map from official report showing the initial positions before attack.

It is also worthy of note that the operational plan stated, 'This plan is for the initial phase of attack and is liable to alteration at any time during initial phase by force commander.' Everyone understood that any plan rarely goes according to schedule.

Another ominous detail of the planning document states that 'burials will be in situ'.

The Greek Sacred Squadron had been trained by their British comrades and were now considered more than capable of taking over operations in the region. This raid was to serve as a parting statement; then the SBS would take some well-deserved leave before redeployment.

The whole operation was under the field command of Brigadier 'Bull' Turnbull, with Lieutenant Colonel Ian Lapraik deputising. The objectives were to kill or capture the entire garrison (some 180 men, Germans and Italians), blow up enemy gun emplacements, and sink any shipping that might be found in the harbour. It would be impossible to hold the island for the enemy airfields on Rhodes and Cos were far too near, so it was to be a quick, shattering blow followed by a hasty retreat. The Germans would, of course, reoccupy, but they would have to completely restock the garrison, carry out extensive repairs and replace their guns. It has been estimated that the SBS, numbering no more than 250 men, were responsible for tying down and harassing as many as eighteen thousand Axis troops in the Aegean.

Simi had been raided many times, the defences were known to have been strengthened, and the defenders had a citadel to fall back on. The enemy, well used to the SBS visits, having already been raided several times, had taken to sleeping round their guns. Despite this, on the night of the 13th of July, the approach and three separate landings went unobserved. As well as knowledge gained from previous visits, Captain Stewart Macbeth had made a personal reconnaissance of the island and had pinpointed the enemy dispositions. He oversaw South Force, which was to assault a monastery position at Panormitis, known to house a detachment of enemy troops. West Force, under Captain Charles Clynes and including the Jock Patrol, had to make the difficult approach to Molo Point. They were to be in position by first light (about 5am), laying up unobserved in the monastery cemetery at Evangelismos, overlooking the promontory above Nos beach where the gun emplacement was situated. (The harbour entrance being about two hundred metres wide.) The plan was for the Jocks to wave a red flag when in position and ready to assault the gun emplacement.

'Fairmire' under camouflage, in Turkish waters, in position for Operation Tenement.

The 'main force' was landed at Agia Marina opposite a small island and close to the mouth of Pedi Bay. Around midnight the raiders disembarked from five motor launches into Carley floats and were transferred to the rocky shoreline. The report states that 'very anxious time' was had when the last motor launch mistook Pedi Bay for Marina Bay. Apart from the delay to the tight schedule, the concern was that the boat contained all the mortars and machine guns.

During the landing, two Greek officers slipped on the rocks and drowned.

Sticks turned to Ken and said, "Here, two of the Greeks have fallen overboard!"

"It was dead of night," remembered Ken, "pitch black. I heard two almighty splashes as the Greeks fell in. Loaded as they were, they went straight to the bottom; one had a radio on his back. As Royal Marines we were used to boats and the sea. But maybe they weren't. But we had to leave them and carry on."

As well as the loss of the two men, a Vickers machine gun also disappeared into the depths. All were extremely anxious about the noise. The fate of the two lost men was superseded by the risk of discovery and loss of surprise.

H Patrol SBS (nine men) were initially to act as a beach party and would land in the first wave. Quickly and as silently as possible, the equipment and ammunition were transferred to shore, no easy task from bobbing craft over slippery rocks in pitch darkness. Then came an exhausting few hours as the transfer of supplies from the shore to a hill overlooking the harbour, town and castle proceeded.

The official report states that:

All the approach marches were over particularly difficult terrain, with big rocks and boulders and no paths. Owing to the impossibility of landing large carrying parties, all ranks were forced to carry extremely heavy loads in addition to their equipment, to get sufficient ammunition up to the battle position for the possibility of a long battle. This was particularly the case with the main force, where the approach was extremely steep, five hundred feet having to be climbed in under two miles. The conditions were of the kind to test the best mountain trained troops.

Ken remembered making several trips carrying loads of three-inch mortar bombs over the rough, boulder-strewn terrain, each time a trip of well over a mile and a climb of several hundred feet. This route has since been retraced by a present-day SAS operative. He did it in the evening when he could see his route, saying, "It was exhausting carrying nothing!"

An official report further comments on the transfer of equipment:

> *Three thousand yards (almost two miles), over most appalling country in pitch black. The average load carried by each man was 80lbs (36Kg). Some indication of the ammunition moved can be gauged that four three-inch mortars and four medium machine guns were kept in action more or less continually for six hours.*

Before first light all forces were laid up in concealed positions, undetected and awaiting the coming onslaught. H Patrol were the foremost troops, situated close to the town's outskirts, forming a first line of defence should the main force be discovered. They were in a covering position for the Greek-manned mortar and machine-gun positions and would be the initial assault troops to enter the town from the north-east.

Ken was positioned about a third of the way down the slope on the opposite side of the bay from Molo Point. He was teamed up with another Ken: Kenneth Eric Joynson from Birkenhead; another good boxer. Together they manned a Bren (a light machine gun). The signal to open fire would be a mortar round fired at the citadel. The pair's task was to direct suppressing fire across the bay onto the concealed seventy-five-millimetre gun position, approximately four hundred metres away. They were to keep it occupied and hopefully out of action until the Jocks waved a red flag from the cemetery. This would indicate that they were about to storm the position from its rear. Best laid plans…?

Bren Gun.

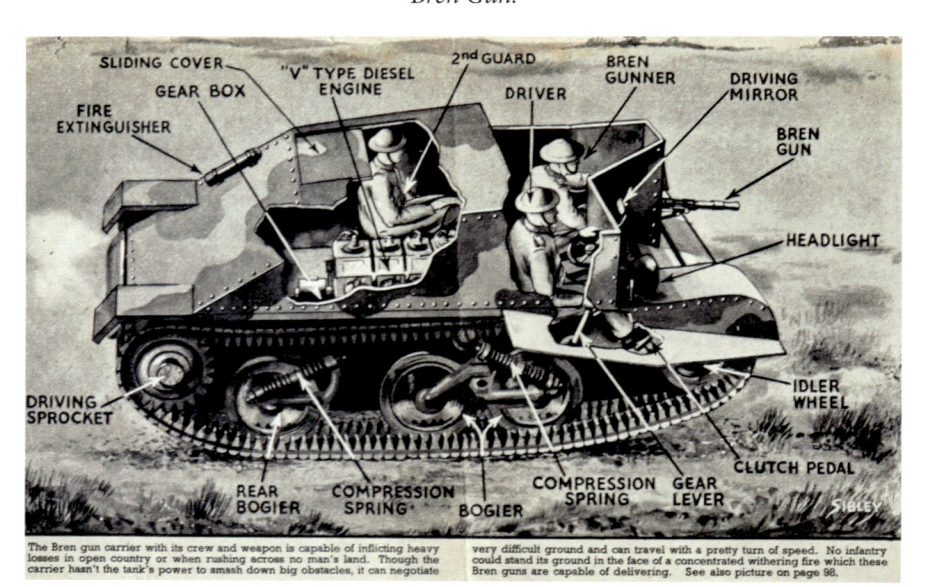

Bren Carrier.

Two differing times were in place for the start of hostilities. Intelligence had learnt that two German Ems barges in the harbour were due to sail at first light. So, a start time of either 0500 or 0600 was scheduled, depending on the situation with the barges. These large craft had voyaged from their home on the Ems River in western Germany, across the river systems of Central Europe, into the Black Sea, and then down to the Greek islands. Here they were being deployed to supply the various garrisons in the Aegean. A naval gun had been mounted on each vessel's foredeck which could cause much damage to the lightly armed raiders.

The first deadline came and went. The two Kens were becoming increasingly concerned as the second deadline approached. They had been unable to locate the heavily camouflaged gun emplacement. Shortly before 0600, the barges slipped their moorings and sailed out of the harbour. The Kens had been taking turns at spotting with a pair of binoculars and manning the Bren. With moments to spare, "the gun crew gave themselves away," said Ken Smith, who was using the binoculars at the time. First one and then the others stood up and stretched the night's stiffness out of their bodies. Smith spotted them immediately and pointed their position out to Joynson, who sighted the machine gun. They watched from their vantage point across the bay as the gun commander formed his men up, pointed at them and began issuing orders. Leaving one man behind, they filed the forty or so metres down to a house at the water's edge on the Harani side of the headland, presumably to have breakfast. For the Jock Patrol this was a blessing as they watched from their concealed position approximately 150 yards away. The gun crew were stood down, giving away their position and the gap in the wire.

The barges were slowly beginning to disappear, and the line of soldiers had just made their way into the rear of the building when the signal for the attack to begin exploded. The first mortar round aimed at the citadel scored a direct hit. Immediately the line of Germans exited the building and raced, in a neat line, towards the gun emplacement. The Bren guns' magazines had been loaded with a mixture of ball, tracer, incendiary and armour-piercing rounds. As Smith spotted and loaded, Joynson sent a stream of bullets arcing across the bay at the line of German soldiers. The shots landed to the side of the line, taken by a slight breeze. As Joynson corrected, the line of soldiers veered and then, still in line, turned and headed back into the house, followed by a line of tracer bullets.

Smith was issuing directions to Joynson. "Put some in through the windows and door." Then, noticing that the sole German manning the gun was frantically trying to work it, "Give the gun a burst!" shouted Smith.

Alternating between the two positions, they were managing to keep the gun out of action. The citadel was under a constant barrage and the Ems barges, having been alerted by the action, were making their way back. Five Royal Navy motor launches appeared on the scene and a small naval engagement took place in the bay. The Allied troops on the hillside had a grandstand view as the navy launches raced around the slow barges in an elliptical orbit, firing a broadside as they went. The Bren was in continuous action, trying to prevent the gun from opening on the Royal Navy and taking them off the hillside.

To add to the confusion, a white flag was being waved in the cemetery. "Take no notice of that; give them a burst, make them keep their heads down," said Smith. The Jocks enjoyed a charmed life. When attempting the assault on the gun emplacement they had forgotten or lost the red flag, and so assumed that a white one would do! Not so – Ken had taken a differing view. "I saw a white flag being waved – wrong one. So, I gave them a squirt as well. Fortunately, it was at extreme range and the Jocks promptly took cover behind the cemetery wall." Another of Ken's insightful comments about his Scottish comrades was, "The thick Jocks had forgotten the bloody flag!"

Throughout the war the marine and Jock Patrols usually operated together and formed a strong bond. At subsequent post-war reunions they would draw together some tables and spend long nights recalling their shared experiences and exploits. A chorus of Scottish insults and abuse would always greet Ken, to which he would reply, "Should have shot the bloody lot of you!" He further enhanced his reputation when he took up brewing his own wine from nettles, elderberries and the like. His Scottish comrades would always turn up with some particularly fine vintage whisky to offer around. Not to be outdone, Ken would produce a bottle of his finest home brew. Comments such as "What are you trying to do, poison us?" were hurled at him.

When the Bren ammunition ran out Ken Smith set off for more, but only made it a few paces before a Spandau machine gun opened on him. Instinctively he dived to the ground and rolled behind a large stone. The Spandau began to remorselessly reduce his cover to chippings. Ken could feel the vibrations of the bullets hitting the rock, later saying that "The Jerry must have thought he'd got me."

"You all right, Smithy?" called out Tansy, who, together with Sergeant Jim Horsefield, was sheltering nearby, behind a wall.

Shouting into the dirt, Ken replied, "Yes, as long as I don't move."

"Hang on," said Jim, "I think I know where it's coming from. We'll give it a burst and you get out of there."

This was successfully achieved, and shortly they began to make their way down the slope and into the edge of town, all the while under enemy fire. Ken remembered a surreal moment as he weaved his way down the hillside with bullets whistling around him. Looking up, he could see in the town girls at windows and on balconies, waving to them.

H Patrol now advanced to within three hundred yards of the castle but could make no further progress as they came under very accurate enemy twenty-millimetre machine-gun fire.

It was now a three-hour journey to get ammunition from Marina Bay. To remedy this, a dory loaded with ammunition was dispatched from Marina Bay to the harbour, but this was sunk by enemy twenty-millimetre gunfire. The SAS then resorted to a tried-and-tested method: they would try and bluff the enemy into surrender.

As the battle had progressed, one of the barges had run aground on a nearby beach. The other, having surrendered, was under Royal Navy escort. The gun position on Molo Point had been overrun by the Jocks, and the town and boatyard were largely under Allied control. But the strongly garrisoned citadel was still in the hands of the enemy. Simi Castle dominates the town and overlooks the harbour. The main enemy garrison were securely entrenched inside and had only to hold out until relief arrived. The Jocks, having arrived at the head of the harbour, had three of their number pinned down behind a low wall, where they were to stay for the next three hours. One of these, Lance Corporal Roberts, had a lucky escape: when raising his head slightly to light a cigarette he received a bullet graze from the temple to the neck. A series of skirmishes had taken place to clear the town and boatyards, miraculously with the assaulting force only suffering a few relatively minor wounds. By 9am a stalemate ensued, and it was decided to move main force headquarters, the Vickers machine guns, and mortar troops to new positions about eight hundred yards from the castle. The remaining Germans were holed up, safely ensconced in the castle, and the Allied force were in no position to storm it.

A series of emissaries were dispatched to the citadel in an attempt to negotiate the Axis force's surrender. As long as the Germans and Italians sat tight, their position was well-nigh impregnable, although accurate mortar and sustained small-arms fire was making their lives uncomfortable. To give the impression of a much larger attacking force, a furious fusillade was unleashed upon the castle, accompanied by a series of loud and spectacular explosions as enemy equipment and installations were destroyed. A German naval petty officer, the captain of one of the Ems barges (now tied up alongside the quayside and hidden from the citadel), was then dispatched to the castle to negotiate its surrender. The subterfuge worked and at about 3pm the garrison marched out, waving a white flag. As Ken so eloquently said, "It was bullshit, a ruse – but it worked."

Ken was then employed helping to supervise the growing number of prisoners lined up along the quayside before taking the opportunity to indulge in a little souvenir-hunting. He leapt aboard the Ems barge and promptly bagged the ship's swastika flag from the stern. Venturing inside, with the aid of his dagger he prised both the officers' wardroom clock and the crews ship clock off the walls. Later he would toss a coin with Sticks for the timepieces. Sticks won and selected the fine-looking wooden officers' clock. Many years later it would stop working and, much to Ken's disgust, Sticks' wife Meg threw it away. The crew's brass clock kept time in Ken's front room until his death in July 2017 and is still working to this day. Continuing with his search, he came across a drawer stuffed full of swastika/Stuka drachmas, the currency the Germans had introduced throughout occupied Greece. He was busy liberating this when a sound alerted him. A quick investigation revealed a German who had managed to elude the ship's search. He was quickly and unceremoniously ushered up to join his comrades on the quayside. "I kicked him up the staircase," said Ken.

The numbers do vary slightly with different reports, but it does seem that around 151 prisoners had been taken, twenty-one Germans and Italians killed, and a fully garrisoned island captured, together with two Ems barges and other miscellaneous craft and vehicles.

Whilst all the prisoners were being lined up and counted along the quayside, Ken Joynson came running up to Ken Smith (who was the patrol's explosives man), urging him to come and look at something. Smith followed him to a building at the end of the harbour where the road narrows. Nowadays, it is from here that a new road heading off and up to Pedi starts. They entered a house and climbed a short flight of stairs. The pair emerged into a dimly lit room where a safe bearing the words 'Made in Birmingham' sat invitingly. Smith opened a large chest and found it contained some heavy, richly embroidered material. With this he thought his mother could make some nice curtains. They sped off to retrieve his rucksack. In Ken's words, "Well, we had explosives, hadn't we; anything you wanted. I had plastic explosive, ammonal, guncotton and time pencils. Well, there might have been some papers with some intelligence value in the safe." As if. Go tell that to the marines!

The SAS personnel came to rely upon the sale of booty, as sometimes they would go over two months without pay. SS badges, flags, anything with German insignia, and especially Luger pistols would fetch a good price, particularly amongst the American troops.

Like two excited schoolboys the Kens were soon rushing back into the room, where, to their dismay, having only been gone but a few short moments, a fully robed Greek Orthodox priest had "appeared from nowhere". The door to the safe was wide open, two candlesticks and a cross were now arranged as if on an altar upon what had been destined to become a pair of curtains, and the priest was offering a brief prayer. He then turned to the stunned pair and, drawing the sign of the cross in the air with one hand, proceeded to bless them. Sheepishly they backed out of the room and ran down the stairs, exchanging recriminating remarks about each other's virtue.

They burst out of the building into the bright sunlight, having to brake hard to avoid toppling into the harbour. At that moment a terrifying *rat-a-tat-tat* rent the air. Two Messerschmitt's had emerged from the hilly island interior and were strafing the town. Where the pair were standing was the narrowest part of the quayside, only a few metres wide; instinctively they threw themselves backwards, pressing their bodies into the house's doorway. As they did so, a line of bullets tore up the pathway in front of them. The paraded prisoners and guards had all been forced to dive and run for cover.

Ken turned to his would-be partner in crime and said, "That's him upstairs warning us to lay off his kit!" Later he would remark, "Having been a good choirboy, I should have known better than to try and rob a church!"

Reports differ as to how many and what type of aircraft appeared. Some say three and put them as Stukas. Ken always insisted it was two Messerschmitt's. The official report records three Arados and three Messerschmitt 109s. One of the aircraft dropped a message into the castle urging the German commandant to 'hang on as help is on its way'. The German commandant was seen to be shaking his head and is reported to have said, "Too bad – you see, that is what comes of being late. I thought they had forgotten about us. I radioed for them five hours ago."

Rhona McPherson has vivid memories from post-war reunions. "I always remember them talking about Jock Cunningham, who was a medic in the SBS in Simi. He was treating wounded Germans on the quayside when an aircraft flew over and started firing at them. The Germans by all accounts jumped on him to protect him."

With the surrender an almost carnival atmosphere descended upon the town and soon a feast was being enjoyed by all, including both islanders and prisoners. The captives seem to have been delighted that they were not about to be executed, and some even revealed stashes of hidden wine. In the boatyard an ox was roasted on a bowsprit. The military food store in the castle and one in the town was distributed to the starving civilian population. This was in addition to twenty-five tons brought in by a relief caique.

The arms etc. captured or destroyed were:

One seventy-five-millimetre gun.
Seven twenty-millimetre Breda guns.
Sixteen medium machine guns.
Thirty-nine light machine guns.
Six 45 mortars. All rifles and pistols.
Two large arms dumps (estimated fifteen tons).
One explosive dump (estimated five tons).
Instillations destroyed.
Wireless telephone station.
Baggage room.
Telephone exchange and twelve phones.
Cable cut (Piscopi to Nisiro).
Diesel fuel dump (approximately fifteen tons).
Fortifications at castle and Molo Point.
Caique yard and shipbuilding facilities.

Nineteen craft were destroyed. Their estimated tonnage:

Two of 150 tons, reliably stated to be EMS hulls.
Two of ninety tons, in water complete.
One of seventy tons.

Fourteen of average thirty tons each.
Total: 970 tons.

Two EMS craft were captured complete and serviceable. The prisoners were then loaded aboard the two Ems barges in preparation for a departure under the cover of darkness. Ken was instructed to get some rest. Whilst he was asleep, "some matelot" (seaman) made off with his flag and hoard of drachmas.

The trip back to the British-held island of Castlelerosso was uneventful. Ken took the opportunity to get one of the German prisoners to write out the words to the song 'Lili Marleen', made famous by Marlene Dietrich. Originally a poem and first recorded by Lale Anderson. This song became a favourite of both sides and was adopted as an unofficial anthem of the wartime SAS. Sticks entertained himself by trying to entice a prisoner to swim to freedom in Turkey. The convoy hugged the coastline for safety, at times being barely a hundred metres or so from the shore. Although tempted the prisoner turned down the offer, indicating (by mimicking the actions of someone firing a machine gun) that he would be shot for trying to escape. When questioned if Sticks would have done this, Ken thought for a moment before answering, "Maybe."

One patrol, under the command of the New Zealander Captain 'Stud' Stellin, was left behind to offer a warm welcome to the anticipated arrival of the enemy relief force. Having first bombed the town, two German launches sailed into the harbour. They were greeted with such a fusillade of accurate and intense fire that they were forced to withdraw, ablaze. Stellin's patrol then withdrew to the mountains to await darkness and a rendezvous with a pickup launch. As they watched from a distance, the town was again bombed, and the German flag eventually hoisted over the citadel at 3pm. It was still not over for this patrol. On the homeward journey they were intercepted by an enemy E-boat. Fortunately, every member of the patrol had managed to arm themselves with an automatic weapon. The E-boat was left sinking!

'The Big Raid on Simi', as some have called it, has been recorded in several publications. It has even made it into a book featuring the ten best special forces actions ever! Perhaps the most accurate account was published shortly after the war in 1947, entitled *The Filibusters* by John Lodwick. He was one of the SBS officers taking part in the action. The accounts all record the remarkably low Allied losses: two Greek officers drowned and six wounded. It was not until over sixty years later that another casualty came to light. A former member of the SAS was researching a book listing all the Second World War losses the unit had suffered (*The SAS and LRDG Roll of Honour, 1941–1947* by ex-SAS soldier X, QGM, first published in 2016). After getting in touch with both Ken Smith and Ralph Bridger he became aware of another casualty.

Following the surrender of the main garrison at the citadel, Captain Lapraik dispatched Ralph Bridger with a written note to be hand-delivered to Captain Macbeth, Officer in Charge (OIC) South Force. Having been up all night and involved in the arduous transfer of equipment and fighting in the ensuing battle, to then have to traverse the length of the hilly island, on rough tracks under a blazing sun, was no easy task. When Ralph arrived at the south end of the island the enemy were holed up in a monastery, offering a spirited resistance. He arrived on a ridge overlooking the monastery and was directed to take the message to the foot of the slope. Making his way down the slope, he was fired on from the island and forced to dodge behind a wall. Using this for cover he completed the journey before turning around to see a sign indicating that the route, he had taken was through a minefield. He located Lieutenant

Bob Bury, who was involved in a deep conversation with one of the monastery priests. Bury then gave Ralph a second note to be delivered to Macbeth, who was located at the top of a nearby hill. After a few unprintable words from Ralph, Freddie Moore, a tall, slim lad, volunteered to accompany him. It was a steep hill with a series of walled terraces. They set off on separate routes, arranging to meet at a prominent group of trees. Soon the pair came under accurate machine-gun and sniper fire. Progress was made with a succession of sprints followed by a dive for cover. An ex-member of today's SAS retraced the route, saying, "It was bloody hot and with no cover from where the Germans were firing." As the pair neared the trees a sniper bullet hit young Freddie in the buttock. Ralph pulled him under the shade of one of the three trees on that terrace and, with no medical kit, covered the wound as best he could with the only dressing available, which was his shirt. Freddie was in a great deal of pain, and before Ralph left to get help asked him if he would visit his mother and sisters and explain to them what had happened. Ralph assured him that he would be fine, then left to get help and deliver the messages. He had only made about four more of the terraces when he found himself pinned down by accurate machine-gun fire. Lying in a dead spot under a small bank, he was showered with leaves and debris as the machine gun tore up the ground around him. When the firing ceased, he tried to push off but was frozen, unable to move. Eventually he forced himself to move, taking a few more steps before again diving for cover. With this method he made it to the top, where he tore into Macbeth and a Sergeant Geary. They said that they would "see what we can do about Fred", then gave Ralph a note to be delivered back to Lieutenant Bury. Ralph took a much longer but safer route on the return. The enemy were then persuaded to surrender after finding out about the fate of the main garrison. Ralph lamented, "I never knew what had happened to young Freddie", and that he had always felt guilty about him getting shot.

Following painstaking research by the former SAS operative Soldier X, it was revealed that 'Moore had been evacuated to Egypt and that his next of kin had been informed on the 22nd of July 1944 that he had been wounded in action. Diagnosed with both a complicated fracture to the head of his left femur and Sciatic Palsy, Moore died of his wounds on 27th October 1944', over three months later. He was mentioned in dispatches, 'in recognition of gallant and distinguished services in the field'. He has now taken his place on the SAS Regiment's roll of honour. Aged just twenty-one and from Gravesend, Kent, he was believed to be an only son with either five or seven elder sisters.

After Simi one of the patrol, Tommy Tucker, came up to Ralph to say his goodbyes. "I've had enough of this." It seems the Simi raid was too much, and he was RTU'ing himself, adding that he would prefer to take his "chances on the boats". Ken always credited the SAS with saving his life, but not everyone had the same opinion. Tommy obviously thought his chances of survival were much better back in the marines.

In the Aghios Loonis Church graveyard, Yialos Harbour, Simi, are located two memorial stones. One is dedicated to three SBS men killed on the island in 1943. (The three are buried in the Commonwealth War Cemetery on Rhodes.) The other is dedicated to the two Greek Sacred Squadron officers who drowned, and is inscribed with the words:

Here lies the Lieutenants of the Sacred Company, Georgios Menikidis, Evstathios Tsopelas, fallen on the field of honour during the battle of 14th July 1944 on Symi. Let their death be the betrothal for the union of Symi with Mother Greece.

UJ-Boat, (Ems barge), captured during Simi raid.

Simi Harbour viewed from near the castle showing the gradient of the area. In foreground a group of Italian prisoners are carrying a wounded comrade on an improvised stretcher. The captured Ems barges are berthed on this side of the harbour out of sight.

Simi: Molo Point middle far left. On the right side of the harbour the narrow quayside can just be made out from where a modern road now starts and can be seen Switch-backing up the steep hillside heading off to Pedi. The Bren gun position was about midway along this section of road.

The narrow quayside at Simi, showing a mixed SAS, Royal Navy and Greek Sacred Squadron in 'salvage operations.'

Simi

Bill Mayall after the Simi Raid.

*The Marine 'H' Patrol on Castle Lorosso after the Simi raid showing off some spoils of war. It is understood that Ralph Bridger took the series of Photographs with a 'Liberated' camera. He refused to let anyone else handle the camera for fear of not having it returned.
Rear L to R; Ray Iggleden, played for Leeds and Leicester; Ken Joynson; Ken Smith; Albert 'Sticks' May.
Front L to R: Clr, Sgt. Jim Horsefield; Gunn, RTU'ed; Captain 'Tansy' Lees; Bill Mayall, Didcot, Oxfordshire; Tommy Tucker, Norwich, Norfolk.
Witten on the reverse: All marine patrol except Ralph, our officer centre front. How do you like our Jerry sailors' hats. I got mine off a young Jerry who comes from Hamburg. I also captured an Italian flag but had my Swastika pinched, but I got a couple of Jerry badges you asked for mum.*

Clr. Sgt. Jim Horsefield on Castle Lorosso after Simi.
The photos, from Kens private collection, were originally thought to have been taken on Simi after the islands surrender. It is now understood they were taken on the only British held Greek island, The isolated island of Castle Lorosso, (Kastellorizo).

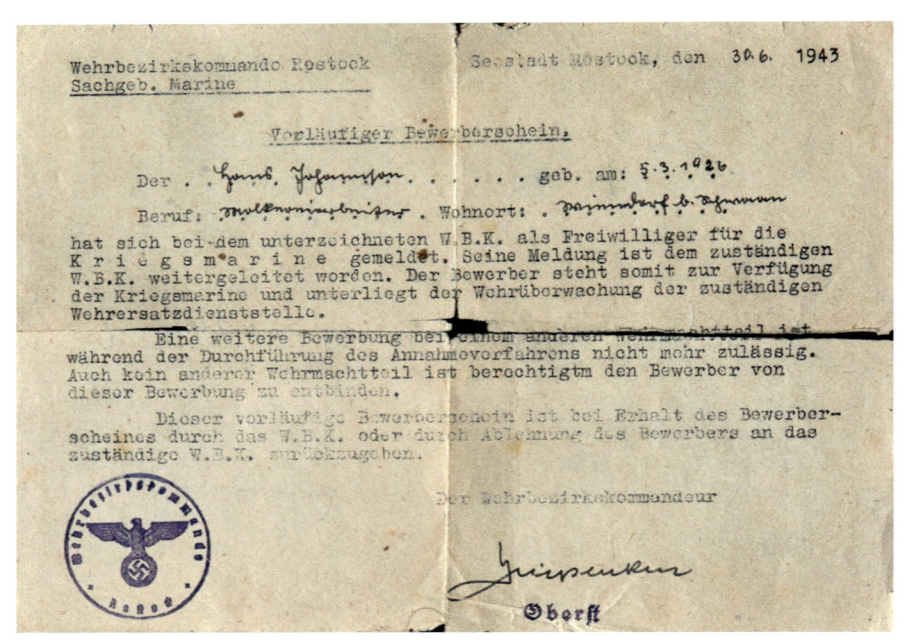

Series of captured German documents, pay books, etc.

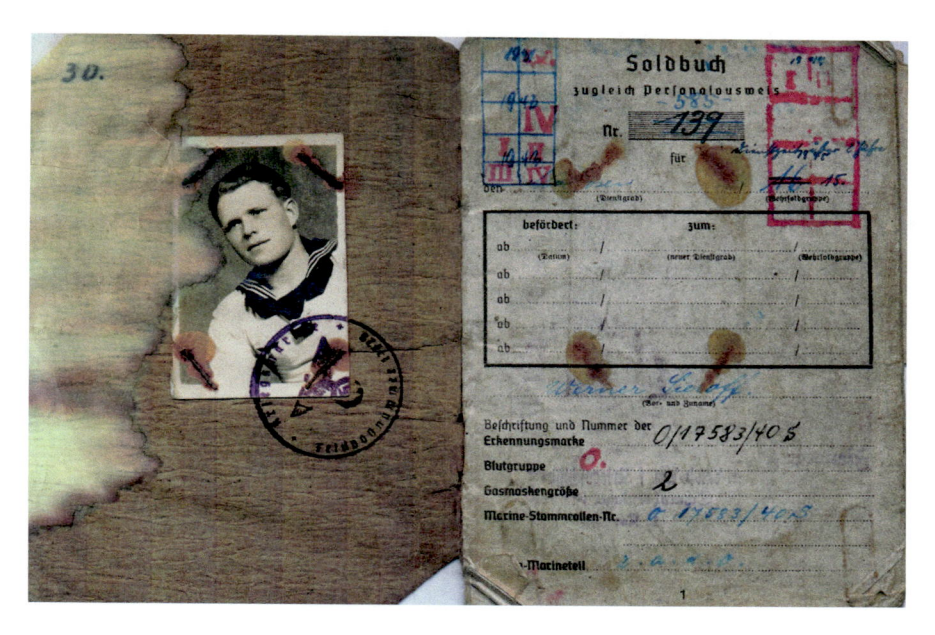

German pay books.

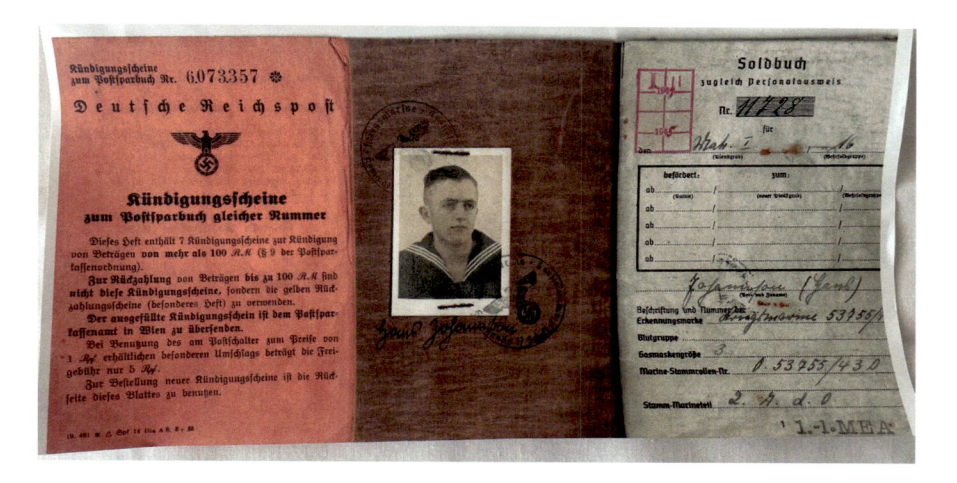

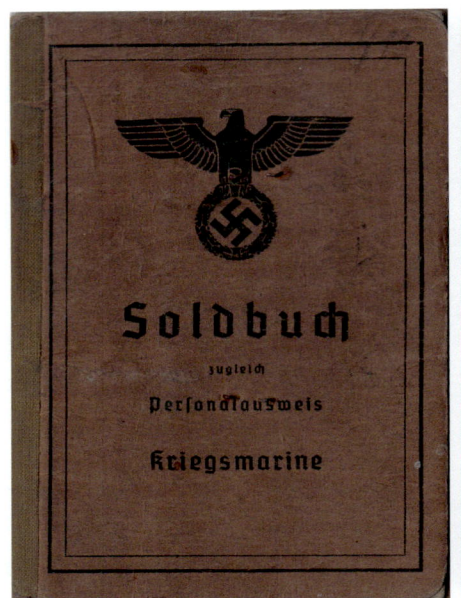

Tommy tucker on Simi, he RTU'ed himself after the raid saying, "I've had enough".

> TOMMY TUCKER. R.M. H.M.S. PENELOPE
>
> Prior to joining the 1st S.A.S. 1st S.B.S. Tommy served on the Penelope and she took a lot of punishment hence her name the Pepper pot. He was part of our H patrol all ex Marines & had done quite a few raids on the Dodecanese Islands. When the raid was staged on the Island of SIMI tommy went through a lot of roughing up & after the raid when we withdrew to an Island called Castle Rossa for a rest tommy came to me to say good bye he had requested to return to the R. Marines as the experience of the SAS had got him down he said his time on the Penny was a cake walk compared to what he just been through & he was going back to a quieter life he was a very brave man & I admired him for his courage and as I never saw him again in life I can only hope he found a bit of peace.
>
> Ralph Bridgers
> 12/5/06

Ralph Bridgers handwritten note about Tommy.

2002, Simi: rusting gun barrel at water's edge, close to the location of the concealed German emplacement.

2002: Ken's eightieth birthday trip to Simi; pointing across the bay to his Bren-gun position.

Summer 2004: Ralph Bridger (seventy-six years) and Ken Smith (eighty-one years), reminiscing.

11

NORTH AFRICA

"Corporal Smith, get four chaps together – you have a very important prisoner to guard."

After the Greek island campaign H Patrol found themselves based for a short while at Mersa Matruh. This lies approximately halfway between Alexandria and Tobruk, on the Mediterranean coast of Egypt. Here they readied themselves for their next deployment. They were accommodated in a former German Afrika Korps field hospital that was partially underground and about as isolated as could be possibly found. As Ken said, "It was in the middle of nowhere."

Intense training took place for an unknown destination. After being "dropped off miles out to sea" there were long swims back to shore. Brutal forced marches with heavy loads, "walking all over the desert" with only survival rations, and "lots of canoeing". Ken, Sticks and Bill proved to be the most adept at this last task, so when a regatta was organised, they were teamed up in a three-man Folbot and ceded last in a race around the bay. Winning convincingly, they were presented with a trophy which turned out to be a polished brass shell casing ("the desert was littered with them") stuffed full of cigarettes. Just try giving that as a trophy nowadays!

Taking some leave in Alexandria, Ken and a few of his comrades were aimlessly wandering around the city. A jeep pulled up alongside; in it were a couple of the unit's officers, who asked them, "What are you chaps up to?"

"Nothing much," came the reply.

"Hop in, we're off to a party."

No second invite was required, and the overladen vehicle lumbered off to one of the 'posh' suburbs of the city. They pulled up at a very large mansion with a walled garden, owned by a wealthy French expatriate. A garden party was in full swing, and the officers immediately joined in. They were completely at ease, whereas the troopers felt "a bit out of place". But not for too long as a group of young ladies came over to welcome them. Ken was amazed as the girls, all French origin, could instantly switch from their native tongue to perfect Queen's English and back. It transpired that the party was to raise funds for their homeland, a large area of which had by now been liberated. The population were suffering and in need of much. To this end, a charity auction took place with the grand lot being a treasured bottle of fine vintage wine. The party's host won the auction with an outrageous bid, then with great ceremony proceeded to uncork the bottle and pour small portions of the contents into numerous glasses, thus enabling many to sample this delicacy. As honoured guests, the SBS were all offered a glass to sip and relish.

Ken promptly quaffed his down and then remarked, "Taste just like that cheap vino down the local bar." It was one of those moments when you speak to a friend in a noisy gathering just as quiet descends. His remarks were greeted by a few moments of stunned silence and an incredulous look upon the host's face. Unfortunately for Ken the hole in the ground did not open to swallow him, and this incident only went on to further add to his growing reputation as a total heathen.

Ken was detailed to go fishing in the bay for the unit's dinner. He was surprised to see, sat at anchor in the cove, a brand-new, gleaming RAF search-and-rescue motorboat. He could not remember the last time he had seen anything shiny and in pristine condition. All else appeared rusting and in desperate need of some tender loving care (TLC). After admiring the craft, he set to with his task and tossed some explosives into the sea; usually six sticks of Nobels 208. Following the explosion he quickly set to gathering the result: a shoal of stunned fish. As he collected dinner he noticed an archetypal RAF officer, complete with handlebar moustache, storming down the beach in his direction. Ken then endured a severe reprimand as he was subjected to a harsh dressing-down.

"You hooligans. Do you see that?" the officer said, pointing at the launch. "The government has paid thousands of pounds it can ill afford, not for you to use as target practice!"

The lecture went on for some time. Upon returning to camp Ken explained to the officer who asked why the meal was going to be late.

"Hooligans? I'll give him hooligans," said the officer as he formulated a plan of revenge. The Marine and Jock Patrols were about to undertake some mischievous training.

The flour used for cooking came in small hessian bags. Empty ones were collected and filled with sand, and a label attached saying, 'This could have been a bomb!' One of the main RAF air bases, some distance across the desert, was paid a visit. The exercise was treated as a mission. Ken remembered a long trek, lying up in concealed and camouflaged positions, observing the target, formulating a plan of attack, and after dark every plane, as well as fuel dumps, ammunition stores, numerous vehicles and buildings, was targeted with a small present.

By daylight the troops were well away, camouflaged and happy with the trouble they had created. The CO of the airfield was surprised to receive an early morning wake-up call informing him that "Us hooligans have just blown up every plane on your base!"

Ken was once woken in the middle of the night. It was about 0200 hours and there were torches outside his tent.

"Corporal Smith, get four chaps together – you have a very important prisoner to guard."

This turned out to be General Heinrich Kreipe, the German officer in charge of Crete. He had been captured by a couple of Special Operations Executive (SOE) officers and local partisans. Having been smuggled off the Cretan coastline by members of Bob Bury's SBS detachment, the general was landed at the Mersa Matruh base, where he was placed in the centre of a room with Ken and three others facing him as guards. No chances were being taken. Dressed in a long black leather coat, the German general stood staunchly upright and stared at his guards with contempt. He was a small, stocky man with an extremely arrogant persona. When a suitable secure location had been found to house the general, a surly Jock, Hans Majury, was detailed to act as his batman (orderly/servant). This must have been a deliberate act of devilment as a more belligerent, cantankerous, foul-mouthed, antisocial person could not be found. The tall Scotsman spoke in a dialect that even his fellow countrymen struggled to comprehend. To be a German officer's servant was not on his wish list, and he made it known. When serving Kreipe food he would smash the serving spoon down on the plate, always accompanied by a torrent of incomprehensible abuse. The general complained about the "unintelligible heathen oaf".

Unfortunately, the entertainment did not last too long as a small convoy of cars, escorted by several Military Police jeeps, emerged from a dust cloud and sped into camp. "They didn't pay much heed to any blackout regulations, coming out with lights on." It was said that "they must have emptied out all the top brass from Cairo". Much fuss was made, and they were soon on their way. Ralph commented, "There was a general, a colonel and lots of military police, (MPs). But no one saluted."

In 1957 a motion picture, *Ill Met by Moonlight*, was released, starring Dirk Bogarde, a Hollywood A-lister. This film tells the story of General Kreipe's capture.

In a moment of peace, Ken found a quiet location to sit and sketch a Polish boat opposite his position, anchored just out to sea. He thought it was a destroyer nicknamed *'Blissky Whisky'*. Close by sat another ship. Suddenly he "heard this sound" he had never heard before. *Whoosh* – a German plane appeared out of nowhere and "dropped a bomb between the two boats. It didn't hit." Ken believed it to be the first time he had ever encountered a jet aircraft, and wondered at the time just what it was.

After a period of intense training the troops were granted a few days' leave, with almost all opting for Cairo. Ken, having spent some time there for his sniper's course, chose Alexandria instead. There he came across a few old navy pals on shore leave. Some Military Police started to "push their authority" on the group. To say that Ken disliked 'Red Caps' is somewhat of an understatement. He saw them as bullies, safe in the rear and away from the fighting, who seemed to gain enjoyment out of intimidating and bullying servicemen. His friends were all in uniform and forced to take a dressing-down. Ken was in civvies (civilian clothes) and took the opportunity to tell the MPs exactly what he thought of them. Unfortunately, his pay book was sticking out of his shirt pocket, the MPs spotted this and knew he was military personnel. A street brawl erupted, with Ken giving a good account of himself before eventually being overpowered by sheer weight of numbers.

He woke up in a cell having received a severe beating, his face "looking a picture", with little identification and unable to provide any details other than his service number, rank, name and where he was based. Escorted by a couple of Red Caps, he was put in the back of a jeep and taken in handcuffs across the desert to their base at Mersa Matruh. At the camp he was handed over (with a stack of charge sheets) for the unit to deal with. The only real punishment was to be RTU'ed, sent back to the marines. Having managed to borrow an ill-fitting cap from a clerk, sporting a swollen and bruised face and black eyes, and fearing the worst, Ken was led before the camp CO, Captain Macbeth. He marched into a spartan room in the concrete blockhouse of the old German field hospital. Dreading his fate, he stood to attention and awaited the inevitable. It took a few moments for his eyes to adjust to the dim light compared to the desert glare. Macbeth was shirtless and moving back and forth between a desk and a metal filing cabinet, busy with routine paperwork and seemingly oblivious to the sorry-looking figure paraded before him. Ken wondered where on earth a metal filing cabinet had come from in the middle of the desert.

Eventually Macbeth looked up and said, "Ah, Smith, I've been hearing some good reports about you."

He then carried on shuffling about as a bewildered Ken, struggled to make sense of what had just been said.

What came next was even more of a shock. "I was thinking about promoting you, but the marines have a different system from the army and it's all a bit confusing."

Not as confused as Ken!

"Tell you what I'll do: I'll make you up to corporal and we'll sort out the details later!" Macbeth then picked up the pile of Ken's charge sheets that lay on the table. "And as for these," tearing them in half and throwing them in a bin, "I'm surprised at you allowing yourself to be caught by the Red Caps!"

Ken left the room not quite believing what had taken place. When his mates arrived back from Cairo to find Ken sporting a brand-new pair of chevrons, and then heard the story of how he had achieved his promotion, they all vowed to spend their next leave in Alex. One of the group, a renowned boxer, even said he thought he could make sergeant!

Bill Mayall, 2nd left, and a couple of the 'Jocks,' Hans Majury and Robbie Drummond.

12

ITALY

"He went down like a sack of spuds."

The SRS had been in Italy since the very beginning of the liberation campaign. In fact, they were amongst the very first troops in. On the 10th of July 1943 they stormed ashore ahead of the invasion fleet to eliminate the gun batteries located on the headland at Murro di Porco, Sicily. This position covered the Allied landing beaches and could have caused much damage to the approaching armada. They continued to fight in advance of the Allied forces, taking on the supposed 'soft underbelly of Europe', which in fact turned out to be the tough old gut.

The author of *The SAS and LRDG Roll of Honour, 1941–47* gives this timeline to events as:

End of November 1943 – SRS embarks at Taranto for Bizerte, Tunisia, and subsequently spends nearly a month at 2nd SAS camp at Philippeville, Algeria (personal diaries).

25th December 1943 – SRS (less advance party) embarks at Algiers for the UK (personal diaries).

7th January 1944 – 1st SAS regiment is re-established in the UK using the SRS as its nucleus (numerous service records).

15th March 1944 – 2nd SAS Regiment returns to the UK via Algeria and joins the SAS Brigade (strength is 640 all ranks – WO 379/79). Due to lack of numbers, it is initially designated as a battalion but soon regains regimental status.

19th July 1944 – First operation in Northwest Europe Campaign (Operation Defoe – WO 218/199).

14th January 1945 – 3 Squadron 2nd SAS returns to Italy to resume operations (WO 379/79). Following D-Day operations.

General Miles Dempsey, the commanding officer of XIII Corps, lavished high praise on the SAS troops in Italy and gave six reasons why he thought them successful:

First of all, you take your training seriously. That is one thing that has always impressed me about you.

Secondly, you are well disciplined. Unlike some who take on the specialised and highly dangerous job, you maintain a standard of discipline and cleanliness which is good to see.

Thirdly, you are physically fit, and I think I know you well enough to know you will always keep that way.

Fourthly, you are completely confident in your abilities – yet not to a point of overconfidence.

Fifthly, despite that confidence you plan carefully.

Last of all, you have the right spirit, which I hope you will pass on to those who may join you in the future.

Following the big raid on Simi on the 13th–14th July 1944, the SBS split, with Jellicoe taking a large force to harass the retreating Germans out of Greece. They helped push them from the islands, drove them from the Peloponnese Peninsula, and played no small part in the liberation of Athens. Anders Lassen, with only thirty to forty men driving commandeered fire engines, managed to compel a German force of several thousand men to abandon Salonica, the second largest city in Greece. This avoided much bloodshed and destruction. He then ruled the city for over a week, before returning to Athens where he lived in the city's plushest hotel. There he would drive his jeep up the stairs and chain it to a radiator outside his room. Someone had stolen a previous jeep, and he had no intention of losing this one. Other elements of the SBS relocated to Italy via North Africa, where they set up headquarters at Bari. One of the unit's officers, Patterson, together with much of their records, was lost in a plane crash in Italy in the autumn of 1944.

To begin with the troops were housed under the terraces of a football stadium before being transferred to an abandoned monastery at Monte Sant'Angelo, Monopoly. From August 1944, the Special Boat Squadron were involved in operations across the Northern Mediterranean theatre in Greece, Albania, Yugoslavia, Istria and Italy. The relatively small forces of a few hundred men were keeping no fewer than six German divisions occupied. A close relationship, first inaugurated in the early days of the SAS amid the sands of the North African desert, continued long after that campaign had ended. The LRDG became a behind-the-lines reconnaissance unit. In Italy both formations were billeted together at the monastery just north of Bari. The intention was to keep the units well away from any other troops.

One evening Ken Smith, Sticks May and Ken Joynson were invited by the LRDG to a quiet social in a small room at the church hall they were occupying. They had a couple of bottles of cheap vino and were enjoying a low-key evening listening to some gramophone music and exchanging stories.

As the evening progressed raised voices were heard coming from the main entrance. One of the LRDG men came over to Ken's group and said, "I'm very sorry but there is a spot of bother outside with a couple of your chaps."

The three SBS men went to investigate and found a drunk pair of troublemakers, Ralph and Iggy, demanding entry and an invitation to the party. Ken, apologising to their host, said, "Leave it to us; we'll sort it out." They started to try and reason with their intoxicated friends, saying it was a small gathering, just chatting and listening to some music. But the two friends were having none of it, so Ken ordered the pair back to camp. An indignant Iggy accused Ken of hiding behind his stripes. A now-furious Ken said, "Outside", unperturbed by his would-be opponent's boxing record as a Yorkshire amateur boxing champion. The pair squared off, then Ken let fly and hit Iggy with a tremendous blow.

"He went down like a sack of spuds," said Sticks.

In the meantime, Ralph had hit Joynson, who disappeared over a small parapet landing badly. Ralph, on seeing what he had done, quickly sobered up and took charge of his groggy friend Iggy, who was slowly coming to, saying, "What hit me?!"

To which Ralph replied, "Smithy."

"Bloody hell. Ken?" said Iggy, shaking his head to clear it.

Sticks jumped down to Joynson and quickly realised the seriousness of the situation. The patient was soon loaded into a commandeered jeep, and they sped off to a nearby RAF base where they knew there was a doctor. The duty guard at the camp's gate was reluctant to let them enter or wake the doctor. He was quickly persuaded otherwise. The doctor was extremely annoyed to be woken and forced out of bed, but he soon altered his attitude after a quick examination of the patient, saying, "It's a good job you made it here; he wouldn't have lasted the night!" Joynson was immediately admitted and operated on. After discharge he was RTU'ed and never seen again.

Ken had driven back to camp to sort things out. Sticks stayed at the hospital and the following day had to walk back to camp through the snow. By the time he made it back he was in a foul mood. The guilty pair were ostracised for a while and forced to keep a low profile.

The nearby Bari Stadium hosted a few events to entertain the troops. One was an exhibition boxing bout between Joe Louis the reigning world heavyweight champion, and the American forces' heavyweight champion, a huge mountain of a man. The serviceman was keen to impress and perhaps gain some bragging rights, but Joe kept him under control and let him know who was boss. The SAS/SBS seemed to be well represented by talented boxers and Joe was good enough to spar with a few of them, just as long as he didn't land any punches. The stadium also hosted an exhibition soccer match between an England touring team that included many national players (Billy Wright, Tom Finney, Stanley Matthews, Frank Swift and Stanley Mortensen) and an army team that included Ray Iggleden.

Bari must still have been in a ruined state when the SBS were based in the area. Not only had it sustained considerable damage during the German retreat, but only a year earlier on the 2nd of December 1943, at 7pm on a dark winter's night, 105 German bombers (Junkers 88s) bombed the port. The harbour was lit up as no blackout was in place and the radar precautions were useless. The SS *John Harvey*, with over one thousand tons of bombs on board, was half-unloaded. The cargo included mustard gas, intended for retaliation if the Germans resorted to chemical warfare! The raid lasted no more than fifteen to twenty minutes and resulted in the worst chemical explosion of World War II. Eighteen ships were destroyed and over one thousand people killed. It was the US Navy's second biggest disaster after Pearl Harbor.

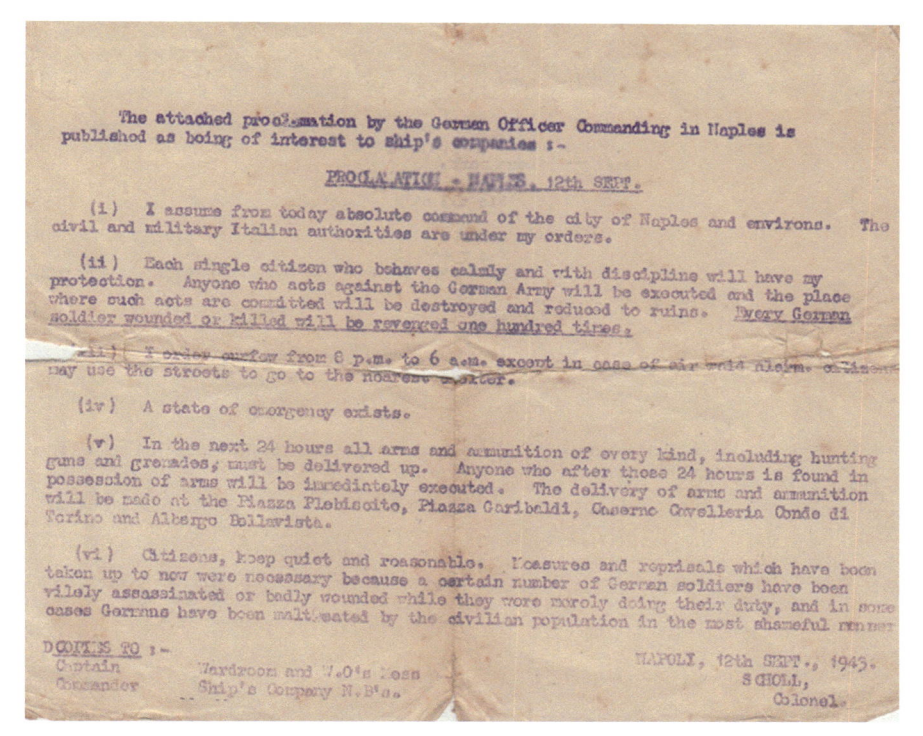

Naples, Italy, German proclamation 12th September 1943.

13

ALBANIA

"Lit up like a Christmas tree."

If you are going through hell, keep going.

On the 23rd of September 1944 the Marine and Jock Patrols departed Bari, travelling via Brindisi, Italy, to be landed at Valona/Vlorë, southern Albania. The Albanian partisans were ill-armed and resistance to Axis forces was largely led by the Russian-trained Enver Hoxha. The next two months would prove to be extremely arduous: constantly on the move, unable to trust the local partisans, low on supplies, behind the lines, and always aware of the enemy threat. Ken said, "All we seemed to do was climb, climb, climb. We were constantly on the go, with local partisan guides taking us on from one area to the next." It wasn't until the 16th of November that the half-starved, dishevelled, flea-, crab- and lice-ridden soldiers were withdrawn back to Bari. Dirty and unkempt, with their uniforms in tatters, and totally exhausted, here they were stripped, and their clothes burnt, showered and shaved, "injected with all sorts", and put on a high-energy diet. They had trekked the entire length of Albania with a foray over the Julian Alps into mainland

Greece, eventually emerging close to the Yugoslavia border. A few of the recorded dates are:

23rd September: Departed Brindisi; arrived in Albania.
27th September: Arrived at base (partisan?).
4th October: Kosinë.
6th October: Left Kosinë via Përmet.
7th–16th October: Izgar.
20th October: Kosinë.
21st–26th October: Marching.
26th October: Korcha, beer factory, Pogradec.
16th November: Returned to Italy.
17th November: Monte Sant'Angelo.

Other Albanian places Ken mentioned visiting were Pory, Palermo, Kue and Tepelenë.

Albania was an extremely impoverished country, with most of its population eking out a meagre living from the mountainous countryside. The rural inhabitants lived an almost feudal life as peasants. The country was part of the Axis Pact, but warlords, partisans and rebels controlled large areas. The SBS found it difficult to trust anyone and for the most part went their own way: blowing up bridges, railways, communications, stores, ammunition and fuel dumps, etc.; harassing German troops retreating from Greece; calling in air strikes; and generally making a nuisance of themselves. There were "lots of actions" as enemy patrols were frequently encountered.

Initially everything had to be carried on their backs. Ken would often demonstrate a well-remembered routine used to don his heavily laden rucksack. Firstly, he would heave, an imaginary pack

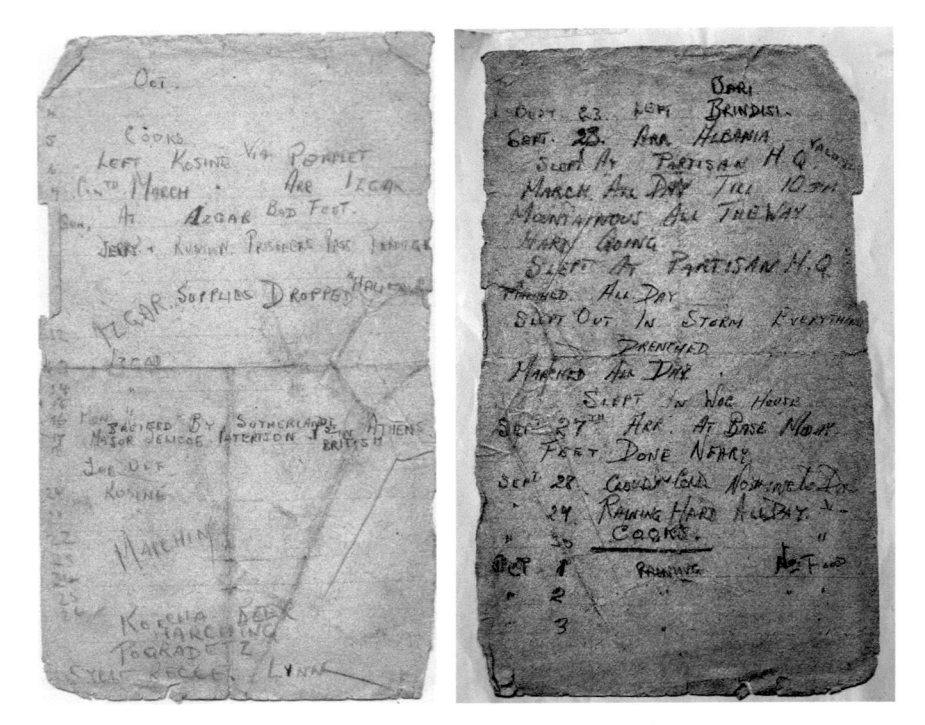

A couple of pages from Ken's Albania diary.

onto a wall, rock, or some other raised platform, grunting under the strain of his envisaged load. Then, balancing it, he would first put his right arm through the strap and then, turning slightly, put his left arm through the other strap; lean forward to balance the load; take the weight, leaning at almost ninety degrees; and with bent legs, trudge forward. He would then say, "We walked like that all day."

According to Ralph, "We walked the length and breadth of that country."

After approximately 150 miles they managed to acquire some mules/donkeys. Even so, the packs were unbearably heavy, and walking remained stooped. Resupply was by parachute drop. It did not take too long for the locals to realise that a triangle of bonfires signalled the drop zone. When the aircrews were later questioned as to why they failed to deliver much of the resupply, they answered that when the locals heard aircraft engines the countryside would be "lit up like a Christmas tree".

Radios were cumbersome affairs powered by large "car-type batteries". Often the acid would spill out as they traversed the rocky terrain. Ralph remembered that after one turn (a day) carrying a battery he said, "I had no skin on my shoulders and back" as the acid had leaked.

Ralph had only one fond memory of that country. Stopping overnight in a partisan-controlled village, they were invited to a party in one of the houses. 'House' might be too grand a description as it was no more than a large "flea- and lice-ridden shack" that "stunk to high heaven." It was a typical Albanian dwelling: a two-storey affair with the animals living below, providing winter warmth for the human inhabitants above. "Everything, and I mean everything" took place in this simple abode. Any women were usually kept well hidden; the only females encountered were "old hags with no teeth". The party resembled something from the Middle Ages. Traditional songs and dancing took place on the upper floor. The floorboards creaked violently, and the animals below complained noisily. A few bottles of rough local wine and spirits livened the night up. Apart from that one night, there was precious little joy to be had in Albania. Although most days the morning ritual of trying to get the packsaddles on the mules (generally accomplished with a vast amount of cursing and swearing) provided good entertainment. Ken gave another demonstration of his language skills when trying to barter with a local man. He couldn't understand why the Albanian would not agree to the trade. He was vigorously nodding his head in refusal (in Albania, a nod of the head means no, and a shake means yes), with Ken complaining that he was "almost giving it away". It was then explained that Ken's version of Albanian, when translated, meant something along the lines of 'Will you have sex with me?'!

Somewhere between Pocadades and Frascia (Ralph said, "It was possibly at Octrovra"), the SBS were 'booked in' for two nights in the monks' cells at a mountaintop monastery. They were following a narrow mountain track and far below them in the valley lay the remains of a burnt-out village. The Germans had torched it after discovering explosives hidden in a haystack. Nearing the end of the day and with only a short distance to go, there was a commotion near the front of the train. One of the mules had fallen off the track and was stranded on a ledge some twenty or thirty feet below. It was Hans Majury from the Jock Patrol's mule; apparently the poor animal was flagging badly so he gave it a couple of Benzedrine tablets! He was left behind to try and resolve the situation whilst the convoy continued to the destination.

Upon arrival Ken quickly unloaded his animal and, together with another man, was sent back to help Hans. Hans, meanwhile, had managed to unload his supplies and they were stacked up on the track, but his obstinate animal was refusing to budge from the ledge. Together they "tried everything" to persuade the mule to clamber back up to the track, but it stubbornly refused. The commotion brought an Albanian, who "appeared out of nowhere", to the scene. It turned out that he had previously emigrated to the USA and worked as a New York taxi driver before returning to his homeland, and he could therefore speak an American version of English.

On seeing the problem he said, "Leave it to me, bud. Where are you staying?"

Normally they would trust no one, but they decided to take a chance as the track only led to one place: the monastery. After telling the man where they were based, they loaded up Ken's mule and headed off, not arriving at the monastery until after dark. The following morning the three were allowed a short lie-in. Ken was surprised to find that he had been sleeping between two female partisans. On venturing outside he was even more surprised to find the errant mule calmly tethered and none the worse for his ordeal. The Albanian Yank had simply grabbed a handful of hay and strategically placed small amounts in front of the animal, in a line, back up to the track. The mule had just followed the food trail.

The troops were issued with a small package of various drugs. The medic who had explained what they were for and when to use them had ended his lecture by advising them never to take any. Ken swore that he always remembered those last words and took the advice. They also had cyanide capsules sewn into the collars of their shirts. If taken prisoner, they had the option of chewing on their collars to avoid torture. By this time the fate of some of their captured comrades had begun to circulate and they were all aware of 'Hitler's Order'.

Near to the capital, Tirana, they rested in a small town controlled by a partisan group. The Germans had built a brewery and now the partisans were using them as slave labour to work it. These poor fellows were in a pitiful state: infested with lice and crabs, dressed in tatters, with no shoes, having to make do with rags tied to their feet. Ralph said, "There was about thirty-five to forty Jerry in the brewery." They tried to surrender to the SBS, begging to be taken prisoner and citing the Geneva Convention.

The troopers explained that they were in no position to take prisoners of war. Reg Seekings, one of the 'original' SAS soldiers, said, "Generally, we didn't take prisoners. I don't mean we shot them out of hand." Depending on the circumstances, they would usually be disarmed and briefly held.

The SBS were able to give the captives a moment of respite by having one memorable night in each other's company. A large amount of the factory's produce was consumed, and the place was filled with singing as a mixture of songs in differing languages were sung. One intensely poignant moment was a rendition of 'Lili Marleen', sung by the German prisoners with tears streaming down their faces.

The following day, "We clinked our way out of the town" as the already overburdened mules struggled under an extra load of bottles. "They had bowed legs with the load," a smiling Ken recalled. He also remembered watching from a wooded slope which overlooked a small town that the enemy was pulling out of. "As they left, we went in."

One action that took place was when a German mountain division, retreating from Greece, was spotted and would the next day be making their way through a wooded valley.

Tansy quickly drafted a message and called out, "Corporal Smith, get this off immediately."

"It always seemed to be Corporal Smith," Ken once said. He, together with a Marine Williamson, was dispatched with the note to an LRDG radio post located a few valleys away on the shore of Lake Ohrid, Macedonia. It was known that they were scheduled to be in contact with command at 0700 the next morning.

Partisans provided an escort, but first they had to get a guide to take them over the mountains. He was in a nearby village and proved reluctant to acquiesce, but his partisan comrades soon persuaded him otherwise. First, he had to go to a neighbour's house for the communal pair of shoes. Ken frequently pressed upon them the urgency of the situation – *"Multi pronto"* ('faster') – but with little effect. Their guide was an old man, the going was painfully slow, and despite Ken pressing for more speed the radio deadline was slipping away. As first light approached, and believing he knew the way, he and Williamson pressed on ahead, desperate not to miss the LRDG regular call to Allied HQ.

His sense of direction proved to be correct. Passing over a col, he spied the radio shack far below. It sat beside a lake and the two operators were having a cup of tea and taking the morning sun outside the hut. Ken rushed down the hillside as the men rose and entered the hut to make contact. With moments to spare he handed over the message: a request for an air strike on the enemy convoy. After a quick cup of tea and ensuring that the message had been sent, Ken and Williamson set off back. He arrived on a ridge line overlooking the valley just in time to see the arrival of some rocket-firing Typhoons. They, dived into the valley, causing carnage amongst the Germans, who had no motor transport; it was mainly horses and mules. At the same time the SBS and partisans positioned on the slopes opened fire. The surviving Germans quickly dispersed into the trees and began to hunt down their assailants. According to Ralph, "We had a ding-dong."

As darkness fell, the partisans and SBS melted away as their positions were overrun. The British soldiers made for a prearranged rendezvous. Ken said, "the countryside was crawling with Jerry" as he made his way to the meeting point. This had already been overrun and abandoned, and a ring of onions had been left on the floor. This was a coded signal meaning, 'Make your way to the previous night's bivvy.' When Ken finally arrived at the rendezvous most of the troops were already there, as was the kit he'd been forced to leave behind to aid his urgent march. He was totally exhausted, having been on the go with no sleep for over two days. He then discovered that his sniper's rifle was missing. It had been drummed into him that this specialist weapon was one of only a few in the British armed forces and he was to guard it with his life. When Sergeant Jim Horsefield came in sporting a large black eye Ken instantly knew what had caused the injury, and demanded of him, "Where's my rifle?"

"That bloody thing? Threw it away," came the blistering reply. Jim had taken the weapon to use in the ambush but, being unskilled in its use, had fired it as one would a normal rifle. The recoil had hammered the telescopic sights back into his eye. He said he had thrown the rifle under a bush as the Germans were about to infiltrate his position. The following day, a search was conducted but nothing was found.

Ralph had a couple of stories to add to this tale. He remembered Sticks manning a tripod-mounted machine gun, blasting away down the slope, seemingly oblivious to the bullets coming his way. He often said, "Sticks was the bravest man I've ever known." He went on to say that during the engagement, Jim was found hiding out in a hut and was to be RTU'ed. Ken always thought it was the loss of the sniper's rifle that led to Jims's discharge. Tansy told Jim he was to be RTU'ed on return and to play no further part in the running of operations. Increasingly, he was turning to Ken and Sticks to help run the patrol.

Ken spotted a strange, out-of-place sight as they trudged into a small hovel of a village (possibly Kossinge): a bright red-and-white barber's pole projected from one of the buildings. As soon as possible he raced back to the 'shop' (which looked like it should be in a cowboy movie), pointed to his hair, and then sat in a vacant barber's chair. The look on the faces of those present was incredulous: a mixture of shock and trepidation as they stared at the dishevelled-looking wild man now awaiting grooming. The bewildered lady barber produced a "froufrou spray" perfume bottle; the type where a small flask of scent has a little rubber ball attached that, when squeezed, propels the perfume in a fine mist. With arms outstretched, and staying as far away as possible, she emptied the contents in Ken's direction. According to him, "We must 'ave stunk" (somewhat of an understatement). "She threw a cloth round us, and she cut my hair from a distance", trying to keep her body, and particularly her nose, as far away as possible.

He strode away from the premises feeling so much better and keen to show off his new clean look. Glancing back, he witnessed a frantic sanitation process taking place at the barbers.

At one stage Ken had to be left behind for a couple of days with the LRDG. His ankle, badly sprained during ski training, was playing up. He took the time to do some sketching and write a few things in a small notebook. Diaries were strictly forbidden in the unit. 'Who Dares Wins' the SAS motto; or 'Who cares who wins.'

The men were constantly tired and hungry, and often wet. As they trekked there was always a pot hanging from the side of one of the mules, and into this would be thrown anything vaguely edible: wild tomatoes, mushrooms and the like. After one particularly hard day's trekking they collapsed into their sleeping bags on the side of a boulder-strewn hill. Then it started to rain, growing ever more intense as the night wore on. Ken fastened his bag as tight as possible but despite his best efforts, water started to seep in. Soon a puddle formed at the bottom of the bag. He was forced to slowly raise his feet as the puddle grew ever larger. It wasn't too long before his knees were drawn up almost to his chest. Enough was enough and he made his way to a pile of stones with the dubious title of a shepherd's hut. On his arrival he found most of his comrades already standing around despondently muttering oaths.

The next morning the sun burst through and all lay naked, warming their bodies, as their clothes and equipment lay scattered on boulders all over the hillside, drying out. Ken glanced across at Sticks and was intrigued to see he was now sat upright, counting aloud as he intently picked fleas off his body, squeezing them between his thumbnails. "I don't know why you're bothering with that," said Ken. "You're going to be covered in them again in no time."

Albert Lewis J. May ('Sticks') died after a long illness in April 1998, aged seventy-six. Ken was at his bedside for his last moments. As Sticks lay there, unresponsive and seemingly unconscious, Meg, his wife, asked Ken to say something to comfort him. All Ken could come up with was to talk about their shared time in the SBS. He reminisced about the hillside in Albania, and when he came to the part about crushing fleas a faint smile appeared on Sticks' face and he gently pressed his thumbs together as if crushing parasites. He passed away with that smile upon his face. Ralph said of Sticks, "He was most fearless – I never knew a braver man."

They made it to the northern edge of Albania, close to the Greek and Yugoslav border. Here, Lassen's patrol from M Squadron was parachuted in, as were some much-needed supplies. Andy's patrol was to carry on and cross into Yugoslavia. A couple of Office of Strategic Services, (OSS), operatives arrived and advised that it was all getting very "political", and it was best "not to mix". Belgrade had been liberated by the Soviets on the

20th of October 1944 and the Russians were advancing into the Balkans.

According to Ralph, "There were only about ten parachuted in and it included some from L Squadron. No sooner had they landed when one of them started to help himself to our meagre supplies. By this time, we were on starvation rations. Ken stormed up to the man and said, 'Do you know what you have taken? That's all we have been existing on for three weeks." He then hit the man, knocking him clean out. "Flattened him."

Lassen's patrol gave the wild-looking bunch of savages a wide berth and were soon on their way over the Yugoslav border.

Ken never talked about the specifics of any military engagements, except to say, "We were frequently in contact with the enemy and always on the go."

The bedraggled, skeletal wild men were withdrawn to southern Italy on the 16th of November 1944. They spent the next three weeks recuperating in a schoolhouse in Monte Sant'Angelo. "Under a roof," said Ralph. "We were in a bad way. Malnourished, underweight, flea- and lice-ridden."

A medical orderly, "a small Scotsman", had them all strip off and their clothes were burnt. He went through their bodies, looking for fleas, ticks, etc., and told them to "Go have a shower; you're all flea-ridden and lousy", and then put them on a high-calorie diet.

After the short recuperation they were sent to Bari, and "billeted under a football stadium, on a dirt floor, in sleeping bags, with big rats running over us. It was considered a rest!"

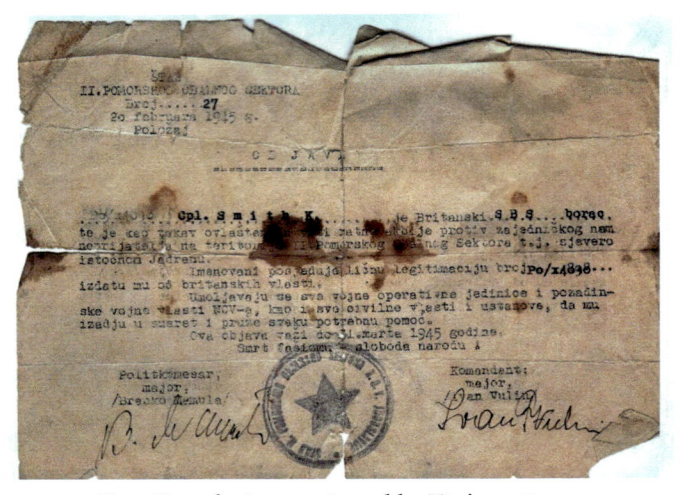

*Kens Yugoslavia pass, issued by Tito's partisans,
showing his blood staining.*

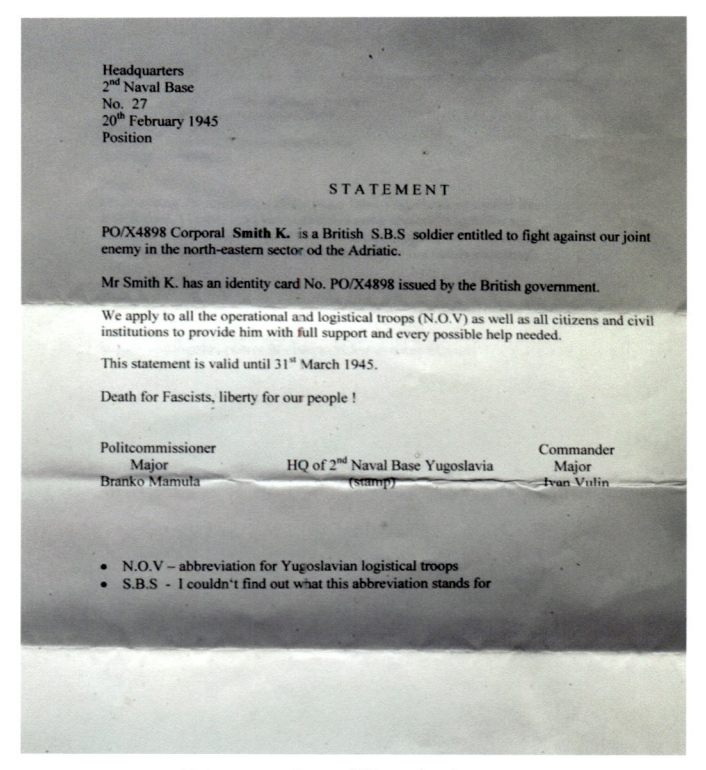

Headquarters
2nd Naval Base
No. 27
20th February 1945
Position

STATEMENT

PO/X4898 Corporal **Smith K.** is a British S.B.S. soldier entitled to fight against our joint enemy in the north-eastern sector od the Adriatic.

Mr Smith K. has an identity card No. PO/X4898 issued by the British government.

We apply to all the operational and logistical troops (N.O.V) as well as all citizens and civil institutions to provide him with full support and every possible help needed.

This statement is valid until 31st March 1945.

Death for Fascists, liberty for our people !

Politcommissioner		Commander
Major	HQ of 2nd Naval Base Yugoslavia	Major
Branko Mamula	(stamp)	Ivan Vulin

- N.O.V – abbreviation for Yugoslavian logistical troops
- S.B.S - I couldn't find out what this abbreviation stands for

Interpretation of Yugoslavia pass.

14

LUSSIN MAP

The island of Lussin as it was known by the troops but also goes by the name Luccin/Losinj/Lošinj.

Lussin is part of the Dalmatian Island chain off the coast of former Yugoslavia (now part of Croatia). The island is long (thirty-three kilometres/20.5 miles) and thin (less than five kilometres/three miles at its widest point). Its main town, Mali Lussin, is approximately a third of the way up its length towards the southern end in a large natural harbour. Veli Lussin is a few miles south-east, on the east coast. Villa Punta guards the entrance to the village, situated inside a small inlet. A high ridge runs the length of the island apart from the narrow stretch north of Mali Lussin. The island is heavily wooded with a few cultivated areas. A road runs the full length, and many tracks criss-cross the island. Large, well-rounded boulders are stacked to form drystone walls that bound the narrow tracks on both sides and form much of the walking surface.

15

YUGOSLAVIA

"If there's any trouble, shoot the bloody lot of them!"

Men can be highly civilised while other men, considered less civilised, are there to guard and feed them.
(George Orwell)

In the winter of 1944 Jellicoe was posted to the staff college at Haifa, Palestine, and David Sutherland took over command of the SBS. Ambrose McGonigal became the new CO of L Squadron following the death of Patterson in an aircraft crash. The unit were not noted for their record-keeping, and a plane crash in southern Italy (possibly the same incident) resulted in the loss of much SAS/SBS documentation.

By the middle of January 1945 the SBS, including Captain 'Jimmy' Lees and H Patrol, were stationed in an abandoned monastery at Monte Sant'Angelo situated on the Adriatic coast of Italy. Could there have ever been a more inappropriate place in which to base them? At the end of the month Milner-Barry, Sutherland's new second in command, was posted to Land Forces Adriatic HQ at Bari, southern Italy. He learned there that 'something was in the wind about our movements which would involve quite a lot of work… operations looked promising' (Milner-Barry). These operations were to be on what David Sutherland had described as 'those jagged splinters of land off the Croatian coastline which rejoiced in such names as Krk, Rab and Pat, Lussin and Olib'. He warned his men that they were garrisoned by the same Germans who had been stationed in the Aegean and were 'well aware of both the strength and weaknesses of the raiding forces now about to attack them'. The Germans were now entrenched behind formidable defensive positions with extensive barbed wire, mines, machine-gun emplacements and sentries on high alert – especially during the hours of darkness.

In February S Squadron established their HQ in Zara, Yugoslavia (now Zadar, Croatia). With the war's end in sight, political and strategic manoeuvring was taking place. The situation was becoming ever more sensitive. In Yugoslavia the Axis forces were conducting an organised retreat, actively harassed by Tito's partisans, a communist legion and by far the most effective anti-Fascist force in the region. The partisan allegiance favoured the Soviets and British forces were finding themselves increasingly unwelcome and forced to operate along the Adriatic coastline and in the numerous Dalmatian Islands.

The enemy were offering a staunch resistance, fiercely defending their positions and unwilling to give up ground easily. Unlike in the arid Greek islands, the SBS now found themselves operating in densely wooded terrain. Instead of a largely friendly and cooperative population, the locals seemed unwilling to help and sometimes even hostile. The Ustaski/Ustashe/Ustasha (a mainly Croatian force) violently opposed the partisans (who were mainly Serbian) and fought alongside the Germans. The SBS learnt not to trust anyone in this harsh environment.

The Italians had formally surrendered on the 3rd of September

1943 but many of their troops had continued to fight on. The Fascists did so willingly, but many were coerced into continuing with hostilities. However, by this stage of the war it was obvious that the war's end was approaching and increasing numbers were surrendering. Two Italians had given themselves up to the partisans, who in turn handed them over to the British. The pair said that their comrades also wished to surrender, and that they were billeted on the island of Lussin in a large, fortified manor house, Villa Punta. This guarded the entrance to a small inlet leading to the fishing village at Veli Lussin. A sizeable German garrison of over two hundred troops was known to be stationed at Mali Lussin only a few miles away. A Royal Navy launch of the Levant Squadron was duly dispatched to pick up the surrendering Italians. They returned to base "badly shot up". Understandably the navy was incensed by this turn of events and, seeking retribution, turned to the SBS (for whom they were providing an extremely effective 'taxi service') and asked if they would "sort them out"!

At this time, (now promoted) Captain Lees, Sticks May and Bill Mayall were away on a reconnaissance mission. A small mixed patrol was assembled comprising seasoned veterans of the Marine and Jock Patrols under the command of a new officer to the unit, Lieutenant Jones-Parry from the Parachute Regiment. A brigadier conducted the raid briefing, which took place on the deck of HMS *Colombo*, a light cruiser tied up alongside the harbour at Zara. A small party consisting of the brigadier, Jones-Parry and a couple of naval officers strolled around the deck. They were closely followed by one of the Italian deserters, escorted by two SBS NCOs, Sergeant 'Jock' Cameron and Corporal Ken Smith. The Italian was to act as guide and liaison with the billet's occupants.

The naive young officer asked what he should do if there was any problem.

"If there's any trouble, shoot the bloody lot of them!" came the curt reply from the brigadier.

It was obvious to the two NCOs that the Italian guide had heard and understood the exchange. Ken thought, *this could be trouble.*

Lussin, *Operation Aniseed*

The raiding party was landed after dark in a secluded cove on the opposite side of the island from the target; the island being only a mile or two wide at that point. Their guide had difficulty finding his way, complaining about how it all looked so different in the dark. The going was laborious: a high ridge divided the island, and boulders were stacked to form walls and pathways. As time went on Ken believed that the Italian, fearful of the fate of his comrades, was purposefully being obstructive and hindering the patrol. Ken voiced his concerns.

The night dragged on, they continued to wander around, and tempers became frayed.

First light was approaching when Jones-Parry turned to an increasingly belligerent Ken and said, "Well, Corporal Smith, what would you do?"

Believing he could make out their objective in the distance, Ken said, "Shoot him," pointing to the Italian, "and go this way."

This had a remarkable effect upon their guide, who immediately became very agitated, full of excuses, and certain of where they were. A short, intense discussion followed, with Sergeant Cameron erring on the side of caution and advising a postponement. Fortunately for the Italian, Ken's advice was not taken. It was decided that it would be foolish to continue with dawn fast approaching and it would be best to return the following night. Some fuel that had been taken to torch the billet was secreted away. The patrol headed for the rendezvous with the naval launch, which was tied up to a small jetty in a cove just to the south of the fishing village. Skirting some habitation, they "roused the local dogs". There was also lots of broken glass, making silent progress difficult.

By first light the raiding party was laid up under camouflage on a nearby deserted island. The weather took a turn for the worse and a storm blew up which persisted for the next few days, preventing their return to Lussin. HQ radioed to find out what was going on, and when the situation was explained they were more than a little annoyed and immediately ordered the detachment back to base. It was not in their nature to be thwarted so easily, and a second, more forceful attempt was planned.

Captain Lees' reconnaissance party had by this time returned. For Sticks there was sad news: his mother was dying, he had been granted compassionate leave and was already on his way home. He managed to get a lift on an American bomber to Italy, and there he learned the terrible news of his mother's death. Unable to secure a flight to Britain, and with the family assuring him that all was in hand, a grieving Sticks made his way back to Zara.

By the time of his return, the second Villa Punta mission had already set off. This was a much larger band of men comprising at least four officers and two patrols (the Marine and the Jock). Ken, who was not known for his diplomatic skills, had told 'Tansy' Lees that the new officer had "no idea", and would he come along?

Villa Punta (Point House)

A force of approximately eighteen SBS operatives was landed after dark at Lussin on the night of the 9th–10th March 1945. They again disembarked in a quiet, secluded cove on the opposite side of the island from the target. No difficulties were encountered during the landing or the subsequent approach: a journey of approximately two miles over the densely wooded and boulder-strewn ridge. About midnight they stealthily emerged from the cover of a high stone-walled pathway onto the gently rising roadway that led up from the village to the fortified villa less than one hundred metres away. On the opposite side of the road was a low stone wall compared to the three-metre-plus wall on the side they had appeared from. In ghostly silence they began their advance when, with frightening ferocity, "All hell broke loose," said both Ken and Ralph. Machine-gun and rifle fire opened on them; bullets bounced off the road and ricocheted from the tall wall. The air was filled with the sound of intense gunfire. Instinctively the raiders took cover and returned fire. Ralph pressed himself into the tall wall, gaining some shelter behind a telegraph pole. Two men reputedly leapt over the small parapet wall into the darkness, falling over two metres onto the rocks below. Ken dived behind the small wall, Tansy lying in front of him.

"Are you all right, Smithy?" Tansy called out.

"Yes, sir, right behind you," was Ken's reply.

"Follow me," cried Tansy and, crawling on their stomachs, they set off for the villa.

Ralph abandoned his meagre cover and raced across the road to join them. By now the SBS troops had recovered from the initial surprise. Their training instinctively kicked in: accurate, well-aimed suppressing fire was being directed back at the enemy, and the tide of battle slowly started to change. One of the Jocks, who favoured a Bren gun, charged forward, firing from the hip and taking out a machine gun firing from the roof. Ken's weapon of choice was the German Schmeisser sub-machine gun; an extremely reliable piece of armament, spare ammunition seldom causing a problem, the opposition being a fertile source of resupply. With much practice and "a light finger, single, accurate rounds could be loosed off". Many SAS troops used non-British weaponry, the Schmeisser being one of their favourites.

The confused and chaotic situation began to resolve itself. Orders were given out, superior skills and training began to give the raiders the upper hand, and enemy fire was being suppressed. "They were expecting us" and "It was an ambush" were common opinions expressed at subsequent reunions. At the very least it seemed as if the defenders were on high alert. Had the fuel dump been discovered, or had the raiders been spotted and reported on their previous visit? Either way, there was no element of surprise and the decision to increase the size of the attacking force was an auspicious one. Sergeant Jock Cameron, 'Brummie' Barlow and Corporal Ken Smith were detailed to go past the villa and secure the road that any retreating enemy would take and by which any reinforcements from the garrison at Mali Lussin would appear.

In the initial phase of the melee Ken had felt a bullet tear into his jacket. Later inspection revealed that it had entered on one side and exited on the other, shredding a neat line across his jumper. He was unaware that he had not been so lucky with another round. Whilst settling into a covering position he noticed that his left hand was sticky and traced the trail of what proved to be blood back to his upper arm muscle. "Here, Jock, I think I've taken one," he said.

An intense firefight raged around and now inside the villa. It was chaos. The order was given to clear the house room by room if necessary. In the confused fighting, both Jones-Parry and another officer, Thomason, were forced to send messages out to stop the firing into the rooms being cleared. On entering a room Jones-Parry was badly wounded, a Marine Kitchingman, who was following, asked him if he was OK only to be picked out and shot dead. Jones-Parry managed to return fire, taking out their assailant. He withdrew from the building to join a growing number of casualties. Flares were fired out of the chimney in an attempt to alert the nearby garrison. Tansy Lees, whilst trying to clear the first floor, was caught up in an explosion, ending up half-buried under the partially collapsed staircase.

Ralph Bridger gave a vivid account of being in the hallway of the building: "I was knocked off my feet by a door being blown from its hinges." With blood pouring from his nose, and slightly concussed, he discharged one magazine from his nine-millimetre Schmeisser, returning fire up the stairs and into adjacent rooms. Then Big Bill Morgan, of the jock patrol, groaned and fell over, someone yelled, "To your left". Ralph rapidly replaced the spent magazine and resumed firing, spinning rounds and continuing to fire when threatened from the opposite direction. As he spun round a few bullets exited the front door and for some time he believed he was responsible for Ken's wound.

It seemed an eternity, but it was no more than fifteen or twenty minutes before the recall whistle was sounded. Someone told Ken that Captain Lees had been hit, and he found him near the building's front door. The pair had formed a strong bond, and it was a bitter blow. The scene was lit by the now-ablaze building. Ken cradled Tansy in his arms. He was unconscious and his wounds appeared to be fatal. Ken always maintained that they "had superb officers", and that "Tansy Lees was the best of them." Now to watch, what appeared to be, his last few spluttering breaths; it was hard to take. In the years afterwards Ken thought that Tansy had died in his arms, but in fact he survived for a few days before eventually succumbing to his injuries. The raid has been recorded as one of the costliest ever undertaken by the SAS/SBS, with two killed in action and up to eight wounded. One of the reasons given was that there were too many 'chiefs.

Ken was abruptly brought back to reality. "Leave him, he's done for! There's a wounded prisoner down there. Take him and get back to the beach," ordered an angry McGonigal.

Enemy reinforcements could appear at any moment, and it was imperative that they beat a hasty retreat. Ken, together with Jock Cameron, leapt over a low wall and slid down a small embankment to where a badly wounded enemy soldier, lying on his back, was desperately trying to toss a stick grenade. Ken promptly kicked the armament out of his hand, the pair lifted and manhandled the wounded soldier up the slope and over the parapet. It was then, in the light of the blazing building, that the prisoner's markings could be seen.

"He's a German, a grenadier, and an officer at that!" cried out Ken.

They were of the belief that the billet was still manned by Italians. Together the pair hoisted the prisoner up and slung him between their shoulders. Grenades had been thrown into the cellars to deal with the enemy hiding out there, and the raiders beat as hasty a retreat as possible, laden down with wounded and prisoners, and leaving the building well ablaze. Ken always maintained that his party was the last away, leaving behind them a scene of devastation: the building partially destroyed and on fire, with dead bodies scattered around it.

His small group had only succeeded in making it the short distance to the path's entrance before there was a deafening explosion close to Ken's ear. The prisoner went limp, becoming a dead weight, Jock let go, and the German crumpled to the ground. As he fell, Ken caught sight of a flash of reflected light, followed by the sound of metal striking the road. He instinctively realised that it was a gun, and that the prisoner must have shot himself in the head. Ken had assumed that Jock had frisked the man; a belief that could have proved disastrous. He turned the dead man over a couple of times to locate the weapon and was delighted to find a pearl-handled Beretta revolver. This magnificent piece of booty was quickly pocketed as it was sure to fetch a high price from the Americans. However, he was destined never to benefit from it. Ralph claimed, in a slightly differing version, to have found the weapon lying on the ground, saying that "Ken must have dropped it."

The shot attracted back a furious McGonigal. "What's going on here?" he demanded.

They quickly explained, and the exasperated officer aimed his revolver and "put three rounds from a Colt 45 into the head of the dead Jerry". The unit had been severely mauled, tempers were short, they were behind the lines and there was the ever-present threat of the enemy.

Ken was ordered forward to help with a stretcher party. He found himself on a rear corner, opposite a tall ex-guardsman. The narrow pathway, the large number of boulders and the uphill gradient made the going very difficult. It seemed to Ken as if all the stretcher's weight was transferred to his corner. His wound was now becoming increasingly painful, it was difficult to maintain a decent grip with his bloodied hands, and his task was proving ever more onerous. "I don't know why we are having to carry this bloody Jerry," he complained.

"That's no Jerry, that's your mate Bill Mayall," came a reply. Bill, Ken's great friend and a good footballer, had served aboard HMS *Penelope* with him.

"Leave me, leave me," Bill croaked; this being a common response from badly wounded men "who just wanted to be left to die in peace".

But despite Ken's own injury, there was no way he was going to abandon his comrade. Soon the load became unbearable, with the wound causing Ken excruciating pain. The stretcher became difficult to manage and grip with his hand now covered in sticky, congealed blood. He only found out much later that the stretcher was in fact a door that had been blown from its hinges in the assault. He was eventually relieved and ordered a short way up the track to take over as a prisoner escort. Considering his earlier experiences, he took no chances with his new charge. Being in great pain, extremely tired and in a foul mood, whenever the prisoner's raised arms began to droop a Schmeisser would be sharply thrust into the small of his back and a brusque voice would harshly order, "*Handi Hoch*" ('hands up'). Ken then went on to use almost his entire repertoire of German: "*Links Horn*" ('left turn'), "*Rechts Horn*" ('right turn'), and his personal favourite, "*Murres Hoiten*" ('shut up').

According to Ralph, "Ken was good at many things, but he was never a linguist!"

They barely made it in time. The sky was starting to lighten as dawn approached and the navy were keen to vacate enemy territory as soon as possible, before they became sitting ducks. They had to be persuaded to wait as more were a short way behind. The crestfallen troops emerged onto the beach. Jones-Parry had made the onerous trek back with a shattered arm and a bullet in his spleen. Ralph maintained that they were the very last to arrive. He and Hans Majury were half-carrying the wounded 'big Jock' Bill Morgan, saying, "We had to call the boat back!"

In the slowly improving light Ken could now see the badly injured German he had been escorting. "Most of his rump had been blown away and the poor fellow had messed himself." He sympathised with the man as "he must have been in sheer agony".

The prisoner indicated to his breast pocket and was allowed to reach in and draw out a couple of tatty, well-worn photos. His eyes glazed over and started to water. Despite what Ken had been through he felt deep empathy for the German and marvelled at how he had endured the forced march to the rendezvous. "If ever there was a hero, it was him. He had seven kids." Ken often wondered what had become of him.

The disconsolate rabble were rapidly transferred to the waiting launch. With great relief the force sped away to leave behind what has become known as one of the SBS's most costly raids. Until that time the Marine Patrol had considered themselves a lucky patrol. That night their luck had deserted them. Ken's final recollection of that fateful mission was stumbling across the boat's deck and looking down a metal staircase. He then collapsed from exhaustion and loss of blood, badly smashing his head as he fell down the stairwell.

It has been recorded that there were at least eighteen SBS troops taking part in the Villa Punta raid, which was reputedly defended by forty-five Germans. Half of the enemy were either killed or wounded but at least twenty survived by sheltering/hiding in the cellars, despite the grenades that had been thrown down there to eliminate them. The Villa Punta raid has been described as the worst SAS raid ever. It was certainly a costly one. Because of Sticks' attempt to visit his dying mother he was the only Marine Patrol member not to have taken part in the raid and always maintained that "If I had been along, things would have turned out a lot different."

Shortly after this action, on the 18th of March 1945 McGonigal led thirty-eight SBS in an attack on the bridge at Osor that linked the islands of Lussin and Cres. The eighty Germans holding this vital and well-protected junction fought off the attackers despite nearly half the garrison being either killed or wounded. The SBS casualties where one killed and three wounded. Raids in this region were becoming costly affairs, and this, coupled with the increasing belligerence of the partisans, led to the squadron's termination of offensive patrols in Yugoslavia.

Those believed to have taken part in the Villa Punta raid included:

Major Ambrose McGonigal (OIC).
Captain Charles Bimrose.
Lieutenant Ivan Jones-Parry (wounded).
Lieutenant Thomason.

Marine (H) Patrol
Captain James 'Jimmy'/ 'Tansy' Lees (killed in action).
Corporal Kenneth Herbert Smith (wounded).
Marine Alfred 'Brummie' Barlow.
- Ralph Victor Cortiss Bridger.
- Bill Mayall (wounded).
- Ray Iggleden.
- Thomas 'Tommy' Kitchingman (killed in action).

Jock Patrol
Sergeant Jock Cameron (Highland Light Infantry).
Sergeant 'Tanky' Geary.
Private Hans Majury.
- Bill 'Taffy' Morgan (wounded).
- Brimming's (London Rifles).
- Robbie Drummond.

There are other versions of this raid included in the appendices of this book, it includes extracts from *The Filibusters* by John Lodwick

(1947), Lady Madeline Lees' letter, and Ralph Bridger's version. Hopefully they will enable the reader to gain a fuller understanding of the confused events that took place at Villa Punta on the night of the 9th–10th March 1945. There are several other versions of what took place, in some instances with widely contrasting descriptions. This only goes to illustrate how the same incident, viewed from differing perspectives, can produce varied accounts.

It is hoped that Ken's version will add to this understanding rather than muddy the waters or cause any upset.

16

TANSY AND TOMMY

"And who are you?"

Tansy

To his troops Captain James Lees was affectionately known as 'Tansy', and as "one of the best officers" in the British armed forces. The Lees family owned a large estate at Lytchett Minster near Poole in Dorset. As the eldest son of Sir John, James, had he survived the war, would have been first in line to inherit his father's seat in the House of Lords.

One of the family forefathers had made a small fortune from the cotton mills around Manchester, but ill health had forced the family to relocate to a more favourable climate. They were offered two parcels of land, one being the four thousand or so acres of prime farmland at Lytchett Minster, the present family seat. The other parcel of land, turned down, is now one of the most sought-after and expensive areas of real estate in the land: It included a marshy district around Poole, which included sandbanks.

When Ken left Tansy, he believed he was taking his last few breaths. In fact, he survived for a couple more days. Together with an Italian officer, also badly wounded at Villa Punta, he was nursed at the local hospital in Mali Lussin. It was initially believed that he would survive and the Italian die. As it turned out, the reverse happened.

Initially buried on Lussin, he was reburied in a military cemetery in Belgrade. The wooden cross from Lussin now stands in the Lytchett Minster graveyard.

In 1950 Tansy's mother, Lady Lees, received a letter from Dr Wasmuht, a German who had served as the medical officer on Lussin, it reads:

The large and trackless island was only held by us Germans in small and isolated posts far apart. We were supported by Italian Commandos. In the South of the Island, about 6km from Lussingrande and halfway between it and Lussinpiccolo, there stood on a rocky promontory, a lonely house set in a large garden. At the time the garden was in full blossom and in the house lived the Italian unit commanded by the newly-arrived Lieutenant Comotti, a lad of about 18 or 19. He was a hot blooded and enthusiastic soldier of the Fascist Militia who had had to take over a very thankless task because his predecessor had been shot in the back a few days previously when in a partisan locality...

This is what happened. Your son, with some of Tito's followers [sic], had landed from an electric motorboat somewhere on the Lussingrande coast and had surprised the post at Villa Punta. He had then himself dashed up to the first floor and suddenly came face to face with the Italian Comotti in one of the rooms. Both had their revolvers. At this moment the bomb that the commandos had brought into the hall of the house exploded. The whole staircase went up, and your son and Lieutenant Comotti were on the first floor and could not get back. From the evidence we have we understood that your son and Comotti shot at each other. The Italian was severely wounded by a shot through one lung and was 'hors de combat'. During the fight the ceiling collapsed, and your son was struck on the head by a falling beam and became unconscious. Tito's Commandos climbed up from the outside – I don't know if there were Englishmen there to – and tried to rescue your son and carry him away with them, but they had to give up as they could not manage it...

All this happened in a very short space of time. A few minutes later I arrived at the unlucky spot and found the two leaders of the opposing units badly wounded men. I could see no trace of Tito's men. Your son's pulse was so good that I believed he would soon recover now that the commotion had died down, especially as apart from a quite slight wound on his right heel there did not appear to be any other injury. I found Comotti at death's door. He had written 'Long Live Italy' on the ground beside him with his blood...

Your son was perfectly peaceful, and showed no signs of pain, but he did not regain consciousness in the days that followed. About two or three days after the fight he died peacefully. He was buried with all honour in the little churchyard at Lussinpiccolo.

N.B. Tito was the communist leader of the partisans in Yugoslavia and became the country's President after the war.

Captain James Lees, King's Royal Rifle Corps, attached Special Boat Service. Eldest son of Colonel John Lees Bt, DSO MC and Lady Lees. Born on the 3rd of March 1920, died on the 11th of March 1945 of wounds received in action at Villa Punta, Lussin,

Dalmatia. His grave by San Martini Church was devotedly cared for by the people of Lussin Piccolo until in 1950 it was moved to St Nicholas Cemetery, Belgrade, and his vase and cross were sent home from Lussin. These are now within the family plot at the churchyard in Lytchett Minster, Dorset.

Tommy

The other SBS fatality on the Villa Punta raid was Marine Thomas Kitchingman, POX 105923, R Patrol, S Squadron. He was just twenty-one years of age. Described as a kind-hearted, very determined, intelligent and resourceful young man. His service records show that whilst serving aboard HMS *Euryalus* he 'attempted to give secret information to a person not authorised to receive' and spent fourteen days in the cells. A nephew, Paul Ogden, later wrote, 'On one occasion during the war Tom dived overboard to save a German serviceman from drowning. Unfortunately, he spent a few days in the ship's brig for his indiscretion.' The son of Harold and Bridget Kitchingman of Rathmell Street, Halton Moor, Leeds, Yorkshire, he was one of seven children.

Much of what you have just read is taken from *The SAS and LRDG Roll of Honour, 1941–47* by soldier X, QGM.

In September 1990 Ken visited the graves of both men, who were by now buried in the capital of Yugoslavia, Belgrade. On the same pilgrimage he also journeyed to the Argenta Gap War Cemetery in north-eastern Italy to pay his respects to those members of the unit who had lost their lives in the Comacchio swamp. Ken revisited Comacchio twice more as well as Simi and Lussin, where he commented on how different it looked in daylight. One of the Italy trips was organised by the British Legion (Ken was at the time president of the Havant branch). At one point on the journey an elderly ex-senior officer, accompanied by an ex-sergeant major, appeared on the coach that Ken was travelling on. The officer, a high-ranking official of the legion, made his way down the vehicle, greeting the old soldiers, asking them how they were, what regiment they had been with, their experiences, etc. When the pair came to where Ken was sat, the old officer said, "Hello, and who are you?"

To which Ken replied, "And who are you?"

Somewhat taken aback, the officer gave his name and old rank, also adding his legion title.

Ken then said, "You should be ashamed of yourself, coming on this expenses-paid trip while we had to have a whip-round just to get the money together for a wreath."

The sergeant major escort quickly ushered the old officer away from the cantankerous man making a nuisance of himself. The years had not mellowed Ken; if anything, the opposite had happened: he was never afraid to speak his mind.

SIR JOHN LEES' HEIR KILLED IN ACTION

DAY, MARCH 29th, 1945

THE news that Captain James Lees, eldest son of Sir John Lees, Bart., D.S.O., M.C., and Lady Lees, of South Lytchett Manor, has been killed in action in the Middle East, has been received with much regret throughout the village of Lytchett Minster, and further afield too.

Capt. Lees, who was the heir to the baronetcy, was 25 years of age. He was educated at Eton and Sandhurst, and received his commission in the King's Royal Rifle Corps shortly before the outbreak of war.

From 1941 to 1943 he served with the 2nd Battalion, attaining the rank of Major, but in 1943 sacrificed his rank to transfer to the Special Boat Service of the Middle East as a Lieutenant, later being promoted to Captain.

He took part in a number of heavy engagements and was wounded about two years ago. The action in which he was killed was one of outstanding gallantry.

Of an especially happy disposition, Capt. Lees was equally as popular with his tenantry of Lytchett as with his wide circle of personal friends.

Captain Lees newspaper obituary.

MADELINE LADY LEES.
LYTCHETT MINSTER.
NR. POOLE.

31st July, 1963.

My dear Mr. Smith,

    I am so dreadfully sorry that I hadn't notified you personally of the Memorial Service, but it had been in the S.A.S. Magazine, and in all the daily papers. Actually, I had been thinking of you, but I could not find your address.

    I have a photograph of you, in a group, wearing German sailors' hats, with the Nazi flag, and I remember very well meeting you at one of the re-unions. How simply marvellous that you have 8 children. I do hope you have plenty of wherewithall, as they are not cheap to keep, are they?

    Well, I enclose a picture of the Memorial and a copy of the Service, which is the next best thing I can send you. It was a perfectly wonderful gathering - Over 21 S.A.S. turned up, and there were lots of empty beer bottles, as usual.

    I had thought that Sgt. Ray Geary was the very last of our people to see my son, but I know that Sgt. Cameron did a "recce" with him, just before that action. I have so much to tell you - I can't write it all in a letter, and also, so much to ask you. Yesterday, I had a telegram from a son-in-law, asking me where James was buried in Dalmatia, as he is cruising there. Well, his grave is actually moved to the Military Cemetery at Belgrade, but, nevertheless, I sent him the Lussine Piccolo address, because his grave there is still looked after and venerated by the people of Lossinje and the girl who nursed him and Commoti, actually brought some soil from the grave which we put on his "grave" here, and planted up with flowers.

                                                 Lt.

The letter goes on to say she would like to meet up with Ken and his family.

17

COMACCHIO

"We were dirty, always wet and damn cold at night." Ralph Bridger

Ken was largely unaware of his passage from Lussin, not fully regaining consciousness until two days later in a field hospital in Bari, southern Italy. He was laid out on a stretcher in a hospital corridor. The building was overflowing with casualties. He had been transferred from the patrol boat at Zara Harbour to HMS *Colombo*, a light cruiser, for urgent medical attention. The bullet was not life-threatening, so for the time being it was left in his arm anticipating it would be operated on and removed later.

Along with the other seriously wounded he was taken to the local aerodrome for casualty evacuation to Italy. He had a vague recollection of boarding an aircraft, possibly a Dakota, fitted out with racks of stretchers. As the airplane's engines roared at full throttle, struggling to gain the necessary height to clear the mountains encircling the airstrip, he glanced across at the occupant of a nearby stretcher. It was an unconscious, wounded German; possibly the same prisoner Ken had escorted off the island. Struggling to focus, he glanced out of the window to see the mountains rushing by perilously close. With a shuddering surge the plane made a dash for a gap between the peaks. Instinctively Ken closed his eyes to await the inevitable impact; then involuntarily he reopened them to see the ground rushing past just below them, so close that he could identify individual stones.

Ralph remembered the arrival at Zara the injured were taken aboard HMS *Colombo* from where a detachment of immaculately dressed marines appeared, accompanied by the ship's band. Had they realised that the ragged bunch of piratical-looking cutthroats that were by now handing around a bottle of hard liquor were in fact British troops, including marines, who knows what would have happened. The ship's marines paraded as reveille was sounded. At one stage the sergeant cast a disparaging look at the motley band of warriors covered in filth and blood and looked as if he intended to come over to discipline them. Ralph, for one, covered in his comrades' blood, was in an evil mood and itching for an opportunity to vent his fury.

Ken said he slept for two whole days before eventually waking up on a stretcher in a corridor of an overcrowded Bari hospital. It was decided to leave his bullet in place as attempting to remove it could have resulted in an amputation. The offending piece of lead was never removed. In later life a check-up at Haslar Royal Naval Hospital in Gosport, Hampshire became an annual pilgrimage. The doctors would make a bit of a fuss and the appointment would take far longer than scheduled as they listened, enthralled by Ken's tales.

According to Ralph, whilst Ken was hospitalised, "the lads enjoyed a short break in Rome", from where they were banned following a barroom brawl! This caused them to transfer their antics to Naples.

One of Ken's tales is that during his stay in Bari hospital, an ammunition ship that was being unloaded in the nearby docks exploded when one of the bombs slipped out of the net and landed back in the ship's hold. The resulting explosion tore the ship in two, with one half landing on a nearby house. Ken said, 'he slept through it'. Mount Vesuvius, just across Italy on the opposite coast, erupted two days later. He often wondered if the two incidents were related. Mount Vesuvius is recorded as being active from 13th March 1945 and on the 24th of March 1944 it erupted creating an ash plume and a pyroclastic flow.

Ken must have felt extremely low: with a bullet in his arm; a massive bump on his head; a swollen, bruised face; having suffered serious blood loss; severely fatigued; with several of his comrades also badly wounded; and having lost two of the close-knit H Patrol, killed in action, including Tansy. Captain Lees was not just his commanding officer but a close friend, hugely respected, someone he'd had complete faith in and been able to rely upon in the most taxing of situations.

When Ken had only been in the hospital for a few days, his pal Sticks paid a visit. "Here, you want to get out of this place; we're all going off to a rest camp."

Desperately in need of cheering up, and not wanting to miss out, when the doctor next paid Ken a visit on his rounds and asked, "How are you feeling?", Ken replied, "Fine; just needed a good night's sleep."

"Are you sure? How is the arm?" asked the doctor, somewhat shocked.

"Yes, all good – a bit stiff but it's OK," said Ken, keen not to miss out on the good times sure to be had.

"Well, if you are sure, you can report back to your unit. There's not a lot we can do for you here now; you can get the bullet taken out when you get back to England." The doctor was a little surprised at the rapid recovery but extremely grateful for a vacant bed space.

The SBS base, in the convent at Monte Sant'Angelo, was high on a hill overlooking the town. At the end of March an optimistic Ken walked into the office, reporting back and 'fit for duty'.

The officer, somewhat taken aback, questioned, "What are you doing here? We've only just loaded you off on a stretcher."

"Just in need of a good sleep, sir," replied Ken.

"Are you sure you're all, right?" said the officer, still somewhat bemused.

"Fine, sir," answered Ken, eagerly anticipating some fun with his mates.

"Well, if, you're sure. Where is your kit?" questioned the officer.

Ken, surprised and beginning to smell a rat, said, "Still in Yugoslavia, sir."

"Right, better take my batman and get yourself down to the stores and rustle yourself up a kit. We're up behind the lines with the Eighth Army tomorrow!"

Ken had been well and truly stitched up. Sticks had known what was in store for them and reasoned that "Ken would not want to miss out." Nowadays the logic is hard to understand, but it was how they operated. They were a close-knit team who relied upon each other, and Ken would not want to be the one letting the side down. Sticks reasoned, and Ken agreed, that with their recent losses it was more important than ever to stick together. He would have felt guilty had he not been there to share the danger with his pals.

The following morning was spent throwing the paralytically drunk and unconscious comrades up onto the backs of trucks, "like sacks of spuds". Much more care was taken when loading up their Folbots, which were waiting for them in Ravenna.

Comacchio, Operation Roast, end of March – 15th April 1945

It was a long and tortuous journey as they bounced their way up the war-ravaged Italian east coast, the scene of many recent battles and much suffering. Their destination, Lake Comacchio, is a place synonymous with heroism; no less than two Victoria Crosses, Britain's highest award for gallantry, were awarded here.

At the end of March, the SAS entourage (which included cooks, clerks, aides, dogs, etc.) arrived at Ravenna, less than ten miles south of the lake. Numbering about sixty, supported by Italian partisans, the motley-looking rabble set up base camp close to the lake. It would seem that the eighteen men often referred to when talking about this operation were the Folbot paddlers, all of whom appear to have been experienced veterans, and this is possibly why the remains of the Marine Patrol were selected for this operation. The unit's new commanding officer was the legendary Dane, Anders Lassen.

The battle in the Comacchio area raged for many days. It was the prelude to the much larger Battle of the River Po, a breakout through the Argenta Gap from the Northern Apennine Mountains and into the expanse of the Northern Italian Plain. As such, it was the last major land battle that the Western Allies fought in World War II. The following Battle of the River Po owes some part of its success to the heroism of those involved at Comacchio, who drew a large part of the enemy forces to their area. The intention was to convince the Axis forces that the Allies intended to break out along the narrow coastal strip that divides the lake from the Northern Adriatic Sea. The lake itself is hardly that; mostly a vast swamp covering up to two hundred square miles, with mudflats, sand islands and large reed beds. It is less than half a metre deep for its most part but has deeper unmarked channels in places. Some of the islands were large enough to accommodate small villages, their main industry being eel fishing. Initially the Germans controlled all but the extreme southern shore of the lake. Brigadier Ronnie Tod, officer in charge of the 2nd Special Service Brigade, had issued orders to the Dane Anders Lassen to paddle out onto the lake and find channels deep enough to transport the commandos. Lassen was the OIC of the eighteen chosen SBS men, gathered from various patrols, who were tasked with 'discovering and charting channels of sufficient depth leading towards the chosen point of landing'. They were to find routes for a large commando force, supported by floating tanks, to land behind the enemy lines. When the attack finally took place the squadron would lead the assault, guiding the main force through the channels by means of lights and other signals. The commandos 'would have to paddle in a small fleet of Goatleys, Carley floats; in a dozen different kind of embarkation normally reserved for the shipwrecked. The draught of a Goatley is one inch when unoccupied. When carrying ten fully equipped men, the draught of a Goatley is nearly two feet... And two feet is the average depth at Comacchio.' (*The Filibusters* by John Lodwick, p. 187.)

The main attack was to take place along the coastal strip, conducted by two full commando brigades, No. 2 and No. 9, supported by tanks and a brigade of the guards. This is where one of the VCs was awarded. It was to a Corporal Tom Hunter, a Royal Marine commando who gained his VC on the 2nd of April 1945. 43 Commando were tasked with securing a long strip of terrain between the lake and the Adriatic coastline. As they advanced, they came under intense fire, and the forward troops became exposed and pinned down by murderous machine-gun fire. Realising the desperate situation, Corporal Hunter charged forward, firing his

Bren gun from the hip at five German gun positions. This valiant act enabled a number of men, who would surely have been cut down, to make their escape. Sadly, Tom fell, fatally wounded. He was posthumously awarded the Victoria Cross. The remainder of his unit held their position until relief arrived the following day.

The SBS were to harry the enemy with raids across the lake, landings behind the lines, and the capture of islands; many occupied by enemy forces. Their forward base for operations would be the islands, on one of which stood a large concrete structure. This proved extremely useful when attempting to navigate the maze of channels and creeks, but also acutely uncomfortable as every enemy mortar and artillery piece in the vicinity used it for 'ranging'. Slit trenches were dug on the islands for defence and cover, but this was more difficult than expected. The ground was so low you could dig no more than two feet before thick black mud oozed into the hole. Someone hit on the bright idea of lining the bases of the trenches with reeds, but this only served to make things worse. Sticks tried his best to brighten the mood: "Women would pay a fortune for a mud bath like this", and, because Ken was sporting a nice white bandage, "What sort of dance do you think you're doing?" and "Stop waving that white flag at Jerry'!" The replies are unprintable.

Once established on the forward island bases, "Commandos would come up in a boat to guard our billets when we were out of a night." For the whole of the Comacchio campaign the SBS troops were "dirty, always wet and damn cold at night", and those that were fortunate enough to survive came away with a permanent reminder of those onerous few weeks: malaria! Lake Comacchio was widely considered "the mosquito capital of Europe".

Upon their arrival at the southern edge of the lake, the SBS troops were forced to pitch their base-camp tents on the grass embankment leading from the lake to the road. The swampy nature of the terrain meant that every bit of dry ground was being utilised. It was here, as they prepared, that Ken noticed some heavily camouflaged shapes, surrounded by tight security. "What are they?" he asked.

"Top secret, very hush-hush; floating tanks," came the reply.

At some stage during the operation, they returned to base camp. The officers and senior NCOs were called away for a briefing. Someone produced a bottle of wine; another version of the story is that the officers' tents were raided, and a bottle of whisky was liberated. Because of their fatigued state they were all soon extremely drunk and fell into a deep sleep bordering on unconsciousness. No one woke until the following morning, and to everyone's complete surprise the convoy, which had been parked up on the road above them, was ablaze and the scene resembled something from Dante's *Inferno*. During the night their position had come under sustained artillery and mortar fire, causing extensive damage. In another version, the road was bombed and strafed by enemy aircraft. Either way, somehow none of their tents had been hit and the troops had slept obliviously through it due to a mixture of alcohol and fatigue.

The SBS spent the first day readying their Folbots and checking equipment. At dusk the troops slid out silently onto the water, disappearing into the night. With great care they set about their task. All night they would paddle, often having to get out of the canoe and push to free it when 'grounded'. As first light approached the craft would be glided into the reed beds and camouflaged with the help of a canvas sheet. When the sun rose, so did a vast swarm of mosquitoes that would briefly darken the sky, forming a great blanket over the swamp, before settling down to feed. The silence was for a short period broken by the buzzing of millions of tiny parasites who then, said both Ken and Ralph, "feasted on us". To break the monotony the troops would burrow headfirst into the

Folbots and have a cigarette, conscious not to let any smoke escape and give away their location. At dusk the mosquitoes would once again briefly rise; a signal for the paddlers to ready themselves and resume the specialist work that had been set for them. "We were miles from our lines," said Ken.

Over the coming days several islands were liberated. All whispered talking ceased, and it was "hand signals only" when approaching an island. Slowly they would glide in, taking care not to splash the water. Once grounded they would crawl forward on their bellies, feeling for mines as they went. On one island a house was situated. Ken said, "Ages were spent crawling ever closer, only to find, when we got there, no one." On another occasion, as they were paddling, the distinct sound of an approaching diesel engine could be heard. Quickly they disappeared into the reeds. Shortly a shallow-draught enemy barge with a Spandau machine gun mounted on a tripod at the bow came into view. It slowly chugged its way past the concealed troops. Sticks was keen to ambush the vessel. With the element of surprise, he was confident of victory. The officer sensibly decided that discretion was the better option, and the craft went unknowingly on its way.

All who knew Ken would undoubtedly have heard the story of the capture of one of the islands, or at least a part of the tale. He believed it to be the night before Lassen was killed – this would make it the 7th–8th April 1945. An island which was understood to be occupied by the Germans was targeted for capture. The canoeists silently glided across the surface of the lake, scarcely troubling the water and hardly disturbing the stillness of the night. Great care was being taken with their paddles to avoid any undue noise and drips; the 'phosphorescence' as it was known, created by any splashes would surely give them away. As they eased closer to the island a ghostly line of figures materialised from the low-lying mist: a line of soldiers clad in German greatcoats topped with the distinctive helmets. Fortunately, their hands were raised, as a few well-aimed bursts of automatic fire would have wreaked havoc amongst the paddlers, who considered themselves 'sitting ducks'. As they clambered out of their craft the surrendering troops said, "*Ruskie, camerad*" ('Russian, friend'), and, indicating the ground around them, "*Minen*" ('mines'). Luckily for the SBS they were captured Russians who had been given two simple options: either fight or be shot. They had chosen a third: surrender. The Russians showed them where the minefields were and escorted them to an old, dilapidated fisherman's hut. The SBS then set about securing the position. The Germans had apparently gone to Comacchio Town to recharge their radio batteries and have a drink, safe in the knowledge that the Russians could do no mischief. Many nationalities fought alongside the Germans at Comacchio: Finnish, Ukrainian, Croat and Italian to name some.

Ken set to at the rear of the hut, digging a slit trench with Brummie Barlow. The defences were quickly achieved, and turns were taken to grab some rest. They were startled awake by the sound of raised voices coming from the other side of the shack – at least three languages, and a combination of them, were being used. Some boats had been spotted approaching the island and a challenge was issued. The SBS believed them to be reinforcements; in fact, it was the Germans returning with the charged batteries. They in turn believed themselves to be challenged by the Russians. A short period of confusion ensued, followed by some intense gunfire as the truth of the situation was realised. From Ken's position he was unable to intervene, and tensely awaited orders or an escalation in the firefight necessitating his involvement.

The uneven match did not last long. Shortly an officer called out, "Corporal Smith, get round here." On his arrival, Ken could just make out in the moonlight a line of Germans, stood with their arms raised, on a sandbank a short distance away. Together with Sergeant Cameron Ken was detailed to go and bring in the prisoners. The pair carefully made their way across the small, shallow channel and covered by sergeant Cameron, Ken went behind the men and frisked them, removing any weapons, maps, orders, watches, etc. They found out that one of the Germans was missing; initially they were unsure if it was one boatload, one section or a solitary soldier. It turned out to be the latter, and he was named Hans.

In something surreally comical, sergeant Cameron, using his arms to mimic an orchestra conductor, called out, "*Eins, Zwei, Drei*" ('one, two, three').

On cue, the line of Germans called out in unison, "*Hans, Caputen, Kommen Sie Raus!*" ('Hans, surrender, come out!') This was followed by several moments of silence.

Quite unperturbed by the ridiculous spectacle being observed by the rest of the patrol, and its dismal failure, Sergeant Cameron gave it another go, and then one more for luck. There was still no response, and the prisoners (about ten of them) were escorted back to the main island on a gondolier type of boat, with Ken even being "offered a drink by a frightened Jerry". Lassen, who was on a nearby island, made contact to find out what all the commotion was about. He quickly ordered the prisoners to be sent to him, no doubt to try and "add to his watch collection". Any prisoners always underwent a thorough search for weapons and papers, and anything of value was usually pocketed.

Dawn was approaching and the darkness began to give way to the first signs of light. Ken was shaken awake by Sticks for his spell on sentry duty. Sticks pointed out something that was beginning to take shape but was unsure as to what it was. After careful examination the officer was woken and eventually the pair were sent to investigate. They launched a canoe and cautiously approached the scene. It soon became apparent that it was the missing German. Rigor mortis had set in and Sticks, at the rear of the canoe, had an extremely awkward and uncomfortable journey back with the stiff dead body draped across the craft and staring up at him. The dead German was a "Gestapo type", and the canoe was redirected to take the body to Lassen's Island, where his comrades would bury him. The journey to the adjacent island was more hazardous: the sun had risen, and much care was taken to keep a low profile. The seating had now been rearranged, with Sticks in the bow and Ken staring at the contorted face of the deceased man. They were extremely relieved to hand the body over to Ralph to organise the burial.

Back at the original island, and later the same morning at about 11am, they were targeted by enemy artillery blowing the reed roof off the hut. The Germans had by now realised the loss of the position and had the 'location, bearing and range'. Ken, enjoying a moment's rest, immediately commenced a well-worn routine: direction, range, bearing, type of ordnance, time of incident and between shells, estimated distance to gun position, etc. He quickly found a pencil and paper to log the incident. Turning to Brummie Barlow, who shared the trench with him, he asked for the time.

"You should know," came the curt reply in a strong Birmingham accent, "you got enough bloody watches last night!"

Quickly Ken fished in his pocket and then tossed a watch to Brummie. "Here, that should shut you up."

Ralph said that "The Germans were targeting from a concrete tower. Every time we were targeted, we would dive in a trench, to be covered in sticky black mud. The depth of the water was constantly changing, determined by sluice gates and tides."

During a torrential rainstorm Ken was teamed up with Trooper Jackson, the one with only one ear. They formed a three-inch mortar team who were detailed to supply a rapid barrage, frantically working with Jackson loading and Ken aiming and firing. The mortar's baseplate started to slip on the sodden, muddy ground, causing Ken to briefly stop firing as he adjusted the weapon before continuing with the salvo. He fired again but was unable to continue as he had not been reloaded. Looking up, he noticed Jackson rolling around on the ground. Assuming that he must have slipped in the mud, Ken shouted above the din, "Stop mucking about and get on with it." He then noticed that Jackson wasn't in fact laughing and was holding his hand – or rather, the stump of it! During the quick adjustment to the mortar Jackson had continued to load; a 'double load' was about to happen. Unknowingly, the weapon was discharged at the very moment Jackson's hand had appeared over the mortar barrel. They had both been operating at maximum when the accident happened. Quickly Ken fumbled for the morphine and plunged the syringe into the patient. He only managed to administer about half the contents before the needle was broken by the patient violently turning, leaving half the point still embedded in the hapless victim. As Ken desperately looked around for help, to his utter amazement a field medic appeared out of the downpour and took charge.

At the subsequent post-war reunions Jackson's first words to all when meeting up with Ken would be "Wherever you go, just keep away from that bloody Jonah Smithy."

Lassen

Major Anders Frederik Emil Victor Schau Lassen was a Dane from an aristocratic family who by the age of twelve is reputed to have stalked and killed a stag, armed only with a hunting knife. He was serving aboard a merchant ship when the Germans invaded his homeland. Immediately he declared war on the Germans and made it his personal mission to do all he could to help liberate his country. A series of well-documented escapades found him as an officer in the 1st SAS/1st SBS. By the time of his arrival at Comacchio he had already been awarded the Military Cross three times, the third highest award for gallantry in the British services; after, he would also receive the Victoria Cross and the George Cross.

Ken believed it was the day before Lassen's demise (this would make it the 8th of April 1945) when Brigadier Tod arrived at the forward island operating base and asked for Major Lassen. He was informed that the Dane was on another island a short distance away. An order was issued for someone to go and get him as the brigadier "wasn't going any further". Sticks was dispatched by Folbot, returning in due course with Lassen.

The Scandinavian was a passionate, driven man; some would say fanatical. He spoke in guttural broken English and often would hammer a clenched fist into an open palm to emphasis a point. A hasty conference was convened in the lee of the ruined hut. Sat on their haunches around a little bank, a plan was formulated. The British wanted the enemy to believe that the main attack, scheduled for that night, was to be on Comacchio Town itself.

The brigadier soon came to the point. "I want you lot to go out tonight and spread as much chaos and confusion amongst the enemy as possible."

Lassen's swift reply was, "We can capture Comacchio, but we are too few to hold it."

"I don't want you to capture Comacchio; I just want you to—"

Before the brigadier had time to finish, Lassen was banging his fist in his hand and with a raised voice said, "But we *can* capture Comacchio."

It was the brigadier's turn to interrupt, and angrily he said, "I don't want you to capture Comacchio. I want you to go out, spread your troops as thin as possible, and cause the Germans as much trouble and confusion as you can!"

As this discussion took place, Ken was fascinated by the fact that Lassen's ribs were clearly visible. They were all shirtless and wearing shorts, so he inspected the other SBS operatives to find that they were all as skeletal: "Skin and bones; not an ounce of fat on any of us." He was crouched opposite Sticks, and they both rolled their eyes in disbelief at what they were hearing. How just eighteen exhausted and battle-weary men were going to capture a garrisoned town who were dug in, alert and expectant was beyond belief!

It was in all probability the same boat that had brought the brigadier and his entourage ("full of brass") that delivered a Yugoslav Commissar. He had made the long and now-hazardous trip to find Corporal Smith and recover the Yugoslav Pass he had been issued. This pass was granted by the Yugoslav communist partisans to enable the recipient passage through the territory they held. Tito, with the Russians now on his doorstep, was collecting in any outstanding passes. The Iron Curtain was already starting to fall. Ken did a quick search of his kit but as he suspected it was nowhere to be found and so he said that it must still be in Yugoslavia with the rest of his stuff. He couldn't understand what all the fuss was about anyway. This left the Commissar extremely disgruntled but unable to do anything. Ken believed that some of the accompanying officers were only there to say in their memoirs that they had ventured 'behind the lines'. Many weeks later, Ken's Yugoslav kit caught up with him. There, in the bottom of the bag, stained with his blood, was the pass that had caused all the fuss. For many years he carried it around in his wallet as a unique souvenir.

He even had it translated, and it mentions 'death for Fascists, liberty for our people'!

The brigadier had his way, and shortly after dark the canoes slid off, splitting into small groups to set about the diversionary plan. Earlier a long line of guncotton charges and cordtex (thirty-odd blocks) had been laid along the side of the lake. These were "to be set off when Andy gives the go-ahead". Hopefully they would fool the Germans into believing that a major attack was under way and draw the enemy to their sector.

The operation that night was to prove a costly one. Young Alfred John Crouch (or 'Freddy' as he was known to his pals) was one of the casualties. He was a twenty-seven-year-old former Metropolitan Policeman from East London. Dick Holmes, one of the originals (someone who joined the SAS and fought in the sands of north Africa), said of him, "Freddy was a great guy, steady as a rock and a very good soldier." There is some confusion as to exactly what happened to him. There are also reports that during the Comacchio campaign someone was swallowed by the mud. Ralph had a version of events which he believed to be true, maintaining, "Crouch drowned recceing." The Folbots were constantly grounding in the shallow water. One or sometimes both paddlers would then be forced to evacuate the craft and push it free. It was during one of these manoeuvres that Freddy began to sink in the soft silt. Unable to come to his assistance in time, his comrades watched in horror as slowly the mire swallowed him. Not once did brave Freddy cry out, for this would surely have alerted the enemy who were close by. After that incident, Ralph, who was the rear canoe paddler with Iggy up front, refused to go overboard to push the craft clear! Up until that time this had been their usual practice.

It is recorded in *SBS: Silent Warriors* by Saul David that 'In the early hours of 9th April 1945, the eleven-man SBS patrol was engaged by fire from multiple enemy machine guns.' By this stage, was the force down to just eleven?

That night, as Ken's canoe approached the shore heavy gunfire erupted "about a hundred yards away", where he knew Lassen's small group were landing. Soon the whole area was alive with action. Chandelier flares lit up the sky and the sounds of explosions and gunfire was all around. Machine-gun fire tore up the water's surface. Ken's canoe was in open water and a sitting duck. They turned turtle when spotted, being forced to swim clear, towing the canoe. They retreated into the darkness, eventually making it to a safe place to remount their Folbot and head back to the forward base. There seemed no point in persevering as with all the pandemonium the aim had been achieved and to proceed would have been suicidal.

Some of the others had already arrived back at their forward base camp, and Ken's party were greeted with sombre news: "Wally's had it." Slowly, in ones and twos as others returned, the reports grew more depressing: "Rocky Roberts bought it"; "Lassen's had it"; "Sean's badly shot up." It was all so matter of fact. Wearily, the casualties were reported and dispassionately accepted.

Lassen died on the fifth anniversary of the German occupation of Denmark. His party landed on a causeway at the very northern tip of the lake leading to Comacchio Town. After being challenged, and their attempt to bluff their way by claiming to be returning fishermen failed, they came under heavy machine-gun fire from a series of pillboxes. Several of the patrol were hit and wounded. The War Office account states:

Major Lassen himself then attacked with grenades and annihilated the first position containing four Germans and two machine guns. Ignoring the hail of bullets sweeping the road from three enemy positions, an additional one having come into action from 300 yards down the road, he raced forward to engage the second position under covering fire from the remainder of the force. Throwing in more grenades, he silenced this position, which was then overrun by his patrol. Two enemies were killed, two captured, and two more machine guns silenced.

By this time the force had suffered casualties, and its fire power was very considerably reduced. Still under a heavy cone of fire, Major Lassen rallied and reorganised his force and brought his fire to bear on the third position. Moving forward himself he flung in more grenades, which produced a cry of "Kamerad". He then went forward to within three or four yards of the position to order the enemy outside and take their surrender.

Whilst shouting to them to come out he was hit by a burst of Spandau fire from the left of the position and fell mortally wounded; but even whilst falling he flung a grenade, wounding some of the occupants and enabling his patrol to dash in and capture the final position.

Major Lassen refused to be evacuated, as he said it would impede the withdrawal and endanger further lives; and as ammunition was nearly exhausted the force had to withdraw.

The War Office also added:

By his magnificent leadership and complete disregard for his personal safety, Major Lassen had, in the face of overwhelming superiority, achieved his objects. Three positions were wiped out, accounting for six machine guns, killing eight and wounding others of the enemy, and two prisoners were taken. The high sense of devotion to duty and the esteem in which he was held by the men he led, added to his own magnificent courage, enabled Major Lassen to carry out all the tasks he had been given with complete success.

For his actions that night Lassen was posthumously awarded the Victoria Cross, Britain's highest award for gallantry. One story has it that his VC was initially blocked, Brigadier Tod being no great fan of the sometimes-abrasive man. However, the unit's old commanding officer, Earl George Jellicoe, had the ear of high command and bypassed some official channels.

The Victoria Cross takes the form of a Maltese cross bearing a lion and a crown, together with the words 'FOR VALOUR'. The recipient's name, rank, unit and achievement appear with the date on the reverse side. It can be awarded to any member of the British armed forces who has shown 'most outstanding bravery or extreme self-sacrifice in battle.' Since the VC was instituted in January 1856 (the medal is made of bronze from a cannon captured at Sebastopol, in the Crimean war) it has been awarded less than 1,400 times, including 626 during World War I and 181 in World War II.

Many years after the war, Ken Smith visited the cemetery at Argenta where Lassen was buried. He stood before his grave to pay his respects. Glancing around at the rows of gravestones, idly reading the inscriptions, he was surprised to see that a grave in the row behind and only a couple to the side was that of Marine Thomas Hunter. How strange to see, in all the graveyards scattered across Europe, two VCs lying so close to each other. Some years later Ken again returned to pay his respects and noted that Hunter's grave had been moved to a section of the graveyard dedicated to the commandos.

The M Squadron SBS roll of honour for those who took part at Comacchio (as can be best ascertained) is:

Major Anders 'Andy' Lassen (Danish, killed in action).
Captain Charles Alan Bimrose (West Yorkshire Regiment).
Captain 'Stud' Stellin (New Zealand).
Lieutenant Turnball.
Sergeant Major Les Stephenson (Guards).
Sergeant Major Workman (Guards).
Sergeant Jock Cameron (Highland Light Infantry).
Sergeant Waite (wounded).
Corporal Edward 'Ted' 'Rocky' Roberts (killed in action).
Sergeant Sean O'Reilly (Irish Guards, wounded).
Fred Greene.
Trooper Alfred 'Freddy' John Crouch (killed in action).
Fusilier Stanley 'Wally' Raymond Hughes (killed in action).
Bombardier T. C. Crotty.
Private Williams (London Rifle Brigade).
Alfie 'Brummie' Barlow.

H Patrol

Corporal Kenneth Herbert Smith (Royal Marines).
Albert Lewis 'Sticks' May (Royal Marines).
Ralph Victor Cortiss Bridger (Royal Marines).
Ray Iggleden (Royal Marines).

Other names that have been mentioned in various publications as either being there or associated with the SBS at Comacchio:

Corporal Watkins.
Hank Hancock.
Private Hunter.
Mick Conby.

Private Medcalfe.
Trooper Randell.
Private Barbour.
Sergeant Patsy Henderson.
Private Thompson.
Michael Patterson (7th Hussars).
Private Shaw.

The details are those available at the time of going to print. It is hoped that further information will be forthcoming to help complete the list.

One would think that the SBS had done enough and their time on the lake was over, but this was not the case. For those that had managed to survive thus far, there was still work to do; they were not yet finished. The last task given to the SBS operatives was to find a channel deep enough to enable an amphibious force to be landed behind the enemy lines. At each turn in the channel a canoe was to be positioned. They were to flash a prearranged Morse signal back along a compass bearing; this would mark the route for the troop convoy's night-time passage. Whilst this was being set up the SBS were forced to lie up on mudflats or amongst the reeds during daylight. The assault was scheduled to take place at the north-east corner of the lake.

On the night of the landings, Ken found himself in the foremost canoe with Captain Bimrose. The pair were immersed up to their necks, positioned at the base of an embankment screened from above by overhanging shrubs. Turns were taken to flash the Morse code letter 'P': *DIT DAH DAH DIT*, pause, *DIT DAH DAH DIT*. This was on a given bearing to the preceding canoe manned by Sticks and his partner. They in turn were flashing a Morse letter on another bearing, and so on through the lake, marking the channel. It had taken two nights of stealthy paddling to get this far. Overhead, a road ran along the top of the bank. Drunken German soldiers could be heard returning in a horse-drawn cart from a night out in the town, singing 'Lili Marleen'. They made extensive use of pack animals due to the shortage of fuel.

At zero hour a terrific bombardment erupted. A two-hundred-yard-wide area around the SBS's position was supposed to be left clear. "You could have fooled me," said Ken. "As far as we were concerned, they targeted us!" Further flashing of the signal was futile as the firing of the guns lit up the night as if it was daylight. All around the ground was erupting and the air was filled with the screams of the wounded and terrified horses. Soon dawn began to break, and across the lake could be seen landing craft and tanks stuck on mudflats and sandbanks and stranded in the shallows, having lost the channel during the hours of darkness. However, sufficient had made it through to force a landing a short distance away, and a fierce battle raged.

"What do you think we should do, Smithy?" asked Captain Bimrose.

"Keep our bloody heads down," came the reply.

Bullets, mortar and artillery fire were being exchanged above them as they lay in the water with only the tops of their heads exposed.

Eventually Captain Bimrose said, "Bugger this – let's get out of here."

Skilfully they readied the Folbot, and as they were about to set off Ken, who was the engine room in the front, turned and said, "It's my twenty-third birthday today, sir."

The captain replied, "Happy birthday, Smithy; now paddle for your life."

Furiously they set off across the lake, knowing that their very lives depended upon it. They were soon spotted, and machine-gun fire tore up the water around them as mortars exploded close by. They gave their all, and every so often Bimrose would drag his paddle hard to abruptly alter course as they zigzagged away, hoping to avoid the enemy being able to zero in on them. Somehow, they survived, eventually arriving back at base camp in a state of total exhaustion, having in the process lost all the skin off the palms of their hands. Unable to summon the strength to move, they lay slumped in the folbot cockpit for ages.

For his actions that night Captain Bimrose was awarded the Military Cross. His citation describes how he 'drew much fire onto his canoes… and in spite of great danger remained within range creating a diversion until absolutely satisfied that the main attack was going in successfully'. It was the 12th of April 1945. At the time the Military Cross could only be awarded to officers of captain rank or below, and warrant officers. Since 1993 the rank system has been removed. The MC is now the third-level award for all ranks of the British armed forces for 'exemplary gallantry' on land, after the Victoria Cross and the Conspicuous Gallantry Cross.

Eventually they summoned the strength and made it to shore. Here they were greeted by a sergeant who announced, "Congratulations, Smithy, your wings have come through." Normally the parachuting wings are worn on the upper right arm. In the SAS, after three (some say five) successful missions behind the lines, they become an award and are permitted to be worn on the chest, above the medals. Ken had long ago lost count of how many missions he had been on, but it had always been his ambition to gain his wings. The lax attitude to paperwork and record-keeping had meant that the formalities had taken a long time to catch up with him.

He was then presented with a bottle of whisky when Captain

Bimrose came into his tent and said, "Here you are, Smithy, happy birthday."

Ken would say, "He got a medal; I got a bottle of whisky and my 'Wings.'" Later he was officially awarded his wings by Earl George Jellicoe.

The wearing of the parachute wings above one's medals is a unique 'award' of the wartime SAS. In later years, 'officialdom' disapproved of this dress code, with many believing it to be no more than 'bravado' by the 'Old Rogues'. One story has it that a group of five ex-SAS Chelsea Pensioners were causing their RAF comrades some disquiet. The RAF considered themselves the only military personnel sanctioned to wear this dress code. Eventually an official letter was produced to endorse the five. This, in ensuing years, was interpreted by some as the five being the only ones legitimately entitled to wear it. There is some discussion as to the exact criteria for the award, but it now appears certain that it was envisaged as a decoration awarded for three successful missions behind enemy lines. It was initially anticipated that the troops would be parachuted in. However, the first ever SAS mission resulted in high losses when the men were dropped in gale-force winds. The unit was fortunate to survive this near disaster, with most survivors making it back only with the aid of the LRDG, a reconnaissance unit. This was the birth of the 'Desert Taxi Service', as they respectfully became known. When the unit expanded into the whole Mediterranean theatre submarines, motor launches, canoes, etc. became the norm, but the unit still maintained the ability to parachute. Being able to wear one's wings on the chest is a source of great pride.

Following the cessation of hostilities in 1945 the SAS was disbanded, and all troops returned to their original units. In Ken Smith's case this was the Royal Marines. He developed the habit of always carrying his pay book around, especially on parade. He was frequently picked up for his unorthodox wearing of the parachute wings, whereupon he would produce his pay book, turn to the awards page, and with great pride proudly explain his entitlement.

Perhaps now is a good time to reflect on what, for Ken, had been a particularly intense and traumatic period, especially the five weeks from early March until the 12th of April 1945:

16th November 1944: Back from Albania to southern Italy, "skeletal, flea-ridden and lousy".

Mid-January 1945: SBS based in Zara, Yugoslavia, recceing and raiding.

First week of March: First attempt on Villa Punta, Lussin.

9th–10th March: Raid on Villa Punta. Ken receives a bullet in his arm; two of the patrol are killed and eight wounded.

12th March: Ken regains consciousness on a stretcher in a hospital corridor in Bari, southern Italy.

A few days later, mid-March: Back at SBS base drawing kit and heading up to north-eastern Italy.

Second half of March: 'Behind the lines' at Lake Comacchio until after the 12th of April.

End of March – 15th April: Operation Roast.

7th–8th April? Brigadier Tod's visit to the forward operating base; briefing; Yugoslav partisan seeking Kens Pass?

8th–9th April: Anders Lassen killed in action; awarded VC. Three others also killed in action.

11th–12th April: Forward canoe flashing in commandos (*DIT DAH DAH DIT, DIT DAH DAH DIT*).

12th April: "Paddle for your life." Ken's twenty-third birthday. Captain Bimrose awarded Military Cross; Ken awarded his wings.

Mid-April: Withdrawn from the front lines.

7th May: VE Day; Germany unconditionally surrenders.

By 13th June 1945: Ken back in the marines and on passage to the UK.

In 2001 Ken attended the funeral of an ex-SAS/SBS soldier. At the wake, as old stories were recalled and memories shared, the Comacchio campaign and Lassen's death were brought up. Initially Ken listened before interrupting, "Yes, I was around when it happened."

Immediately a surprised George Jellicoe said, "You were? We thought they were all dead by now. Would you be interested in a trip to Comacchio around Easter time? The Italians are unveiling a memorial." (As it happened, there was in fact another survivor: Ralph Bridger was still going strong.)

In April 2002 the Earl Jellicoe and Colonel Richard Lea, accompanied by two veterans, Ken Smith and Hank Hancock, were guests of the town of Comacchio and the Italian government. Here Ken had the pleasure of meeting Lassen's sister, a Danish countess, whom he described as "a lovely lady". The group were there to attend the inauguration of a commemorative stone to Anders Lassen and the three other SAS/SBS operatives who died there and are buried in the nearby Argenta Gap War Cemetery.

Ken sat amidst the rubble of northern Italy, watching columns of German prisoners of war streaming past. The odd shape to his front left is the remains of a church bell.

Comacchio

THE MARINE PATROL 1943-1945

M Squadron, 1st SAS / 1st SBS

Greece, Albania, Yugoslavia and Italy.

Capt. "Tansy" Jimmy Lees.	KIA Lussin, Yugoslavia.	Kings Royal Rifles.	Lytchett Minster, Dorset
Sgt. Jim Horsefield.	RTU after Albania.	Royal Marines	
Cpl. Ken Smith.	Wounded, Lussin.	" "	Portsmouth, Hampshire
Albert "Sticks" May.		" "	Portsmouth, Hampshire
Ralph Bridger.		" "	Worthing, Sussex
Tommy Kitcheman.	KIA Lussin.	" "	LEEDS YORKSHIRE
Ray Iggledon.		" "	Leeds, Yorkshire
Bill Mayhall.	Wounded, Lussin.	" "	DIDCOT OXFORDSHIRE
Tommy Tucker.	Voluntary RTU after Simi.	" "	
Ken Joynson.	RTU, injured Italy.		Liverpool, Lancashire
Alfie "Brummie" Barlow		Army	Birmingham
Ben Gunn.	RTU.		

Notable Actions:-

Simi, Greek Dodecanese Islands.   13th, 14th July 1944.

Lussin, Croatia, formerly Yugoslavia.   9th March 1945.

Comacchio, Italy.   End of March to 15th April 1945

[signed] Ken Smith POX4898

[signed] Ralph Bridger POX115247

ACCORDING TO RALPH THERE WERE ONLY FOUR OF THE ORIGINAL PATROL LEFT AT THE END OF THE WAR.

KEN SMITH
STICKS MAY
RAY IGELDON
RALPH BRIDGER.

18

WARS END

"Afraid of a little gunfire are we".

After Comacchio the survivors returned to Monte Sant'Angelo/Monopoly where all SBS personnel were gathering. On the 2nd of May 1945 Field Marshal Alexander issued a 'special order of the day' to all troops in the Mediterranean theatre:

> *After nearly two years of hard and continuous fighting which started in Sicily in the summer of 1943, you stand as victors of the Italian Campaign. You have won a victory which has ended in the complete and utter rout of the German armed forces in the Mediterranean. By clearing Italy of the Nazi aggressor, you have liberated a country of over forty million people. Today the remnants of a once proud army have laid down their arms to you – close to a million men with all the arms, equipment and impedimenta.*

Field Marshal Alexander's letter to the SBS in Italy at the war's end reads, in part:

The reputation you have made for yourselves in your successful operations in the Mediterranean, the Aegean Islands and the Adriatic coast will never be surpassed, and I would wish you all good luck and God speed wherever you may go.

Within two months the SAS, the SBS and the LRDG had all been disbanded.

When on the 7th of May 1945 Germany unconditionally surrendered it sparked off huge celebrations across the globe. A little-known incident now took place. According to Ken, Lebanese stevedores were being employed at one of the south Italian docks. They had been promised repatriation at the war's end and expected to be on their way immediately. The day after Germany's surrender, this did not take place, so they went on strike, refusing to unload the desperately needed food and supplies or to move from their barracks. The SAS/SBS troops, who were stationed nearby, had their automatic weapons exchanged for rifles and bayonets and were sent in. This proved to be a most effective strike-breaking method.

The talk of redeployment to the Far East, to participate in the ongoing bitter fighting against the Japanese, perhaps added to the sometimes-wild partying by the unit. A barrel of wine on the back of a cart was dropped off for all to enjoy. The extremely boisterous celebrations included pig wrestling. Piglets were released into a muddy compound and drunken servicemen were encouraged to try and secure one of the squealing animals. Both Ken and Sticks managed to grab a pig, and Ken quickly knocked up a crude pen out of old pallets. At mealtimes they would fill their canteens with the barely digestible "grey slurry" masquerading as their food and promptly feed it to the pigs; they at least found it appetising and rapidly gained weight. Most of the troops opted to make their way to the nearby town and buy or barter for a meal. Here Ken once again demonstrated his translation skills by repeatedly calling a local a piece of poo, having mixed up some similar-sounding words. Much to his friends' amusement, he then accused the man of not understanding Italian! Despite his past record and many heroic failures when attempting a foreign language, it must be said that Ken never let this deter him in endeavouring to converse with foreign nationals. After all, "It couldn't be more difficult than trying to talk to the Jocks!"

When at a post-war reunion it was announced that a few members of the French wartime SAS would be passing around and would all make every effort to welcome them and make them feel at home, alarm bells should have been ringing. Ken's table was approached by one of the Frenchmen. In an attempt at polite conversation Ken asked, "Where are you from, Paris?"

It was obvious from the puzzled expression on his face that the Gaul was an equal to Ken in foreign language skills.

Undeterred, Ken persevered, slowly pronouncing, "Parie?"

The guest's face now took on a totally bewildered look. By this time the bustling talk at the table had died down and all watched in eager anticipation.

They were not to be disappointed. Ken produced his master stroke, placing his elbows, forearms and palms together, pointing upwards and then raising them, he slowly said, "Eiffel Tower."

The Frenchman's face registered total bewilderment and he glanced around for help. Ken then resorted to his tried-and-tested response by accusing the Frenchman of not speaking French! The gathering of onlookers erupted in gutsy laughter as someone took the hapless Frenchman aside to explain that they were not laughing at him but rather at a master of detente at work.

One of the abiding memories Ken had of that brief hiatus in southern Italy was "sitting around with the local villagers" who "had nothing; they were dirt poor". Of an evening, with a tiny glass of wine, they would sing beautifully, slowly sipping at their meagre drinks and savouring each taste "as if it were their last".

One of Ken's favourite sayings, "Idle minds are dangerous minds", proved to be especially apt, as much mischief was undertaken by the redundant troops. Ralph had a couple of tales. One occurred when he and Iggy took a PIAT anti-tank gun out onto the cliffs for a spot of target practice. It was nearing dusk, and the local fishing fleet was returning to harbour when they were subjected to a barrage of anti-tank missiles. The pair thought it great fun as the near misses exploded close to the vessels, causing great waterspouts. The entire fleet was forced to hurriedly sail back out to sea. Others took to sniping from the hills at staff cars passing by on the winding mountain roads. After a few days a contingent of Red Caps arrived at the camp to keep order. Ken marvelled as they all had new blankets. Over the following days locals would be seen resplendent in brand-new suits and dresses tailored from what looked suspiciously like service-issue bedding. The MPs disappeared as suddenly as they had arrived, leaving the officers to restore some semblance of order.

Just as the pigs began to reach a good size, the marines were without warning discharged back into the Royal Navy. Hostilities only (HO) troops were already being repatriated and the Royal Navy were keen to get their enlisted marines back. At this stage it was still unsure if the SAS would be deployed in the Far East against the Japanese. The unit had tried to keep hold of at least the twelve with wings but the navy overruled them, demanding the return of all their personnel. Ken, for one, had no desire to return to the rigid discipline of the Royal Marines as he enjoyed life in the relaxed atmosphere of the SAS/SBS. Ralph, Sticks, Iggy and Ken were the only ones from the original Marine Patrol to see out the war.

From the 13th of June until the 7th of July 1945 Ken is recorded as being on passage to the UK, and from the 8th of July to the 5th of September he was based at Eastney Barracks in Portsmouth. The Royal Marines for many years had a regimental museum at Eastney which housed Albert 'Sticks' May's medals. They are at present trying to find another location.

When the SBS marines returned to Portsmouth they were paraded for inspection. A nearby car backfired, and automatically the ex-SBS troopers dived to the ground, only to be ridiculed by the drill sergeant. "Afraid of a little gunfire, are we? Haven't you heard a gun before?" Under their breaths, the troopers muttered oaths about the drill sergeant having not been out of the UK and spending the entire war marching around the parade ground, shouting at recruits.

Ralph recalled being placed on a charge for catching malaria and not taking his tablets. He tried to explain that taking tablets daily in the middle of the Comacchio swamp was not possible. He was surprised to be told that no marines were there.

The ex-special forces troops were finding their integration back into conventional military life somewhat disagreeable. On the 11th of August Ken was transferred to the Royal Marine Tradesmen unit as a junior carpenter, and at some stage he also qualified as a physical training instructor (PTI). He was working out in the gym when a new piece of equipment arrived: it was a springboard to go with the vaulting horse. The apparatus was set up and Ken decided he'd best test it out. Taking his customary run-up, he gave an extra-hard launch to his vault. To his amazement he sailed clean over the horse without touching it, flying over the mat, landing on the wooden flooring, and sliding across it and out through the gymnasium's double doors, ending up in a heap in the adjacent corridor.

The Second World War ended abruptly when on the 6th of August 1945 an American B-29 Superfortress bomber, the *Enola Gay*, dropped a five-ton atomic bomb on the Japanese city of Hiroshima. This was followed on the 9th of August by another at Nagasaki. Japan announced on the 15th of August that they were willing to unconditionally surrender.

There were approximately five million service personnel in the British armed forces at the end of the war, with the vast majority keen to return to civilian life. A demobilisation plan was put in place. The release process began about six weeks after VE Day, and by the end of 1945 over 750,000 personnel had been released. By 1947, about 4.3 million men and women had returned to civilian life.

As Ken had enlisted rather been conscripted, he was not eligible for discharge at the war's end; the priority being given on a first-in-first-out basis for the conscripted men. Having been demoted back to an ordinary marine on his return to the service, he was now promoted up to corporal PTI (physical training instructor).

Kenneth Herbert Smith married Joyce Winifred Galloway on the 12th of January 1946. Joyce had spent most of the war serving in the Women's Royal Air Force (WRAF). It was a very short honeymoon as on the 31st of January Ken boarded HMS *Rajah* bound for Hong Kong, arriving on the 7th of March to join 3 Commando Brigade as part of the engineering troop.

During his time in Hong Kong, for some reason unknown, he was busted back down to marine. His demotion did not last long, as when the brigade turned up for the morning workout no one was available to take the session, so he was given back his two stripes. One of Ken's tales was that "Three times I lost my corporal stripes and three times I was promoted back."

In Hong Kong Ken was posted to a small commando engineering detachment of about twenty men (with a few local Chinese cleaners, labourers and cooks) based in Kowloon. Every evening the officer and the sergeant would return to their respective messes, leaving Corporal Smith in charge. Ken saw no reason to discontinue his SBS-learnt bartering skills, and many loose items that were not nailed down disappeared off base. He had his eye on a large dynamo lying neglected under a desk, and approached one of the Chinese cleaning ladies, Nancy, whom he had become quite friendly with, asking if her uncle, a well-known local trader, would be interested in it. She came back to him saying yes, and that he would be willing to pay a good price. One evening after the officer and the sergeant had left, a truck pulled up and Ken enlisted all the marines on base to help manhandle the dynamo onto the back of the vehicle. A dynamo is a machine for converting mechanical energy into electrical energy, and this was a particularly heavy specimen. Being paid in large notes and wanting to equally divide the spoils (thus making all complicit in the scheme), Ken was forced to go to the local market and buy some goods to obtain the necessary small change. A Chinese embroidered tablecloth and napkins, that subsequently always came out for special occasions in the Smith household, were a souvenir of that shopping trip.

Shortly after this, Ken was sent back to the UK for some leave. He smoked a pipe at this time and would dangle it from his mouth through a gap in his teeth. As the troop ship was about to transit the Suez Canal, he leant overboard and his pipe slipped out, disappearing into the depths. Luckily, he had a spare, but he managed to repeat the feat as the ship exited the canal. He would say that in years to come, if ever the canal was drained, archaeologists would puzzle at the coincidence and its meaning.

Upon his return he half-expected to be met at the Kowloon docks by some MPs and was pleasantly surprised not to be. However, back at the engineering depot all the troops were paraded, and the officer asked if anyone had any information about a missing dynamo. All remained quiet, which surprised Ken as one marine in particular had an intense dislike for him, the pair having crossed swords on a few occasions. Corporal Smith was then called into the office to see if he could shed any light on the matter. Innocently he said that it was possibly some Chinese coming over the wire at night. The officer agreed, saying that you couldn't trust them at all.

As all commandos are required to be in good condition, it fell to Corporal Smith to maintain the levels of fitness by taking routine physical training sessions. One man possessed very little physical ability. He was extremely well spoken, wore thick-rimmed glasses, and reminded Ken of a bit of a swot. The punishment for being last on the regular runs was being detailed to do some unpleasant tasks such as cleaning out the toilet. The swot always came last, and on one occasion, in a posh Oxford-type accent, said, "Corporal Smith, you are a proper bastard!" Ken was proud of this, taking it as a great compliment.

One of his duties was to act as guard to Japanese prisoners of war that were being tried for war crimes. One of those found guilty was sentenced to be hanged, and Ken was made responsible for delivering the man from the courthouse to Stanley Jail, where the gallows were situated. The man was led away in handcuffs and transferred by jeep to the prison. Ken banged on the heavy wooden gates and eventually a couple of Chinese sentries appeared. Bowing profusely and apologetically, they accepted responsibility for the condemned man. With Ken only just having handed over his charge, and with the jeep in the process of negotiating a three-point turn, a shot rang out. The sentries, not wanting to be bothered with the formalities of a hanging, had simply shot the man in the head.

Ken was next posted to Malta in May 1947. Expecting it to be a lengthy stay, he arranged married quarters and furnishings. Then on parade, he dropped his rifle. The bullet still embedded in his arm was playing up. On the 27th of November 1947 Ken was diagnosed with 'Osteoarthritis of the left shoulder; bullet in the left arm, shoulder trouble; physically unfit for Royal Marine service.' The medical officer recommended that Corporal Smith be immediately medically discharged as being unfit. Hurriedly Ken drafted off a telegram to Joyce, who was about to board a ship at Southampton bound for Malta. He could see the pair crossing paths as their respective ships sailed past each other, going in opposite directions. Luckily the message arrived just in time.

Ken arrived back in the UK at the end of 1947, where he was assessed and finally discharged on the 6th of February 1948, having spent seven years and 301 days in the British armed forces. Ironically a naval gratuity of two pounds is paid for each full year of service, so being sixty-four days short of eight years, he received fourteen pounds. Those sixty-four days saved the British taxpayers two pounds. Ken was about to be welcomed back into civilian life, but just how would he adapt? How would society cope?

Whitfield Barracks, Kowloon, Hong Kong, 11th March 1947. 'The Sports page you sent and me, dear. All my love Ken xxx'.

'Barracks, Malta. Engineer Troop, Brigade HQ, July 1947.'

*Wedding photo 12th January 1946.
Standing L to R; George Smith; Albert May; Ken Smith; Joyce Galloway; Alfred Galloway; Ginger Williams.
Seated L to R; Iris, George's wife; Ellen Smith; Christina Farley/Galloway; Roy Galloway.*

1961 photo of the eldest children; Alan; Colin; Barry; Susan; Eric; David.

*Christmas 1975, the only photo of the entire Smith family'
Standing L to R: David; Colin; Susan; Eric; Alan.
Seated L to R: Geoffrey: Joyce: Ken; Barry.
Front L to R: Kieth; Derek; Micheal.*

19

AFTER THE WAR: CIVILIAN LIFE

"No, but something like that."

And once the storm is over, you won't remember how you made it through, how you managed to survive. You won't even be sure, whether the storm is really over. But one thing is certain. When you come out of the storm, you won't be the same person who walked in.

(Haruki Murakami)

Where do you start? It could be unfair to try and characterise Ken as those that best knew him have such widely contrasting views. He lived by what he considered simple rules: straightforward and reliability. He was extremely hard-working, definitely stubborn, and uncompromising, with some quite complex issues. Not being in any way materialistic, never suffered fools gladly, all he ever seemed to crave was a simple, quiet life.

His wife Joyce had a good heart and was the eldest of nine children: three boys and six girls. She was possibly from a previous relationship of her mothers, as no father is registered on her birth certificate; also, she had recollections of her father bringing home a present – a doll – for her sister but receiving nothing herself.

The marriage was a volatile one with frequent heated arguments. Joyce often insisted on having the last word, and this resulted on numerous occasions in her sporting a black eye or bruising. This sort of behaviour was not uncommon in the post-war years, when men mostly considered themselves the breadwinner and that the woman's place was in the kitchen. Joyce endured much on her children's behalf, often being blamed for any misbehaviour or indiscretion: "It's your fault", "You're too soft on them", and even being told, "That one's yours to raise", saying that she would mess it up and the child would turn into a delinquent! Stony silences and not speaking were almost monthly experiences. Joyce suffered for her entire married life, living by the adage 'You've made your bed; you can lie in it.'

The children were always kept clean, tidy and fed, although their plates were usually spotless at the end of a meal. They were taught good manners, to be polite, courteous, to give up your seat for an elderly person and to do work for no reward. But with that number of boys there was always mischief afoot.

The couple lived all their married life in the Portsmouth area; to begin within the city, where their first child, Alan, was born on the 11th of September 1948. David was born less than a year later the 18th of August 1949, and by July 1967 they had a large family of nine boys and one girl. A standing joke was that the parents were attempting to complete the alphabet in children's names, with the next three boys being named Colin, Barry and Eric. A bit out of sequence but the conclusion was drawn that the next child's name should begin with the letter F, especially when the seventh child was named Geoffrey. However, number six, the only girl, was christened Susan: Susan Ann Smith (SAS). The boys, being boys, took to calling her Fanny, which she was none too pleased about, and this resulted in the lads receiving many a smack from their parents for teasing their sister.

Alan was born in St Mary's Hospital (at that time the city's main hospital), christened in St Mary's Church, and first lived in St Mary's Road. Ken found work as a carpenter for a small building company. Wood was rationed, requiring a chit for its supply, with most building timber coming in from Canada. The city, like many across the country, was a maze of bomb sites and the ever-expanding family was fortunate to be rehoused in a 'prefab' on the slopes of Portsdown Hill: 50 Faversham Road, Wymering, Cosham (the site is now part of the city's main hospital car park). A prefab is a prefabricated bungalow made in concrete sections that can be transported on the back of a lorry for erection on a site. Hundreds of thousands were constructed in the post-war years to ease the desperate shortage of housing. They were notoriously cold, damp and draughty, but for many they were a godsend, a home. Some have stood the test of time, still being lived in into the twenty-first century.

In November 1952 Ken started work with the Southern Electricity Board (SEB) in their carpenters' workshop. He worked for 'The Board' until retirement on his sixty-fifth birthday, the 12th of April 1987, he never drew any unemployment benefits; and despite some hard financial times he always managed to keep his family fed and housed.

In the early years of married life, and with an ever-increasing brood, he would spend hours teaching them skills; in particular football skills: how to pass, trap, dribble, use both feet, and kick the ball forcefully and accurately. All the children, except for Barry, who had Down's syndrome, could execute press-ups, forward rolls, handstands, etc. When in 1956 the family was rehoused on the new estate of Leigh Park, Havant, there would be timed races around the block, and a crude set of parallel bars, fashioned from some bent metal tubing, was cemented into the backyard. Ken endeavoured to keep his children active. He insisted they learnt their times tables, often reminding them that "An idle mind is a dangerous mind."

The Leigh Park estate was built to accommodate the overflow from Portsmouth; large areas of the city having to be bulldozed after World War II. By the early 1970s it was reputedly the second largest council housing estate in the country, after one in Glasgow. At that time, it had two large secondary modern schools and a grammar school. Most of the Catholics attended the city's Catholic secondary school, plus half of the pupils at a nearby secondary school came from the estate. In those days most children finished education at sixteen. Oak Park Secondary Modern, one of the estate schools that Ken and Joyce's eldest children all attended, had over a thousand boys and eight hundred girls. However, the estate continued to be expanded and it was said that it eventually became the second largest in Europe, after one in Paris.

There were never the funds to pay for a holiday, so the children would take advantage of youth organisations to go on summer camps: Scouts, Boys Brigade, Army Cadets and the like. On a few occasions a family trip to 'the beach' would be organised. This would take the form of loading up the big pram (usually with a baby at each end), a pushchair for the toddlers, and a home-made handcart for supplies: canvas groundsheets, pegs, mallet, buckets, various tools, a few bottles of 'corporation pop' (water), and some jam or paste sandwiches. The excited children, herded by their parents, would set off on foot for the shoreline at Brockhampton, a few miles away. At high tide it is a pebble beach which quickly gives way to dirty black silt as the tide drops. A small pile of stones would be erected and after a short period of time, half an hour, it would enable you to work out the exact state of the tide. The walk to the beach was an experience: first having to pass the sewage treatment works and its associated odour, proceeding a little further, avoiding the bin lorries on the potholed track with no footpath, then passing the entrance to the main council refuse dump. The tip was located on the same shoreline as their destination, and the family would walk a short distance away before setting up camp. The excursion would be timed to coincide with high water and the children would soon be hobbling across the pebbles to play in the brackish water. Then as the tide dropped it would be time to go cockling in the black, silty mud. The final icing on the cake, so to speak, would be loading up the cart with cowpats and seaweed, both excellent sources of fertiliser for the garden and allotment.

Ken's allotment increasingly became his refuge. It was here, he said, that he was able to find the peace and quiet he craved; to be alone and free to lose himself in his thoughts and recollections. Of a weekend he would leave straight after breakfast, not returning until the evening. His children would be sent down with some sandwiches and a hot flask of tea. One of the sons was practising for an upcoming cross-country race. Ken had shown him how to vault a five-bar gate by throwing the body onto the top rail, reaching over to grasp the lower bars, and bringing the legs over with a twist to land, enabling the exponent to keep forward momentum. When done at speed it hardly breaks one's pace. Unfortunately, he hadn't shown his son how to do it when delivering a lunch pack. The son decided to practise the vault on the allotment gate; improvising, he tossed the lunch bag over, stooping to collect it as he landed. When he picked it up there was the telltale sound of glass and liquid sloshing around in the glass-lined thermos flask. Seeing his father busy amongst the lines of vegetables, he quickly delivered the packed lunch and hurried off with some excuse about not being able to stay and help with the weeding, desperately hoping that by the time Dad made it home he would have cooled down, (and forgotten about it,) following his discovery of the broken flask. When Ken was well into his nineties he still went on about the incident.

Large families were not that uncommon in those days and the children considered their life to be normal. Many families struggled to get by, and harsh discipline was common, with smacking and caning being just a fact of life. The Smith family may have been amongst the last to get a television (black and white in those days) and own a family car, and never had a family holiday, but to some extent the saying 'You don't miss what you never had' is a truism. Ignorance is bliss and there were others they considered were far worse off.

Every Christmas the house would always sport the street's largest Christmas tree. A few weeks before the day, several trees would arrive in the back of Ken's SEB truck, his works transport. Ken's work entailed him travelling around the local countryside, repairing gates and fences on Electric Board substations. Many of these were located conveniently close to Christmas tree plantations. As time went on, he increasingly worked alone, preferring it that way. In his early years with The Board a gang of half a dozen or more would go out for the day. Once, sat in the front of the vehicle, Ken listened to a new man boasting about his time in the SAS. He let the man brag on for a while before asking a few pertinent questions, silencing the man, who obviously had not been part of the unit.

Post-war children would sometimes boast about their fathers' wartime exploits. One of Ken's boys had a friend who often went on about his father being a commando. The son asked Ken what he did in the war – was he a commando? "No, but something like that" was the answer, with no further elaboration.

Ken's method of trying to calm a distraught child cannot be found in any parenting skills book. If one of his children had hurt themselves and was crying, he would say, "I once saw a man with his hand blown off and he didn't cry."

When schools were on holidays, sometimes one or two of Ken's children would go to work with their father. One December day in the 1960s, after having a day's work experience, one of the sons was surprised when the large works van the pair were travelling home in suddenly stopped in the middle of nowhere. Ken jumped out of the van, grabbed a handsaw and turned to his startled son, saying, "Stay here and keep watch." He then disappeared into the nearby treeline. Soon there was the sound of frantic sawing, with treetops swaying and then disappearing. It all took only a few minutes before Ken reappeared, dragging what appeared to be half the forest. He threw open the back doors and loaded in half a dozen Christmas trees. When they arrived home the best one was selected, which usually entailed chopping a bit off for it to fit into the front room. The other trees were gifted to various neighbours. This particular year, one was left over. Ken sent his son down to a house at the other end of the street, where another large family lived, to see if they wanted a Christmas tree. This family were considered poor; the father was a dustbin man, the children's clothes were usually tatty, and the house always looked a mess. The father came to the door and, although surprised, readily accepted the offer. The tree in question may have been the last of the collection but by anyone's standards it was a fine specimen. When the tree arrived, the whole family came out to admire it with an unrestrained, sincere show of gratitude. Ken's son always remembered that incident and how small gestures can mean so much to others.

Although Ken always seemed strong and indestructible, he did have a few incidents of ill health. Occasionally he would be laid up with a malaria attack; one moment sweating profusely and the next wildly shivering. Once when pushing some knotted wood through a large bench saw, the wood slipped, and his hand went into the revolving blade. He never wore any jewellery, including a wedding ring; if he had been wearing one, the blade would have gripped the ring and dragged his arm into the machine. Even so, his right hand was permanently disfigured. Ken disapproved of adornments, including tattoos, saying you don't need them and considering it a weakness. He also deemed swearing a sign of weakness and would recite an old maxim, "Where ignorance predominates, vulgarity invariably asserts itself!"

Another time he slipped a disc in his spine and was laid up in bed for a couple of weeks. A letter from the council was dropped through the door saying that an abandoned car parked on the street outside would be towed away on a certain day unless claimed and removed. Although delighted to have the car taken away, Ken needed the engine for his vehicle. Someone had dropped it off for this purpose. Still struggling to move, he dosed himself up with aspirin and donned a tight surgical truss. By strategically placing a series of wooden blocks and using heavy straps around his head and neck, he managed, by himself, to raise the engine, slowly adding more blocks until the engine was free and clear and he could then move it to his alleyway. Before the car Ken owned a motorbike which he always parked in the alleyway. Of a night the family all knew to walk through the dark tunnel hugging the opposite wall; this was to prevent a painful collision between the ankle and the bike's foot pedal.

One morning Ken was driving into work when he passed his brother Henry waiting at a bus stop. He quickly braked to offer him a lift. Because of an earlier motorbike accident Henry walked with a pronounced limp, but he made his way to the parked vehicle as fast as he could. Henry was a senior draughtsman in the dockyard and a very capable chess player. Ken reached across and threw the door open and Henry, looking at Ken to say thank you, stepped inside. He then gave out a loud exclamation as he found himself stood on the road: the car had no floor! Ken tried to explain, saying, "Just keep your feet up", but Henry was having none of it, stepping back out, shaking his head and saying, "You're mad, crazy, a fool." He stormed off back to the safety of the bus stop, still muttering about his deranged brother. Ken's workshop at that time had a vehicle pit. His car was due an MOT test for roadworthiness, which it would fail due to its badly corroded floor. His solution was to remove the offending areas and replace them using some panelling from old metal filing cabinets, pop-riveting in a new floor. It was a slow process, being undertaken every evening after work, so for many weeks Ken drove around with no floor to his car!

One story that became folklore occurred at his local pub, The Swan in Bedhampton. There are several versions of this story but what follows is generally accepted as what actually took place. Never let the truth get in the way of a good story.

For many years, Sunday lunchtimes would find Ken at his local for a few beers and a game of darts. One warm Sunday he was especially pleased to be sporting a new cardigan, hand-knitted by Joyce. It was a warm day and the door, near to the dartboards, was propped open. In walked Jockey Thompson and the Smith twins, well-known troublemakers on the estate. Jockey was celebrating his recent release from prison. He kicked the door jamb away and went to the crowded bar, where a space suddenly appeared. Ken replaced the doorstop, but Jockey had noticed and immediately went back to kick the doorstop away. A deadly hush descended on the noisy bar as Ken told him to leave it in place. An argument developed and Jockey threatened Ken. Ken didn't back down, and said to Jockey, "You think you're big with your mates; I'll take you all on, one at a time, outside."

The group moved outside, Ken realised that his opponents were not going to play by the Queensberry Rules, so he backed himself against the pub wall. People were still piling out to witness the action when suddenly Ken was hit hard as a fist flashed in from the side. Seeing stars and shaking his head in an effort to clear it, he immediately raised both fists to defend his face. Crouching behind this defence, more blows thundered into him, but he was now braced. Through the small gap afforded him by his clenched fists he could clearly make out Jockey's face. His right arm shot out, catching his opponent square on the chin and (according to several witnesses) lifting the man off the ground and clear over the bonnet of a car parked behind him, where he lay unconscious. One witness, a keen boxing fan, said he had never witnessed a blow like it. Ken's brother George had by this time made it outside and had one of the twins on the floor. The other twin held his hands up in a gesture of surrender and was told in no uncertain terms to take his friends away.

The victorious locals noisily trooped back into the bar to celebrate the incident. The story was the talk of the estate for some time. But upon Ken's return home he received no hero's welcome; rather, a severe telling-off. When he had let fly with the punch it was so forceful an action that it ripped apart the stitching across the back of his brand-new cardigan. Joyce was not pleased. The following morning "two coppers" (policemen) knocked on the Smiths' front door. Joyce was worried that her husband was about to be arrested but this was not the case: they were interested to find out who "the grey-haired old man" was and to congratulate him. Ken's hair had turned grey at an early age, no doubt due to his wartime experiences. The story that circulated around the large estate was that an old man had bested a local bully!

Ken is credited with possessing an extremely powerful right arm. There are several examples of this, such as when he knocked out Iggy in Italy and the member of Lassen's patrol in Albania, and you could in all probability add to this list several Military Police. He put his ability down to spending many, many long hours as thirteen-year-old apprentice rip-sawing lengths of timber to form staircase stringers; the long side supports to a flight of wooden steps.

Many years after the war, he was out in Portsmouth for the night. One bar he visited had a mixed-race man taking on all challengers at arm-wrestling. He was the area's champion. After some persuasion Ken reluctantly agreed to participate. The rules were explained, grips taken, tensed, and then to everyone's surprise Ken pushed his opponent's hand down flat on the table. There followed a brief stunned silence before a cheer went up. The shaken champion immediately demanded a rematch, muttering about not being ready and being in a bad position. The second contest was as short as the first, with the same outcome. If ever Ken recounted the tale he would say, "It was so easy." It was not said in a boastful way but as a matter of fact.

In another story Ken came across his daughter, Sue, when she was about fifteen or sixteen. She was in the back of a car in a pub car park with a boy. Ken dragged the young man out and incensed, drew his right arm back with such force to strike the poor lad that he pulled his shoulder out. The would-be victim later said to one of Sue's brothers, words to the effect of, "I know he's your dad but if he had struck me, I would've been forced to hit him."

The knowing reply was, "You would have had to find your head first!"

After the war Ken continued with his love of football, but if the truth be known he was no fan of the modern game where prima donnas roll around on the ground feigning injury, often saying that the game is now played by "a load of fairies". In later years he would watch televised games with the sound turned down rather than listen to infuriating commentators who were just as bad as, if not worse than, the players. His soundtrack to a match was largely a series of tuts and sighs, with the odd disparaging comment.

In the early '70s he was overheard saying that he could do better with the local pub team. Someone, not expecting a response, challenged him to prove it. So, Ken took on 'The Rovers' (now 'The Heron') team for a couple of seasons. Under his guidance and strict training regime they went on to win a prestigious cup. They were the first Havant team to win the Hampshire Junior Cup. Before a game he would spend ages pumping up the ball, bouncing it until it gave a high-pitched ping. Once the opposition stopped the game shortly after kick-off, complaining to the referee that the ball was too hard. Ken could not believe his ears, especially when the same complaint was levelled at the replacement he offered. Eventually, much to Ken's disgust, some air was let out of the match ball.

He had been brought up on the old, heavy laced-up leather footballs. As centre forward, he was often called upon to head the ball. If it had been laced up wrong or you caught the ball at an awkward angle it could cause a nasty gash to the head. In a post-war game after heading a cross and connecting with the laces he was forced, after the match, to attend the A&E department at the local hospital. The forehead wound required several stitches and the nurse told him not to play again for a few weeks. The following weekend found him back in A&E with the same wound. The nurse given the job of stitching him up remembered him and said, "Didn't I tell you not to play for a few weeks?"

His excuse that "We were short, and I couldn't let the team down" fell on deaf ears. He believed she was particularly aggressive with her needlework to show her displeasure and reinforce the message.

Traditionally football was a winter game, with cricket being played in the summer. So, every summer Ken would don his whites and play the genteel game, although, true to form, he played it his way. He was not recognised for his batting skills as it was either a four or out, but he was acknowledged as a demon fast bowler. With his speed and pace, the ball would strike the wickets so hard they would fly down the ground, turning end over end and sometimes flying past the wicketkeeper. He was even known to break wickets. Often the captain would remove him from the bowling to give the opposition a game and knowing that some of them were terrified of having to face Ken. In Hong Kong he had been the opening bowler for the Commando Brigade, the team being otherwise all officers. After matches, refreshments would be laid on in the officers' mess, and Ken would have to sit outside and wait!

His eldest son Alan, himself a noted fast bowler as well as an extremely talented goal-scoring footballer, well remembers his father on several occasions telling a particular cricketing tale. Ken had been selected to open the bowling in an invitation match. Johnny Arnold, a onetime opening batsman for England and one of only twelve people to have ever represented England at both cricket and football, was first up to face him. Ken's first ball was unceremoniously dispatched to the boundary for four runs. Feeling annoyed with himself, he took an extra-long run-up and let fly with a delivery at maximum speed. It took the middle stump clean out of the ground and the bails flew over the wicketkeeper's head.

The Portsmouth team he later played for went on to win a prestigious trophy. Ken stayed on to enjoy the celebrations, missing the meal Joyce had prepared and arriving home not only late, but slightly inebriated. He ended up being hit over the head with a saucepan, and with blood coming from the wound he reputedly said, "I suppose you're happy now."

Following one cricket match, the players all retired to a nearby inn. Ken sat outside, not having any money for drinks. One of his teammates asked if he would join him to make a double pairing at darts. Ken said he couldn't play the game or afford it; the losing pair having to buy the victors a half-pint of beer. The man was eager to play and explained that it didn't matter he would buy the beer and do the 'chalking', and all Ken had to do was aim for the centre of the board. With nothing to lose, and the remote chance of a free drink, Ken agreed; his new partner put their mark on the board. The procedure was that victors stayed on the board, and challengers awaited their turn and had to chalk (score) the match before their game. It turned out Ken's partner was a highly skilled player, never missing his doubles, and the pair stayed on the board, unbeaten, for the session. A bonus was that his new friend was a non-drinker! Ken asked him how did he get so good? The man explained that he was a teacher in a city school and that the boys found maths less than entertaining. He had hit on the idea of using darts to encourage the classes' interest: they would score, having to work out doubles and triples, addition and subtraction. The novel method of tuition was a great success. Ken replicated the idea, with a dartboard being hung in the family front room. He used heavy, thick darts, and over the years would replace the tips when worn down with sharpened carpentry nails. The old-style flights would often delaminate, and much time was spent over a steam kettle, regluing them. Eventually Ken became a top local darts player and a member of The Rovers pub team. They became Portsmouth area champs, going a whole season undefeated.

One of the highlights of the Smith year was the Electric Board's annual sports day. This eagerly anticipated event took place at the firm's Drayton depot near Cosham. Many of the larger employers of the day had leisure facilities for their employees. Drayton had a large social club; sports pitches for football, cricket and the like; it even boasted an indoor shooting range. Much time and effort went into the sports day, with a marked-out sprint track which hosted running events, sack races, egg-and-spoon races, wheelbarrow races, etc. Around the grounds, various games and stalls were located: coconut shy, skittle alley, wooden trolley ride, carousels, etc. The day also included a large buffet lunch. When it came time to leave the Smith entourage would troop what seemed like a mile or so to the main road for the bus ride home; Alan and David laden down with prizes they had won.

A carnival atmosphere had been encouraged, with many novel events designed to include all. One year's 'family race' started with a child sprinting fifty or sixty metres to the father, who would 'piggyback' the youngster back to the start, where the mother was waiting with a needle and thread to tack a patch of cloth onto the seat of the father's pants. The Smith family team was led by Alan. He had inherited a good degree of his father's DNA, being not only a highly talented footballer but a gifted athlete, twice representing the county of Hampshire in running. He easily pulled away from the field, some of which were mere toddlers. When he leapt onto his father's back, they were in the clear by half the course. Ken arrived back at the start line with the rest of the field only just setting off on their return journey. He bent over for the patch to be attached, only to suddenly and violently jump into the air, uttering a loud scream and clutching his backside. Much to everyone's amusement, he paced around in great discomfort, letting all know of his predicament. Joyce, meantime, was exhorting him to stay still as she desperately tried to complete her task with the remaining half of her needle. The excitement and adrenaline had gotten to her. Acting in haste, she had plunged the needle through the patch and pants to sew the small piece of cloth to Ken's backside! His violent reaction had broken the needle in half. There is some speculation in the family as to whether this incident was the accident it is reputed to be.

If not at his allotment, Ken could usually be found in his handbuilt wooden shed at the bottom of the small garden. Here he would craft various items from wood including furniture and toys; the latter often being Christmas presents that were shown to the recipient on the day with the rider, "Don't touch. The paint's still drying." He was especially known for his bowls, vases and plates, all made from small scraps of wood painstakingly glued and clamped together before being turned on an ancient lathe. The shed was powered by a long extension lead fed from a kitchen socket. When Joyce had made a cup of tea, to attract Ken's attention she would switch the power on and off a few times. A standing joke amongst 'the boys' was that dad would appear one day for his cuppa minus a finger or two.

A selection of Ken's woodwork.

Over the years many people would visit the small, unassuming terraced council house to talk to, interview and record Ken. Much SBS documentation had been lost in an Italian plane crash, and so historians and authors would increasingly seek him out. To the family this was all taken for granted and only in later life was the significance of these visits realised.

It could be said that during his life Ken had three great friends: his brother George, his comrade-in-arms 'Sticks', and his fourth-born child Barry. Barry was born with Down's syndrome and spent his first years in the Leonard Cheshire Home at Dorchester, Dorset. When he was about five or six Ken insisted that he should rejoin the family, saying that if Joyce could babysit for neighbours she could look after Barry.

There are many stories that bring smiles to the faces of those fortunate enough to have known Barry. He was an innocent, gentle soul with a great sense of humour. He would spend hours with his younger siblings cradled in his arms, rocking them to sleep. The family for many years always had a large black double pram in the hallway; this being the daytime resting place for the current baby/babies, usually one at either end. One day Joyce heard the babies crying and upon investigation discovered that Barry had climbed aboard and was sat in the middle of the pram with a bottle in each hand, drinking the babies' feed.

Ken once built a small rowing boat in the back garden. Nearing completion, he needed to establish the balance point for the seat and rowlocks. Barry did not like water and would never have entered the car if he had known his father's intention. The pair, with the dinghy, drove to a quiet creek that had a slipway. The conditions were perfectly calm, and Ken floated the craft in barely knee-deep water. It took a huge amount of persuasion and even more threats to coax Barry into the water and then, supported, to step into the boat. Trying to balance Barry and make slight adjustments to the seat caused the craft to rock slightly, which rapidly developed into a violent commotion as Barry panicked and burst out of the dinghy. He flew up the slipway, leaving his father surrounded by the wreckage of his masterpiece. The stern of the boat had only been clamped into position and Ken was desperately trying to salvage the sinking craft; all this accompanied by an exchange of insults, the word 'plonker' being freely used by both. Ken managed to fix and refloat the craft but this time no amount of cajoling would get his son to move from his entrenched position some twenty or so yards from the water's edge. The running debate ensued for several hours, with Barry calling his father "nuts", "stupid" and an "idiot", to which Ken replied, "That's rich coming from you." Insults continued to be exchanged as the now-wobbly boat was loaded up and the pair returned home.

In later life a routine developed where Barry would come down the stairs from his bedroom at about 9pm. Ken would hear him and quickly change the TV channel to the most inappropriate programme he could find ballroom dancing, the news, etc. Barry would plonk himself down in his chair and announce with a certain amount of disgust, "You can get this rubbish off." The pair would exchange banter before switching to a football channel.

The end was sudden and tragic for Barry, and it devastated his parents. Having risen in the middle of the night to use the toilet, he must have become disorientated on the landing at the top of the staircase. There was a loud commotion, and he was found crumpled at the foot of the stairs; he did not cry out in pain. At the hospital they discovered he had broken his back, and he died later that morning, aged fifty-five, on the 26th of November 2010.

All expected and secretly wished that Ken would go before Joyce, worried about his ability to look after himself. This was not to be as Joyce suffered a severe stroke in the summer of 2012 and passed away on the 14th of March 2013, having never recovered or regained the ability to speak. With Ken now living on his own he increasingly became somewhat of a recluse. Although many tried to help, he insisted he was OK. When he talked about his wife Ken would sometimes praise and vilify her in the same sentence.

His eldest son Alan had earned himself, by virtue of circumstances, the unenviable title of his father's carer. Ken took to doing his laundry in a plastic ice-cream container. Despite having numerous clean and brand-new clothes he insisted on wearing the same ones for weeks on end. When challenged about his behaviour or asked if he needed a hand he would answer with remarks like "When we were in Albania…"

Alan tried hard: changing the dressings that covered open sores on his father's back, sneaking away clothes to launder them even though the best thing would have been to burn them, changing bedding, etc. It was usually a thankless task, and when asked how it was going, he would remark, "He won't help himself." The most used adjective to describe his father was, by far, "awkward".

At one stage during Alan's daily visits Ken started to complain about a toothache. For several days it grew worse, but no amount of cajoling would persuade him to visit a dentist. One morning Alan turned up and asked his father how the tooth was. "Oh, OK," came the reply. "Fixed it." It turned out that Ken had gone down to his shed, picked up a rusty pair of old pliers and pulled out the offending molar. He was well into his nineties at this stage! Even at this age he would proudly demonstrate his fitness level: bending over and with straight legs touching the floor with the palms of his hands was a trademark exhibition.

No one could remember the last time Ken had seen a doctor. All ailments and injuries were dealt with by the comment, "It's all mind over matter", and "rubbing it with a wet lettuce leaf" was a cure-all. One of the sons did manage to get him to the doctor's surgery once. Ken insisted on being early, and as the scheduled appointment time approached the frequency of checking his watch increased. By the allotted time he was up and pacing the waiting room. As a generalisation, doctors' appointments run late. Eventually Ken was called in, only to re-emerge in what must have been record time to rush out of the surgery. When his son caught up with him and asked how it had gone his father replied, "A waste of time." The doctor had suggested he make an appointment for a blood test at the hospital, which of course would have been a further waste of valuable time. Not that Ken's appointment diary was ever busy.

Ken increasingly became even more awkward. At one stage he even locked Alan out of the house, ostracising him, but his son persevered with the difficult task. In his final weeks Ken became bedridden, and a local doctor was persuaded to make a house call but there was little he could do. Ken was by this stage saying he just wanted to go to sleep and not wake up, but his strong willpower would not let his body give up. Yet the inevitable did happen: Alan arrived early on the 6th of July 2017 to find that his father, Kenneth Herbert Smith, had died at the age of ninety-five years.

Just how do you attempt to describe the man? Many adjectives have been used in this volume. One of his sons once said, "He must have been a brilliant soldier, but he was a lousy dad!" This is not entirely true but there is another volume that could be written about his children: how they survived and matured, and their very differing life stories.

Ken's story is in so many ways typical of his generation, although his war years do somewhat set him apart. They defined his post-war years and his uncompromising attitude. His children were equally proud of and embittered by him. He loved small children but found it hard to show emotions. Many found his stories enthralling and were impressed by his strong character. Those that knew him well have widely differing opinions. His wife and children endured much and, in many ways, paid the price for his war years: two of his children refusing to have children of their own, several still bitter about him in their old age, a few being heavy drinkers, and most being resentful of the way he treated their mother. She endured much in her selfless devotion to her children. Was this a price worth paying for having a hero as a husband and father? Some would say no!

Whatever one's thoughts on the subject are, it must be remembered that Ken too endured much. His generation refused to yield when all seemed lost. To personally survive, having witnessed such seismic events and lost so many friends and comrades, himself being wounded, must have been deeply traumatising.

It is now hoped that his many descendants will be able to learn a little about their forefather and his life and feel some pride in being a continuation of that story.

Ken and Joyce with seven of their children on a rare family day out.

20

GEORGE SMITH

"We had to use ack-ack to shoot the bloody things down!"

Young George

Ken had two younger brothers, George and Henry. George is remembered as a big, strong, handsome man and as one of Ken's closest friends. In the early war years, at the age of fifteen, he was employed as a dockyard boy in the Royal Navy yard at Portsmouth. Early in 1941 the Prime Minister, Winston Churchill, paid the yard a visit and all staff were under strict instruction to stay out of sight. George was working below decks when his foreman called for him, sending the young lad on an errand to get "five Woodbine" cigarettes, adding, "Stay out of trouble." But George was spotted and taken to meet the Prime Minister. Churchill shook the young lad, with the chirpy grin's, hand as a photographer captured the moment. George said, "I was just going down the Gangplank when I was grabbed by a very senior officer, who wheeled me to the quarter deck. I thought perhaps I was in trouble and had no idea that Churchill was on the ship. The officer asked if I was the youngest boy in the dockyard and I said I wasn't. 'Yes, you are' he said and pushed me through for a photo.

"The Prime Minister put his hand on my shoulder, and the photographers asked him to shake hands with me, which he did. I can't remember whether he said anything to me: it was all over pretty quickly.

"Latter I received two guineas for the copyright. I was called to the Admiral Superintendent's Office and given this big envelope with my picture inside and the offer of two guineas if I would sign away the copyright. I was advised to stick out for much more than that, but two guineas was a lot of money to me, so I signed. That photograph has cropped up several times in my life. Being only fifteen I was overawed by the whole thing, but it was a great honour to shake Winston Churchill's hand."

George was then invited to meet Admiral Sir William James, the Commander-in-Chief. "I learned later that even the highest of high-ranking officers might have to wait days to see him. But there I was, a scruffy little dockyard boy, waiting cap in hand in this really grand office. There were four senior naval officers waiting too, but his secretary came out and asked if Mr Smith was present; no one had ever called me Mr Smith before. Then I realized it was me.

"I was taken into his office and spent about five minutes with him. Sir William told me he had also experienced a moment of photographic glory in boyhood: as Bubbles in the Pears soap advertisement. He said some people became famous because they worked hard but I had become famous overnight. It was all a bit above my head; I couldn't see how I had become famous.

"I lived in Hilsea then, and after my picture had been seen all over, my mother had several indignant mums tell her that I was not the youngest boy in the dockyard. She took a bit of stick over that, but it was not our fault."

After his handshake with Churchill his foreman gave him a severe dressing down for getting caught and threatened him with the sack. A few hours later the Senior Foreman called for him saying, 'I just want to shake the hand that shook the Prime Minister's hand.'

A relieved George then asked if he wasn't going to be sacked? A slightly puzzled senior foreman said to explain himself. This resulted in the under foreman being sent for.

"I was told to wait outside, but the senior foreman was so mad I could hear him shouting at the under foreman. I can remember him saying: 'Can you imagine what the papers would make of this – a boy sacked for shaking hands with the Prime Minister!'"

The picture subsequently became a poster widely distributed in the USA with the caption 'Give us the tools and we will finish the job.' Afterwards the foreman took his revenge by giving the George one of the yard's least liked jobs: lagging the ship's boiler (blue asbestos was used in those days).

George went on to serve in the Royal Navy, surviving North Atlantic and Russian convoys. He was posted aboard SS *Empire Pickwick*, a liberty ship, this being a Defensively Equipped Merchant Ship (DEMS). He said, "me and my mates used to tell the girls it stood for Devastating Equipment for Miget Submarines, and they liked the sound of that.

The Allies were desperate to keep Russia in the war, sending them large convoys of war materials through the Arctic Ocean to Murmansk and Archangel. These convoys are considered to have been amongst the most difficult of the war. The merchant ships would have a small complement of Royal Navy personnel on board to man a gun welded on the foredeck. George said, "The Russians thought they were doing us a favour taking the cargo from us."

One of his favourite stories from this time was that on a Russian convoy the ships had been fitted out with a new top-secret anti-submarine weapon. Large barrels had been placed on board, and when a submarine was detected, these barrels were opened and the contents, a thick black tar that floated on salt water, were emptied overboard. This formed a film over the surrounding sea. Slowly periscopes started to emerge, their vision obscured by the tar. George would finish off the story with, "We had to use ack-ack [anti-aircraft guns] to shoot the bloody things down!" The adage 'Never let the truth get in the way of a good story' comes to mind.

George also saw action during the D-Day landings as a naval gunner.

After the war Ken and George teamed up as a formidable darts pairing. They made the *News of the World* finals, winning the pairs with Ken going out on a 157 last throw. Many at that time considered this championship to be the world's premier darts competition.

George died on the 14th of May 1992 at the age of sixty-eight, from pulmonary fibrosis: asbestosis!

Liberty ships

Liberty ships were a mass-produced, basic-design cargo vessel, the brainchild of design staff at the Joseph Thompson Shipyard in Sunderland, UK. The first of the wartime vessels to be built in Britain, *Empire Liberty*, was launched in August 1941.

Eventually they were mass-produced in Britain, Canada and the United States. The ship's name usually identified where it had been built. Ships built in Britain were immediately recognised by the prefix '*Empire*'. The names of Canadian-built vessels were either prefixed '*Park*' or prefixed '*Fort*'; the former for those crewed by Canadians and the latter for those under the Red Ensign with British or mixed crews. American-built Liberty's carried either the prefix '*Liberty*' or the prefix '*Ocean*', but some were named after prominent US citizens.

George shaking hands with Winston Churchill.

Fame from a handshake,' the poster with Abraham Lincoln's Memorial as background.

21

RALPH BRIDGER

"Dear Ken, when you get to the foot of the last mountain wait for me there and we will both go over it together."

Ralph Victor Cortiss Bridger, born on the 3rd of June 1925 at Portslade, Brighton. A noble name, and one that well suits the gentleman that he was. Ralph could trace his ancestry back to Jane Seymour, one of Henry VIII's wives, (some sort of distant cousin). His grandmother had had an affair with the son of the local squire. She gave birth to a son in 1890, and the squire forbade any marriage but allowed the baby to take the family name of Bridger. This was Ralph's father, an illegitimate son of the aristocracy.

Ralph Bridger in his eighties.

Ralph's father joined the Coldstream Guards in 1908. Whilst on guard duties at Windsor Castle he met Ralph's mother, and they were married in 1915. On the 23rd of June 1916, in an early encounter of the Battle of the Somme, Ralph's father was awarded the Distinguished Conduct Medal (DCM) for bravery. The citation reads:

For consistent and conspicuous gallantry, notably when in charge of his gun in an important but exposed position. The emplacement was three times blown in by the enemy's bombardment, but, although slightly wounded, he rebuilt it each time, and was fully prepared to meet the enemy when the attack came on.
9331 Lance-Sergeant A. G. C. Bridger, Coldstream Guards
(attached 1st Guards Brigade, Machine Gun Company).

After the Great War he became a hard drinker and would often beat his wife and children. Life was extremely hard for the family and young Ralph quickly learnt how to survive. Being the eldest sibling, he took on the responsibility of helping his mother look after his brothers and sisters, doing a newspaper delivery round, chopping and selling bundles of firewood etc, and giving any earnings to his mother. He would even go to the local market to scavenge for dropped and discarded vegetables.

Ralph spent much of his time up on the South Downs, where he befriended an old drover and was fascinated by his stories. From him he learnt how to forage, how to catch and skin a rabbit, and which berries and fungi were edible. Bathing in the sea and rivers was a naked affair, so when he was loaned a pair of trunks, he believed he could now swim. He jumped off the end of the breakwater; luckily a passing rowboat plucked the young lad from the sea, but not before he had gone under a couple of times!

When Ralph was about thirteen his father, in a drunken rage, pinned his mother to the bed and started to set fire to the bedding.

Ralph quickly grabbed an axe and rescued his mother, at the same time threatening his father. From that moment the frequent beatings ceased.

His father finally abandoned the family home. This compelled Ralph to leave school and take on various jobs, giving all his wages to his mother. In the course of time, he secured work as a coalman; the work was hard but well paid: nineteen shillings and sixpence (less than a pound) a week! The coal sacks weighed between one hundred pounds (45.36 kilos) and 140 pounds, (63.5 kilos). He was only fifteen years of age.

In 1942, at the age of seventeen, he enlisted in the Royal Marines. Getting three square meals a day easily overcame any hardships encountered. After training he was put on a troop ship bound for Alexandria, Egypt. There he languished, awaiting a posting. A bulletin – 'Volunteers for Hazardous Duties with Small Boat Skills Required' – caught his eye and he immediately put his name forward. Whilst awaiting an interview he met Ray Iggleden, another marine. He had been on board HMS *Birmingham* when on the 28th, November 1943 the ship sustained major damage after being hit by a torpedo fired from *U-407* off the coast of Cyrenaica. The forward magazine was flooded, and the ship listed eight degrees. Speed had to be reduced to twenty knots. The *Birmingham* put into Alexandria for temporary repairs and Ray was assigned the same tent as Ralph; all he possessed was the clothing he stood in. He had only just arrived and exchanged pleasantries with Ralph when the Tannoy system announced that all recently arrived survivors from HMS *Birmingham* were to report to the parade ground immediately. Upon his return Ray was incandescent with rage, having been placed on a charge for turning up to parade improperly dressed.

Ralph said, "You ought to do what I'm doing; this lot aren't big on bull."

"Where do I put my name down?" said Iggy.

This was the start of Ralph's lifelong friendship with his best mate and so often his partner in crime. Together the pair were usually up to mischief.

Both passed the interviews and found themselves on the back of a truck to Palestine. They arrived at what looked more like a refugee centre than a military camp. The canvas flap above the truck's tailgate was thrown open and a couple of unshaven, scruffily dressed men with no badges of rank or insignia poked their heads inside and said, "Any of you play football?"

Totally perplexed, Ralph immediately pointed to Iggy and said, "He was a professional with Leeds United and I was offered trials with Brighton & Hove Albion." Although not particularly tall, Ralph's position was as goalkeeper for Shoreham United.

"Quick, get your gear and throw it in that tent." According to Ralph, Marine Ken Smith had selected them for H Patrol, M Squadron, 1st SBS, 1st SAS.

On leave in Italy early 1945. Ralph; Sgt. Scott, Royal artillery; Iggy.

SBS/SAS

The following account was recorded during Ralph's life and at times it obviously replicates Ken Smith's story. It has been decided to include it in its entirety to help authenticate Ken's version and as an acknowledgement of Ralph's endeavours.

The SAS training was hard in the extreme: of the twenty-six that started, only seven passed. Ralph had only just turned eighteen and earned himself the nickname of 'Wallard' (Arabic for 'boy'). He was naive: did not drink, smoke or womanise. All that was about to change. Ralph possessed an excellent memory, and this, coupled with the ability to quickly learn a new language, were attributes that well suited his new unit.

After successful completion of their training Ralph's patrol was sent to the Cedars Mountains, as they were called by the troops, on the Syria/Lebanon border to train for a secret mission in the Alps. Luckily the operation was cancelled, for it was widely regarded as a suicide mission. During their mountain training, together with Ray Iggleden and Buster Aubery, Ralph was caught out in a blizzard. The trio were forced to take refuge by digging themselves a snow cave. After the blizzard they were snowed in and unable to free themselves. Rescuers finally dug them out some twelve hours later. Ralph remembered them lying there with frayed nerves, wondering if they would ever be found, when a probe appeared through the snow, hitting him. He grabbed hold and they were released from their would-be tomb. The three men were wrapped in blankets and taken by sledge to a hut to recover.

Ralph often mentioned Buster, saying he was a walking mountain who had spent six years out in India, where he was a heavyweight boxing champion. As Buster transited through the Suez Canal on his way to the UK, he decided to try out for the unusual unit. As strong as an ox and reputedly able to dead-lift a railway axle, complete with wheels, as if it were exercise weights, Ralph and Iggy quickly adopted him as a useful minder. The pair were in Sue's Bar in Beirut when Buster walked in. "Watch out, double-decker bus just arrived!" they called out.

Soon afterwards a big French Senegalese African came into the bar and spotted a girl sat on Ralph's lap. "What you are doing with my girl?" he cried out, then hit Ralph, slapped the girl in the face and pulled out a knife.

Buster picked up a chair, broke it and quickly dealt with the assailant.

When Buster became drunk, he would strip off naked and walk back to camp singing. On leave in Palestine a shoe-shine boy flicked black polish onto his best dress uniform after Buster had refused the offer of a shine. The lad thought his slight wouldn't be noticed, but Buster spotted the offence and smartly brought his clenched fist down on the lad's head as a mallet, killing him outright. Buster was immediately RTU'ed and never seen again.

Ralph had a tale of a Paddy Nolan, who went on leave to London. Finding his wife having an affair with a Yank, he killed them both, then quickly made his way back, went out on a mission and got himself killed. Although it is an interesting story there is no one of any such name on the regimental roll of honour.

While the unit was based in the Palestine area, elements of the Lebanese Army mutinied. Ralph said they were tasked with quelling the rebellion. "It didn't last long. We went in like a dose of salts in the middle of the night, threw them out of their beds and shook them up. Some of them had hairnets on! Many had small sachets of gold coins." Ralph ended up with a radiogram for his disturbed night's sleep.

The unit was deployed to raid the Greek islands, operating out of a secluded cove on the Turkish mainland. Many months were spent in the area, with most being visited on at least one occasion. Before leaving the islands, one last action was planned. This was to be the third raid on Simi. A combined force of SBS and Greek Sacred Squadron soldiers captured the heavily fortified island.

As the war progressed, the SBS were tasked with harrying the retreating Germans through Greece, Albania, Yugoslavia and Italy. The Marine and Jock Patrols were next landed in southern Albania. For two long months they fought their way up the entire length of the country, operating behind enemy lines with the local partisans. At the end they were on starvation rations, skeletal, filthy, and flea- and lice-ridden. Following a short recuperation, they were next sent into Yugoslavia. It was here that the Marine Patrol's luck ran out. A raid on Villa Punta on the island of Lussin resulted in heavy casualties, with over half their number being either killed or wounded. Captain Lees, the patrol's commanding officer, was one of those killed. "It was an ambush" and "They were waiting for us" are comments the survivors often said when talking about Lussin.

The aftermath of this mauling was a repatriation to Italy. The men believed this to be for some well-earned leave. All could see that the fighting in Europe was nearly over and perhaps the unit would be able to draw breath. They could not have been more wrong. After rearming and equipping the survivors were sent up to north-eastern Italy, becoming part of an eighteen-strong task force. Lake Comacchio was one hundred square miles of mosquito-infested swamp. For several weeks they were again behind the lines, paddling canoes around the vast marsh, capturing islands, taking prisoners, launching diversionary or probing attacks, and charting a course for the commandos to land behind the enemy. It was here that their latest commanding officer, Anders Lassen, was awarded the Victoria Cross. This was the last action of the war for the SBS.

On the 4th of October 2003 a dedication service was held in a London church to inaugurate the SAS and LRDG Roll of Honour for 1941–1947, commemorating those from the special service units who had lost their lives in World War II. At that time 340 names had been recorded, and since the end of those hostilities a further 155 personnel had been lost. Ralph attended that service. He was not a religious man, having lost his faith during the conflict. Halfway through, from a balcony to the rear of the church, a lady sang 'Lili Marleen'. This song was a favourite of the troops on both sides and was adopted by the wartime SAS as their regimental song. Ralph's eyes welled up and tears streamed down his cheeks as he remembered his lost comrades. He was not alone: the hall was full of old soldiers all doing likewise.

After the death of Ken, Ralph believed himself to be the last survivor from Comacchio and the last World War II marine SBS member. He said of Ken, "You could always rely on him. He would have your back and was always calm under pressure. His likes would be hard to see again."

After the SBS/SAS

After the war's end and the disbandment of the SAS, Ralph returned to the Royal Marines. The rigid discipline and unrelenting bull proved too much, and he was eager for discharge. Several bad bouts of malaria, contracted at Comacchio, enabled him to be demobbed. But after a year of civilian life with no work and little chance of employment, he re-enlisted, this time in the Royal Tank Corps, ending up as a sergeant. He had no intention of walking to war again. In the Tanks he saw service in Hong Kong and Korea.

Ralph and Kathleen 1945.

He married Kathleen in 1947. They had met prior to the war, courted during his year as a civilian, and now, with a regular income, the couple were able to wed. Ralph was very much in love with his wife and always talked fondly of her. Together they had many years of happiness. Following a short career in the Tank Corps he took up bricklaying, earning a good wage. They had one son and put everything into raising him, living a quiet life to afford the fees for a private education. Sadly, their son ended up dropping out of school with no qualifications.

When his wife was diagnosed with cancer Ralph dedicated himself to her care, even though by now the years of hardship had taken their toll, with Ralph having himself had a heart attack in 1975 at the age of fifty. He was forced to subsequently give up work after several angina attacks. It wasn't until 2006 at the age of eighty-one, and thanks to contacts through the SAS Regimental Association, that he finally had a triple heart bypass.

Kathleen had passed away on Christmas Day 2002. By this time the couple had been forced to sell their bungalow in Northampton and move in with their son and his second wife in Worthing, Sussex. Following the death of Kathleen Ralph's relationship with his son and daughter-in-law soured and he was forced to move out. A few weeks later the son's first wife, now living in North Devon, took Ralph in. Approximately two years later in 2006, he was again homeless; by this time his worldly possessions reduced to an old, battered suitcase and a black bin bag. His old wartime corporal, Ken Smith, had become aware of Ralph's circumstances and asked one of his sons, who lived nearby, to look out for Ralph. Together with his wife he befriended him, and the couple were able to house Ralph for almost a year until his favoured sheltered housing complex had a vacancy. For Ralph's final twelve years the couple, (and Barbara and Ken Sawyer, [Barbie and Ken]), the son's sister-in-law and her husband, looked after and cared for him. Ralph called the women the daughters he never had, and their families looked upon him as an extra father, grandfather and great-grandfather. His new extended family liked to believe that Ralph found some contentment and peace of mind and that his final years were happy ones.

An SAS motto is 'One more mountain to climb.' Ralph said upon Ken's death, "Dear Ken, when you get to the foot of the last mountain wait for me there and we will both go over it together."

Six months later, on the 6th of January 2018, with his two adopted daughters, sisters Barbara and Lyn, at his bedside, Ralph peacefully passed away, finally to be reunited with his beloved wife Kathleen. After so much hardship he is now at peace.

It was said at his funeral, "A remarkable life led by a truly remarkable human being, the like of which will rarely pass through our lives."

Post war re-union: Sticks May; Ray Iggleden; Philip Bridger; Ralph Bridger; Ken Smith; Robbie Drummond; Hans Majury.

Italy 1945, Iggy back row 2nd from left; Ralph lying in front.

Early post war re-union. Ken middle second row down; Sticks four to his left.

Appendix 1

'Lussin Stories from The Filibusters: The Story of the Special Boat Service by John Lodwick (Methuen Books 1947)'

Villa Punta, 9th–10th March 1945

"Are you all right, sir?"

A very much more difficult objective was now engaged. At Villa Punta, on Lussin, existed a strongly held post now housing no less than forty-five men. These men were Germans. Under McGonigal an expedition sailed to attack this post. Jimmy Lees and two newcomers, Lieutenants Thomason and Jones-Parry led sections. The striking force totalled twenty-one.

Landing unobserved and with local inhabitants acting as guides, the raiders approached the target area. Here McGonigal ordered Jones-Parry and his patrol to advance along the seashore to the south of the villa. Unfortunately, Jones-Parry was observed, challenged by a sentry and fired upon.

Since all chance of surprise had now been lost, McGonigal ordered the general attack. The enemy, who at first had attempted to make a sortie, were driven back into their billet.

The billet was surrounded.

Jones-Parry, Jimmy Lees, and Thomason, with their men, were now sent into the house with orders to clear it room by room if necessary: Jimmy Lees, on the first floor, had almost accomplished his part of the task when he was hit and fatally wounded by a man firing from behind a sofa. He died in German hands the next day, never having regained consciousness.

Elsewhere: "I saw," stated Jones-Parry, "two or more persons moving about in the corridor. I threw a grenade, but it was a dud, so I threw a phosphorus bomb and opened fire. I went in. I went up to a door and listened. No sound, very dark. Rushed in, paused. No movement. I went into a second room. Marine Kitchingman followed me, covering my back. Sergeant McDougal covered the corridor. Suddenly, Kitchingman asked, 'Are you all right, sir?' I replied, 'Yes.' At that moment there was a burst of machine-gun fire from some point in the room which we must have overlooked. I was hit in the arm and chest. Kitchingman collapsed. He had received a burst through his head. My thinking then began to get a bit confused. I changed my magazine and slung my 'tommy-gun' round my neck to make myself more stable. Then I opened fire on the point from which the burst had come, traversing along the wall and floor. I am certain I got the man as there was no reply, only groans. I reported to Captain McGonigal, who sent me on to the road for dressing. Very weak now, so lay down until told the wounded were to move. Finally, walked back to the motor launch."

This report was dictated by Jones-Parry from a hospital bed. If this officer survived to sleep between sheets again it is owing to his courage and endurance in walking two miles to the embarkation point with a shattered arm and a bullet in his spleen.

Meanwhile, McGonigal, with all available remaining men, made the decisive assault. The enemy fire slackened. Finally, it ceased altogether. With their house wrecked by Lewes bombs and on fire, it seemed unlikely that many of the garrison had survived. SBS casualties, though, had not been light for, apart from Jimmy

Lees and Marine Kitchingman dead, eight men, including Jones-Parry, had been severely wounded.

Opinions differed concerning the results obtained on this raid. Some maintained that the price had been too costly, and this argument was reinforced when it became known that no less than twenty of the enemy had escaped unhurt by hiding in the cellars or in the garden. The truth is perhaps that it is extraordinarily difficult to manoeuvre and deploy more than fifteen men, under night conditions, and against a fixed objective, when more than one officer is involved.

There were too many officers at Villa Punta, and though they led the attack with considerable verve and dash they were frequently at cross purposes. Both Jones-Parry and Thomason, for example, had at various times to send messages out to other patrols begging them to cease firing into parts of the villa which friendly personnel were clearing.

Villa Punta must stand as an indecisive action… and in SBS an indecisive action is synonymous with a defeat. The loss of Jimmy Lees and of Kitchingman were particularly grievous, for both these men had served with the unit for a long time and with great distinction. Modest and unassuming almost to a fault, Jimmy Lees had always been unlucky in the operations allotted him. The spectacular captures, the actions which draw immediate attention, had never, somehow, come his way.

Among 'Now it can be told' books, *The Filibusters* must surely earn a special place. For this is fact, not fiction: the Special Boat Service, authentic descendants of Grenville and of Drake, harried, pillaged and destroyed Germans through five long years of war. They came in the night: by parachute, submarine, surface craft and even by canoe. They struck in the desert, in Sicily, Sardinia, twenty times in Crete, more than two hundred times in the islands of the Aegean. They maintained a 'pirates lair' in Turkish waters. Almost alone, they liberated half of Greece.

Appendix 2

RALPH BRIDGER'S LUSSIN STORY

"Don't think the lads ever got over the death of Captain Lees."

A version of events following interviews with Ralph Bridger in the early 2000s.

M Detachment had already been involved in several earlier raids whilst stationed at Zara, but by far the most memorable mission for Ralph was the raid on the island of Lussin, a German stronghold. At the southern end of the island M Detachment's objective was the Gestapo headquarters at the Villa Punta. A team of eight men led by Lieutenant Jones-Parry, a relatively new member of the squad, was detailed to carry out the raid. Their guide on the island was an Italian deserter.

The team were transported to the island on board a naval harbour defence motor launch (HDML) vessel. The location for the landing was a deserted, rocky coastline which enjoyed a deepwater mooring, allowing the boat to pull up close to the shoreline. When the men landed on the beach, they made their way up to the villa, up over a forested mountain which skirted the nearby village. On their way to the villa, disaster occurred. The so-called 'knowledgeable' Italian guide managed to lose his way and the team found themselves wandering aimlessly for some time before deciding to abort the mission. It was far too late in the day to contemplate carrying on, so they returned to the naval HDML boat that was waiting for them offshore and withdrew to a nearby uninhabited island about four miles away. Weather conditions got worse, and the sea was too rough to recommence the raid the following day. After the third day on the island the men began muttering that this was a bad sign. The Germans had obviously become aware of their presence on the island and were well prepared for any attack.

The team was then called back to their base at Zara to prepare for a return match on the island. This time it was decided that there would be a squad of eighteen men taking part in the raid. Captain Jimmy Lees, Lieutenant Ambrose McGonigal and Lieutenant Jones-Parry were put in charge of the men. The strength of this squad was not typical of what had evolved in the formation of raiding forces during World War II and was considered sizeable by normal standards; something the men were not too happy about, but nonetheless they still got on with the job in hand.

At about 0100 hours the raiders arrived at the villa. Unknown to them at the time, the Germans were waiting to spring a trap. The only way up to the villa was by way of a rough track with a ten-foot wall on one side and an eighteen-inch wall on the other side which dropped away onto rocks and the sea below. Ralph and his mates were about halfway up the track when a German soldier who was positioned on the roof opened fire with a machine gun. They all dived for cover behind a low wall and wriggled their way up to the villa on their bellies. The element of surprise was well and truly lost and quick thinking was required on the part of those in command of the troops. The team swiftly split into two, with both squads positioning themselves to either side of the villa. Ralph went to one side of the villa with Captain Lees and about eight other men. Sergeant Cameron and Corporal Ken Smith went to the rear to provide cover. There was a garrison of six hundred Germans stationed about half an hour up the road.

As Ralph and his colleagues entered the front entrance of the villa they broke off to their left and right. It was at this stage that all hell broke loose. Bullets were dancing off the walls and grenades exploding. Ralph was sent to one of the side rooms, and as he got there a grenade exploded. The door blew off its hinges, hit him and sent him flying. He sat dazed and bleeding, but the door had saved his life. Ralph staggered to his feet and made it into the main lobby, where he commenced firing. Someone had called out a warning to Ralph and he immediately emptied the magazine of his much-loved Schmeisser through the adjacent door. He then heard running feet and started shooting up the stairs and onto the landing in the direction of the noise.

Unknown to Ralph at the time, his friend Corporal Ken Smith had just received a bullet in the arm. Ralph had thought that in the confusion he may have been responsible for the bullet in Ken's arm, but Ken assured him that it could not possibly have been him as he was not in Ralph's line of fire. Ken still carries the bullet in his arm today as a reminder of his visit to Lussin and the pair remained lifelong friends.

Ralph then heard someone shout that Captain Lees had been badly hit and was dying. This was, of course, a major blow for the men, as Captain Lees was a well-respected officer and highly regarded by his men. In a fitting tribute to the man Ralph was later to say, "Don't think the lads ever got over the death of Captain Lees. He was the finest officer and man that I have ever met in the armed forces, and we had some damn good officers in our unit."

Another casualty was Tommy Kitchingman, who had been killed in the action. Lieutenant Jones-Parry was badly wounded. He had been caught in machine-gun crossfire but managed to retaliate by killing the gunner responsible for his wounds. Despite this, he managed to get off the island in the subsequent retreat.

Bodies were all over the place and the signal to withdraw was given. The force picked up their wounded and decamped from the scene of the raid. One of the men, Billy Mayall, was so badly wounded in the stomach that he had to be carried off on a door that had been blown off its hinges. Total casualties on the operation were two killed and eight wounded.

During the raid, Germans stationed in the villa had set off several flares in an attempt to raise the nearby garrison. It was imperative that Ralph and his colleagues got away as soon as possible. In their hasty retreat they had the treacherous, mountainous conditions in the forest to contend with. The ground was littered with rocks and boulders. They also had to deal with the two wounded German prisoners that had been captured during the raid. During the retreat, one of the Germans whipped out his Beretta pistol and shot himself in the head. The other prisoner was so badly wounded that he had to be carried off by Sergeant Cameron and the wounded Corporal Smith.

Ralph, along with his Scottish mate Hans Majury, assisted another one of the jocks, Bill Morgan, (although in the Jock patrol Bill was in fact Welsh), who had been badly wounded during the raid. They had no medical kit available at the time; nor could they give medical attention to the man. Their objective was to get away as soon as possible as they knew what the consequences would be for them if they were captured by the Germans. It would be certain death. The difficulty for Ralph and Hans was that they were caring for a wounded comrade and had to be cautious in their movements.

Conditions were not ideal and the quickest way to the pickup point was through the nearby town. It was whilst they were moving through the town that they heard a gunshot going off. Ralph told his mate Hans to hang on to Bill whilst he surveyed what had gone on. On the ground was the body of the German prisoner who had just shot himself. Next to him was the Beretta pistol. Ralph, always the magpie, eyed the weapon with envy and quickly picked it up as a souvenir of the event.

The naval HDML waiting for them offshore was pulling away when they arrived at the pickup point. They were the last to reach their destination. Ralph and Hans shouted and waved frantically at the boat to attract attention. They were spotted by the crew and the boat reversed to pick them up. All the men were, of course, exhausted when they got on board the boat. Many were injured with blood streaming from their wounds. They were not a pretty sight. The naval personnel on board the HDML tried to give assistance as best they could. The sight of the wounded German prisoner who was with the raiding force caused a bit of a stir amongst the crew of the HDML, but after a few words of explanation from the men the situation was calmed down. The crew understood that the German had been taken for information purposes only and it was important to get him back to base for questioning. The boat then sped off back to Zara.

The two young patriots fought against each other. One died. But for his bereaved mother there was no bitterness, no hatred for his enemy. Just forgiveness and love

MY SON, MY SON...

ROBERTO COMOTTI: he lived

JAMES LEES: he died

I felt about Roberto as I would for my own boy

by VERONICA SNOBEL

It was a bitterly cold night. The lone Englishwoman, wearing a man's flying suit, huddled closer into the corner of the compartment as the train thundered towards the Yugoslav frontier.

She had been warned not to make this journey behind the Iron Curtain. She couldn't speak a word of the language, and she had only twenty pounds in travellers' cheques.

But Madeline, Lady Lees, was too preoccupied with her own thoughts to worry about the dangers and problems she might face in Communist territory.

For she was on a pilgrimage to find out how her twenty-five year old son, Captain James Lees, died a few weeks before the end of the war.

All she knew was that her eldest son had been killed while leading a group of commandos on the island of Losinj, off the coast of Yugoslavia.

"He had come through so many battles and adventures, including the North African campaign that I felt he would return safely to us in the end," she told me.

"But when I heard he had been killed, I thought I had to find out for myself what had happened. I longed to see his grave in Lussinpiccolo, on Losinj—whatever the risk."

Her welcome

After that grim eleven-hour journey through a rainy January night in 1949, Lady Lees found that everyone was kind and helpful.

"I had a British passport and a letter from the Yugoslav Embassy," she recalled. "But my real passport was the picture of my son and of his grave, which the War Graves Commission had sent me."

When she reached the island, she found the grave beautifully kept and covered with flowers.

Lady Lees was introduced to Maria Damiani, a young Italian who had been a Red Cross nurse in the hospital where James had died.

Maria gave her the names and addresses of Dr. Klaus Wasmuht, the German doctor who had cared for James, Sister Ubalda, an Italian nun who had nursed him, and Roberto Comotti, an Italian officer with whom he had shared a hospital ward during the last few days of his life.

Lady Lees wrote to all these people, and from them she tried to piece together the extraordinary story of her son's last battle.

James, who served with the Special Boat Service, a commando-type force, was the officer commanding a party—trying to capture the Villa Punta, a house overlooking the bay, which was held by an Italian platoon commanded by Lieutenant Comotti.

During the attack, a grenade injured both James and Roberto. When the British force retired, they had to leave James unconscious beside his Italian enemy.

The wounded men were taken to the local hospital. The Italian recovered, but James died.

"I have never been able to forget that they were both young patriots fighting for their own countries,

A medal for peace ... the award they made to Lady Lees for her supreme act of forgiveness

sharing the little white-washed hospital room," Lady Lees told me. "Somehow, when I heard all this, I felt about Roberto Comotti as I would for my own boy."

So Lady Lees wrote to him. Soon they were corresponding regularly.

Last year, Roberto was sent to this country by the Milan oil firm for which he works. Lady Lees immediately went to London to meet him, and invited him to her home.

The rest of the family—she has five children still alive and nineteen grandchildren—took to him at once.

Her reward

Over in Italy, Lady Lees's supreme act of hospitality to her son's former enemy did not go unnoticed.

A few months later she was told that she had been awarded the Premio della Bonta gold medal, an annual prize presented by a committee in the Italian town of Salo to someone who had contributed to reconciliation between nations.

And in June this year, she went to Salo to receive the medal. First, she stayed in Milan with thirty-six year old Roberto and his family, his wife Katerina, and their two children. Then, Roberto accompanied her to Salo, which is only seventy miles from Verona, where Sister Ubalda was now nursing.

From Sister Ubalda, Lady Lees heard the final chapter in her son's life.

"James died in her arms," Lady Lees recalled. "He had been unconscious for two days. Then he woke, took off his signet ring and told her to give it to Roberto as a token of peace."

Just before he died, James whispered: "My mother will come here to look for me. Give her my last kiss."

"I always felt that he might have left some last message for me," said Lady Lees softly.

Though Roberto remembers having the signet ring, it was taken from him in a Yugoslav prison camp.

"The ring belonged to James's grandfather and great-grandfather," said Lady Lees, who was widowed seven years ago. "I'm sure I shall find it again."

At the beginning of next year, a memorial to James will be unveiled in the little parish church a few hundred yards from his mother's home at Lytchett Minster, in Dorset.

Lady Lees hopes that Dr. Wasmuht, Maria Damiani—and, of course, Roberto Comotti—will be there.

"My son was a man of peace. He always cherished his fellow men," Lady Lees told me, her voice full of love and pride.

"In the early days of the war, before he went abroad, we used often to discuss how we could devote our lives to the cause of peace.

"Now something has started with endless possibilities for good...."

How Jessie helps unknown authors ... Turn the page

73

Lady Madeline Lees magazine article.

Appendix 3

LADY MADELINE LEES' LETTER

"They had to leave him there."

Extracts from Lady Madeline Lees' letter regarding her pilgrimage to Villa Punta, Lussin in January 1949.

We followed a path close to the sea. A violent wind raged, sea spray dashed over the rocks and salted our faces as we pushed along, in and out, wherever the coastline led.

I thought of the first attempt on Villa Punta, when they must have been prevented by breakers like these. There are several lonely Villas along this coast; They must be fun in the summer, but now they are shuttered and deserted. I have never experienced anything like that walk and the thoughts that poured through my heart, and the unseen companions who were with me.

We rounded yet another corner of rock – was this the Villa at last? I was looking at a small bungalow, standing in its own garden. I had a strange feeling that we had arrived, but this was not like it. Then I looked up through the pines and there above us, gaunt and terrible, stood the Villa Punta, with its seaward side ripped right away. It was exactly as Taffy [*Bill Morgan*] had described it, and exactly as it was left after that terrible night of March 8th–9th, 1945.

Here is the main road from Lussine Piccolo to Lussine Grande, and the two gateways of the villa garden with the low wall between them, where James helped the seven wounded men while he awaited orders to go in himself. Here is the spot where he stood, and these are the front doorsteps where he fetched Taffy, badly wounded, and took him to join the others at the wall. Here is the garden wall over which Taffy and his patrol dropped into the garden, because the approach from the sea was found to be impassable – certainly it was and is – and the trees and rocks behind which they sheltered as the machine-gun fire poured down from that top window.

Now up the front door broad stone steps and into the room on the right, which they had cleared without loss and behind it the room where Taffy was shot through the lungs, and the door post behind which he hid when in the room opposite Thomas Kitchingman was killed.

I stood there and prayed for them… Then went to the stairs. I suppose no one has been up those stairs since James went up four years ago; They are shattered and cracked and before they reach the first floor they are entirely demolished; Here it was that James met the Gestapo with their stick bomb; nothing remains but the heap of rubble below, and here under it James was found by McGonigal. He was already in the deep sleep from which he was not to wake until he was safely in heaven.

They had to leave him there, they heard the German reinforcements coming down the road from Lussine and they already had seven badly wounded men to carry over a rough stony mountain track to the cove on the opposite coast. How they ever accomplished that climb with such burdens after so terrible a night is a marvel of human will and endurance for love of their fellow men.

Out of time again I went with them, I saw Taffy walking the whole three miles supported between two friends until he reached the boat and lost consciousness. He had promised his mother he would return, and by sheer will to live he eventually recovered. And so, they all got away except James and Thomas Kitchingman. I stayed with them too. I saw them at last put in a horse-drawn cart and taken back down the road Lussine Piccolo to the Hospital convent on the quayside. There is someone else in the cart badly wounded and unconscious. Who?...

...It is a beautiful little hospital. The nun opened the door of a large room...it was not to this ward that he had been carried: she opened another---a little room for two beds only; I knew at once---yes, I must have been here before. End of letter.

An Italian who had been badly wounded in the Villa Punta battle had been brought to hospital in the same cart as James and put in a small room alone with him. This young man turns out to have been a Subaltern in the Fascist Militia.

By all accounts James was expected to recover and the Italian die. However, the reverse happened, and James passed away on March 11th.

Kens postcard to Ralph from Lussin, July 2004.
"Hi Ralph, to say wish you were here would be an understatement. Villa Punta is still here, they have replaced the door you damaged. Also, they have built a lovely holiday complex surrounding it. The weather is supper. Haven't seen any English – Full of Germans, Croats and Italians. All the best, Ken."

POSTSCRIPT

It must be said that there are several accounts offering differing versions of what transpired on that fateful night, the 9th of March 1945, at Villa Punta. Some reputable authors have contrasting interpretations of events, which only goes to illustrate 'the fog of war'.

Several report that Captain Lees was in fact shot from behind a sofa whilst room-clearing and subsequently died from his wound. This could possibly be confusing Kitchingman's death with his. Others state that the assaulting force was aware that the defenders were expecting an attack, and that Germans were now stationed at the billet and had positioned four two-man patrols in the nearby village. To counter this threat SBS troops had been sent to eliminate these patrols before commencing operations against the villa.

Some say that:

The SBS split their force into two for a planned assault from differing directions.

Hostilities started when an alert guard, posted in the villa grounds, spotted the approaching raiders, issued a challenge, and only opened fire when the correct password was not forthcoming.

A force emerged from the villa to assault the raiders.

Two men leapt over the low sea wall to avoid gunfire and fell to their deaths.

Lees' body could not be found and retrieved by the assailants.

The SBS numbers vary widely, from eighteen to twenty-one and even twenty-seven.

McGonigal asked the enemy to surrender.

Lees' patrol had been held in reserve.

These are some of the anomalies between the differing accounts. If, as stated, the garrison had been reinforced, was it due to the previous visit, the discovery of the secreted can of gasoline, or the dogs barking – or had the raiders been spotted? What if on the first attempt the raid had gone ahead; would there have been that vital element of surprise, or could the result have been even more disastrous?

Appendix 4

2004 LUSSIN TRIP

"Should be all right when they put the roof on and finish it."
Never let the truth get in the way of a good story. (Old sage, Ken Sawyer)

Ken undertook another trip to Lussin in early July 2004. The adage 'third time lucky' does not apply when talking about Ken and Lussin. He was chaperoned by one of his sons, who for reasons that will become obvious would prefer to remain nameless, so let's just call him Colin. He recorded the trip, and what follows is his monologue:

I found myself smiling; that warm inner smile that radiates. It was a smile of relief and satisfaction – no, more than that: so many emotions. I glanced sideways at the eighty-two-year-old gentleman sitting alongside me in the window seat. They say we revert more and more to children in our old age, and at that moment he reminded me of an excited young boy, craning his neck around, looking initially out of the adjacent window and watching the ground slowly become a patchwork as the aircraft climbed; then, as it banked, quickly turning to scan the opposite windows, catching glimpses of the now-receding islands; then turning sharply back as the plane levelled, cranking his head for an improved view. The ground gradually became obscured; initially by wisp-like clouds which slowly thickened to form a blanket of white.

As this scene unfolded, the flight attendant's telephone fell from its housing, dangling on its coiled line only a few rows in front of our seating. Then, with a small crash, the pilot's cabin door flew open to reveal a confused dashboard of dials and instruments. The lack of any response or movement from the crew indicated this to be a common occurrence. My face broke into an open smile. Were we about to embark upon yet more adventure? Surely nothing further could happen.

A mere nine days previously, on a bright Saturday morning in early July, I had kissed my wife goodbye and set out on this expedition. Well, that is how it had eventuated rather than the week's holiday originally envisaged.

It seemed that Ken Smith's visits to Lussin were always destined to be an experience. So much had occurred, and in a small way what had happened mirrored the reason for this journey (although I hasten to add that there can be no comparisons drawn between the past week and what had transpired some sixty years previously). My father, the gentleman sitting alongside me, had then been in his prime, selected from the vast resources of the British armed forces, hardened by years of warfare, trained to near perfection and with the fitness level of an Olympic athlete. He had been a dedicated member of an elite unit that history would recognise as one of the most effective fighting forces to emerge from the Second World War.

Two years previously I had accompanied my father, and eldest brother Alan, on a pilgrimage to the scene of a small battle that has been described as one of the greatest actions ever undertaken by special forces: the Simi raid of the 13th–14th July 1944. Dad had fought in this engagement. He really appreciated and enjoyed the experience of being able to revisit the scene in peaceful times. Inspired by this undoubted success I'd organised a trip to Lussin, Croatia, the scene of a much maligned and significant episode in Dad's life. It was here that my father received the bullet which is still embedded in his shoulder. I had read somewhere that the Lussin raid, Operation Aniseed, was one of the SAS's most disastrous missions. It was certainly costly, and I do not believe the full story has ever been recorded.

My original plan had been for a party of four. Ralph Bridger was to join our party. Ralph had recently moved to North Devon and had become a regular visitor to my home. He was the only other living survivor of the Marine Patrol and the Lussin raid. His body was now frail, but he possessed a healthy mind and admirable recollection, and as such had proved an invaluable source of information. Regrettably, neither Ralph nor Alan was able to make the journey. So, on the 5th of July 2004, accompanying my father I set out for the island of Lussin in Croatia (formerly Yugoslavia). Had I known then what I do now… Well, I guess I would still have gone! Ralph and Alan must be mightily relieved that they did not have to endure my 'well-organised' holiday with its scenic detours. The story has entertained many, usually at my expense, and must now say that I am no longer sought after as a travelling companion, if ever I were.

I did know that it was not to be a straightforward package holiday, the island being somewhat off the beaten track, isolated, and at the end of a long chain of Dalmatian Islands stretching from the mainland into the Adriatic Sea. It had taken much research to find a tour company able to offer us a package. Initially, this was hampered by the fact that I had the incorrect spelling: Lussin rather than Luccin or Lošinj; Lussin is what the troops at the time knew it by. Eventually my persistence was rewarded, and I located a small firm specialising in holidays to obscure locations in Croatia. I was excited: we were able to book into the Hotel Punta at Veli Luccin. This seemed too much of a coincidence as the raid had been on Villa Punta (Point House). Dad and Ralph had spent much time scanning the brochure and speculating as to whether this could be the very same location. But, as they pointed out, their previous visit had been in the dark, sixty years ago, and they "didn't hang around"!

So, it had been with eager anticipation that I set off, excited by the prospect of my father's pilgrimage. My route: via the family home on the outskirts of Portsmouth. Both my parents emanated from this historic nautical city. Dad had been a choirboy on HMS *Victory*, Nelson's wooden flagship at the Battle of Trafalgar and to this day still commissioned in the Royal Navy. I believe it to be the world's oldest naval vessel still on active service, theoretically. I spent a night at my parents' home, caught up on family gossip and dined on home cooking. No one boils vegetables quite like my mother!

The following morning, Sunday, overflowing with the inevitable six cups of tea, we set off for Stansted Airport. The flight was scheduled for early the next day. After a leisurely and uneventful drive, we arrived at our overnight accommodation. It was one of those pub/hotels, located close to all major airports, that specialise in parking your vehicle whilst you are away. Bright and early the next morning the hotel owner dropped us at the airport. We proceeded through the formalities of booking in, security and customs, then found ourselves a small cafe in the departure concourse where we breakfasted on croissants and coffee. With plenty of time to spare we took turns in looking after the luggage and wandering around the myriad of shops, stalls, cafes and bars that filled the busy mall.

So far, so good. At the appropriate time – or so I believed – we collected ourselves and proceeded towards our boarding gate. This is where the alarm bells started to ring.

We had been unable to find seating with a view of the overhead departure screens, and it was only now that I noticed that there was no record of our flight on display. Heading for our gate, we were confronted with a monorail system that transported us to a further departure lounge. I must confess, I had never flown from Stansted before. The seating area around our departure gate was ominously deserted. Resting my father, I went in search of assistance. Confronting some members of staff, I was informed of the news I now dreaded: the plane had left! I had confused the boarding time with the departure time. It's not easy to do but that is not how I made it appear. I have no defence, take full responsibility, and any seasoned traveller credibility I may have possessed is now well and truly shredded. Having travelled around the globe several times, negotiating many difficult situations, how could a simple thing like this catch me out?

We were very professionally dealt with and transported back to the main terminal, reunited with our baggage, taken back through customs, and directed to a help desk. Although very polite, they said there was nothing they could do and to get in touch with our travel agent. I went in search of a telephone, leaving Dad to look after our luggage. He was taking the situation remarkably calmly; content to sit amid the confusion, serenely rolling a cigarette, unaware at this time of how often this scene was to be repeated over the coming days. Whenever my spirits lagged, my father's unflappable attitude gave me confidence to soldier on.

Desperate to try and salvage something, my pride in tatters and my brain in overdrive, the limited options were presented to me. The travel agent was as helpful as he could be. There were only two flights per week to our destination: Sunday and Monday. This was Monday, and we had just missed that. However, Croatia airlines had a daily flight and could get us to a nearby airport to our destination at Pula. I was ignorant of the geography but was assured that if we could get ourselves to Pula we would be met and transferred to the hotel. Not bad; only a day late. We had missed that day's flight, and it flew from Heathrow anyway. The options were presented to Dad, who was for pushing on. Further telephone calls were made, booking a flight from Heathrow, via Zagreb, to Pula, and confirming that we would be met and transferred. With the decision made, there was now a chance that I could salvage some face from this disaster. I began to see a light at the end of the tunnel. Foolish me!

It was during the taxi journey back to our hotel (and car) that I discovered the first flaw in my plan. We were still booked to fly back into Stansted, so it would be pointless to leave the car parked at Heathrow. The hotel owner was surprised to see us back so soon; however, he rapidly came up with the solution to our current dilemma: leave the car where it was and catch the airport shuttle. He even phoned ahead, booking us into one of the hotels that surround Heathrow, and ordered us another taxi to take us back to Stansted Airport. Whilst the predicament was being resolved Dad took another cigarette break. I shall live forever with the image of my father sitting in various locations around Europe, surrounded by baggage, contentedly rolling up. Just what sort of tobacco was he using?

That day dragged slowly on, with hours spent in London's main parking lot: the M27. But by the afternoon we were settled into a hotel overlooking the landing area at Heathrow. I left Dad rolling up yet another cigarette and went in search of sustenance as we hadn't eaten since our meagre breakfast. My father always says he prefers to go hungry, citing Albania (another story), as that way the food tastes better, but my stomach disagreed. Many consider a Big Mac a treat; however, I do not subscribe to that school of cuisine, but times were desperate. We had passed a McDonald's restaurant only a short time before arriving at the hotel, so it wouldn't take too long to fetch us something to eat. A quick walk turned into a marathon hike, having completely misjudged the distance. However, the burgers were still warm when I returned and Dad, who confessed to having enjoyed his first 'Big Mac'.

We whiled away the time idly watching the seemingly endless stream of jets approach and land. My father was fascinated and timed them to one every seventy-five seconds. As one touched down three more could be clearly seen, spaced out, on the approach route.

The weather was gorgeous and by late afternoon a beer was in order to celebrate such an eventful day. Not wishing to have a drink at the sterile hotel bar, we set off to stretch our legs. McDonald's had been to the left, so knowing the distances involved we took a chance on going right, which turned out to be a good decision. Within two hundred yards we came upon an oasis: exactly what we were seeking, and serving good, hearty meals. If only I had known this a few hours earlier. We settled in and spent a few comfortable hours meeting some good company at the bar who were in awe of Dad's stories. In high spirits we made our way back to the hotel, happy with the progress since the earlier debacle and confident that tomorrow we would eventually be leaving the country.

On Tuesday morning (I had left Devon on Saturday), we were at the forefront of the Croatia Airlines flight queue. By lunch we were seated under a large canopy sipping cool beer, having negotiated customs at Zagreb Airport. It was an extremely agreeable port of call: a large tree-shaded park is situated to the front of the terminal building with a pleasant continental bistro bar at one end. We sought shelter in the park and found a bench near to a fountain. Dad rolled the customary cigarette, and we people watched. The simple package holiday had now taken on the air of an adventure, and my father had relaxed into the experience. Our first impression of the Croatian people was very favourable. They appeared to be well mannered, friendly, tall and athletic looking. Frequently when travelling I am embarrassed by my fellow countrymen, who often come across as aggressive and rude.

Ken Zagreb airport, 'rolling up'.

Our connecting flight to Pula took off on time just as dusk was falling. The aeroplane was small; Dad banging his head every time he stood up. We were having quite the adventure, but it was time for it to end. I dared not think of the consequences should we fail to be met. Shortly the saga would be over, and my burden lifted.

It was dark when we touched down at 21:50 local time. The walk to the terminal was thankfully short. I scanned the faces at the barrier, trying to pick out our likely courier, but no one returned my gaze. The few other passengers rapidly vacated the terminal and an ominous silence descended. The lone lady attendant at the information desk thankfully spoke excellent English. I explained our predicament. She resolved the situation, booked us into a city centre hotel, and arranged a lift with the man from the lost property office who was closing and headed that way. He squeezed our baggage, a work colleague and us into a small two-door saloon car and we set off. I have a vivid memory of the airport lights being extinguished as we pulled away.

Our accommodation was a family-run affair in the centre of the city. We quickly registered, dropped our bags, and joined the lost luggage man at the bar. Dad rolled up and was soon entertaining the locals with tales of his last visit to Croatia. He seemed to be thriving on the situation and despite the circumstances we made our way to bed in very good spirits – after all, we were at least in the correct country and confident that tomorrow we would be sleeping in Lussin. Our new friends at the bar had furnished us with several options should a courier fail to show up. Yes, we were closer to the destination, but unless the ferry schedule was sympathetic (which it wasn't), or the company had a boat laid on, the best solution was to take a coach trip halfway back towards Zagreb and then another which island-hopped to Lussin. But that was a problem for tomorrow. Throughout my travels I have often relied upon the advice of the locals and invariably found it to be most reliable.

Wednesday morning, and a phone call to the hotel confirmed that we still had our room, but as for getting there, we were on our own. Having been abandoned by the tour company we took the advice from the previous evening and called a taxi for the short journey to the bus station. Whilst the driver and I loaded the bags into the vehicle's boot Dad sat himself down in the front passenger seat. Well, it would have been, were we in the UK. Our driver let out a burst of laughter as Dad made his way around the taxi commenting on, "Bloody foreigners driving on the wrong side of the road." By the time we pulled away friendly banter was flowing; the driver spoke good English and he proceeded to point out sights along the way. We rounded a large coliseum built by the Romans and he told us that Pavarotti had performed there a few weeks before to an audience of several thousand. Drily Dad said, "It should be all right when they put the roof on and finish it." It took a moment for the translation to register before the driver roared with laughter, adding that it also needed some windows and doors fitted.

All too soon we arrived at the bus station, and our new best friend helped us to the ticket office with the bags and started to negotiate with the clerk about the onward trip. He then turned to us and said that the bus that had pulled out as we'd arrived was the one, we needed and there wouldn't be another for an hour, but if we liked he would try and catch it up. There was no question: let the adventure continue; give it a go. The next ten minutes or more was like something from a Hollywood movie: racing through the city and out into the countryside; the driver flashing his lights, sounding the horn and attempting to use his mobile phone whilst steering one-handed. Exhilarating stuff. I realised that Dad was thriving on the experience, by now fully engrossed in the surreal situation. It took some time to catch up with the coach and then to persuade it to pull over, but eventually, after bidding a fond farewell to the taxi driver and leaving him with a tale to tell, we were comfortably seated in a plush air-conditioned vehicle and winding our way through the beautiful mountainous scenery of the Istrian Peninsula, bound for Rijeka. It is a spectacular drive with massive tunnels burrowed through towering peaks, hidden valleys with finely manicured fields, and precariously winding roads twisting through gorges and snaking along steep hillsides.

We passed tranquil hamlets, villages and small towns that radiated a quiet, peaceful and unhurried way of life. We caught glimpses of the crystal sea dotted with tree-covered islands, and all the while my father sat, serenely contented, taking in the magnificent vistas.

It was a sharp contrast to this when we were dropped into the bustling tourist resort and busy port of Rijeka. The streets were thronged with people industriously going about their business. The heat was oppressive, and the atmosphere tainted with the smells of diesel, fish, seaweed, oil and car fumes. The coach station was in the city centre, surrounded on three sides by a mixture of tired but once-impressive buildings juxtaposed with brash modern structures. The fourth side led directly onto the waterfront. A diverse array of vessels lay moored in the bay or tied up alongside the many quays and jetties.

I found Dad a seat, surrounded him with our baggage, and set off to book tickets on what would hopefully prove to be our final leg of the journey. Having been schooled by an expert I was becoming adept with the language: a bit of arm-waving, shoulder shrugs, finger-counting, and the knowledge that a vast percentage of the population spoke passable English, and seemed to find my efforts entertaining, got me through. With tickets for our destination safely purchased we spent a sweaty couple of hours awaiting the coach. Taking turns, we stretched our legs, wandering through the packed streets or along the waterfront. By early afternoon a shabby-looking coach pulled into the bay indicated on our tickets and a full complement piled aboard. With a thankful sigh the vehicle pulled away and warm air coursed through the cramped company. Women fanned themselves with glossy magazines as the air-conditioning unit sat useless and inactive. Once out of the city conditions marginally improved – this was due in the main part to the increase in speed providing a stronger breeze. We were, however, delighted by more panoramic vistas.

We departed the Croatian mainland over an impressive new bridge linking it to the island of Krk. Halfway down the island we passed the Rijeka airfield where we should have arrived two days previously. The scenery continued to impress with views across the water to the peninsula we had travelled that morning. Crossing the length of Krk we arrived at a small, isolated bay. Somewhat out of character with the beautiful location sat a large concrete quay and modern filling station that dominated the tranquil inlet. With a long hiss from the tired brakes the coach joined the assortment of traffic neatly aligned awaiting the ferry. Many of the other vehicles were loaded down with the paraphernalia for holidaying and tired travellers wandered around stretching their legs, awaiting the arrival of the ferry that had just set out from Cres Island some three or four miles away. Gratefully we joined them, eager to alight from the metal oven we were travelling in. Dad sat on a large rock, rolled a cigarette and smiled, seemingly unperturbed despite our sweaty condition. Glancing at the coach, all that seemed to be missing were a few crates of chickens squawking loudly on the roof.

In time the ferry berthed, discharged its cargo, and as the neat lines of traffic orderly embarked, we strolled aboard as foot passengers, following the mass up one level to the luxury of an air-conditioned restaurant lounge. The relief from the afternoon heat was tangible; I stood feeling slightly guilty for using up the cooling air, for we'd made no purchases. Refreshed, we made our way onto the outer balconies, located a shaded spot and took advantage of the cooling breeze to view the approach into Cres.

The voyage lasted about half an hour. We docked in a small cove overlooked by high wooded slopes. A steep road, lined with the ferry's return load, traversed away around the shoulder of the bay. Making our way to the stairs we found they were blocked by passengers; unable to progress, we watched in disbelief as the first vehicles began to disembark. Barely in time did we make it back; the coach's engines were running and the traffic in front moving.

The journey the length of Cres was a tedious affair: by now we were overwhelmed with fine views, our clothes were starting to stick to our bodies and the pervading odour was unpleasant. It was way past the time to be showered and fed. A few pastries since breakfast had been our only nourishment; Dad had on several occasions refused the offer of food, and it was no surprise that he was beginning to wilt. It was a marvel that he had kept going.

The western tip of Cres is separated from Luccin island by a narrow channel excavated many centuries ago by the Romans. A swing bridge connects the two islands; this was, of course, open upon our arrival, a line of pleasure craft negotiating the short passage. The other passengers poured out from the coach, eager for some respite. We followed a little apprehensively, keeping a guarded eye on our transport, keen not to repeat previous experiences. A stall was doing brisk business; we purchased a refreshing ice cream, enjoying the coldness and savouring the sweet flavours, then washed our hands and cooled our faces under the spring water from a nearby fountain. Before the first movement of the swing bridge we were firmly seated, eager to set off on the final leg.

It came as no surprise to find that our destination was where the coach terminated its journey at the distant end of the island. The main town, Lussin Mali, was only a mile or so from Lussin Veli, where we had a short stop to unload some passengers, which was frustrating, being so tantalisingly close. Late on the Wednesday afternoon we were dropped off at a small car park on the outskirts of the former fishing village that is Lussin Veli. Tourism now seems to be its prime industry. Dragging the luggage, we set off through the narrow-cobbled alleys in what I confidently believed to be the correct direction, triumphantly emerging into the bright sunshine that lit the tiny harbour. Dad needed a rest – he is human after all – so I sat him at one of the tavernas that ring the anchorage, leaving him with half the baggage, a cool beer, and casually rolling a cigarette.

I set off in the direction I perceived the Hotel Punta to be. A wide track led off from one side of the harbour the short distance to what proved to be our hotel. A walk of no more than one hundred metres. Finding reception, it came as an anticlimax when, with no fuss, I booked us in and was handed the keys to our room. It was 19:30 on Wednesday 7th July 2004; four and a half days after leaving my North Devon home. The hotel was a '70s-style concrete-and-brick complex, sprawling away from the rocky shore to lose itself in the pine-covered slopes. Multiple terraced tennis courts continued further inland. The room was comfortable and more than satisfied our needs.

I returned to collect a rejuvenated Dad with the good news that we had finally made it. As we progressed up the gently rising track, memories started to flood back to my father. He recalled the low parapet wall, the telegraph pole, and pointed out the direction the fire came from, searching for details stored deep within his subconscious. He sat down, bathed in the evening sun, on the wall at approximately the position where he and Captain Lees had dived for cover. Deep in thought, he 'rolled up'. Some thirty feet below, the rocks were being gently washed. I started to feel that the trip was beginning to be worth all the hassle we had endured.

Then dad said, "This is where it happened!"

Our short stay at the Hotel Punta was an intensely moving experience, with my father often immersed in deep thought. We explored, Dad pointing out features, gazing in fascination at the now-restored villa last seen as a blazing ruin. It was surreal that now it stood surrounded by a holiday complex; split into a couple of luxury rentals. The ground over which soldiers had stormed now housed a swimming pool. Tourists bathed where they had battled, strolled where they had struggled, and laughter and song filled the air instead of explosions and screams. My father slowly digested the scene, retracing the course of the engagement, seeing for the first time in daylight the location where his many vivid memories originated. What had transpired sixty years previously had taken but a few frenzied minutes.

Dad often sat reflecting with a distant look upon his face. I tried to give him the space I believed he required, taking long swims, exploring the area, walking the short coastal path to Mali Luccin where the island's main garrison had been billeted. On one occasion he tried to locate the footpath they had used. Following the track a short distance he declared, "I think this is it", then demonstrated the plight of his German captive trying to negotiate the footpath with his hands above his head. Just what emotions were coursing through his mind was hard to comprehend. He could go no further, so we returned to the bay and, leaving him to reflect, I set off in an attempt to retrace the route.

Following the path, it soon became apparent that it could not have been the one used as it petered out after only a short distance. Soon I was clambering over stone walls and piles of boulders, pushing through brambles and undergrowth, skirting dense thickets, several times reaching an impasse and having to retrace my steps in favour of an alternative. This obviously was not the correct track. I pictured my father sat outside a cafe, rolling up and sipping a cool beer. I cursed and soldiered on.

Emerging from a particularly thick clump of bush, I stepped onto tarmac. A road ran the entire length of the ridge; I could have taken a taxi. Did I hear my father chuckle? Later he would insist he had made it halfway up the ridge. Walking a short distance along the road I located a building visible from below and it turned out to be an ancient chapel with spectacular views over the Adriatic. Both sides of the island were visible: wooded slopes ran down to the sea; the Italian side scribed by beautiful bays dotted with yachts. In one of these, the SBS had landed. I resolved to complete the journey, picked one of the many tracks that led off the road, and headed in the direction of the isolated bays. Well-rounded boulders were piled up to form drystone walls that bounded the footpath on both sides and for much of the way they formed the walking surface. It was awkward trekking; so easy to turn an ankle. My thoughts strayed to those men who had negotiated this journey in the dark, exhausted, anxious, some wounded, others struggling under the burden of injured colleagues, shattered by their losses, and all the while under threat of discovery or ambush.

By late afternoon I was reunited with my father. Finding him had proved easy. He was seated at one of the bars, a mere fifty metres from where we had parted, smiling contentedly with a cool beer, I joined him, having earned my reward. He had strolled out to the opposite point of the inlet and spent some time gazing across towards the villa. We passed the time in quiet conversation, slowly sipping our beers, people-watching and putting the world to rights. Every so often a motor scooter would harshly disturb our tranquillity. Dad would smile and go into what was becoming a familiar discourse: "I'm going to stand for Mayor of this place; there will be no more of that." Pointing to the scooters, "I'll make a parking lot for them," indicating the centre of the harbour, "right there." By the end of our stay, he had compiled an extensive list of mayoral dictates, including the gem, "I'll ban all foreigners." His dry sense of humour was working overtime.

Every evening, we would end up in the complex's auditorium, a large open-air venue adjacent to the swimming pools. A good-quality local band would go through their repertoire and the many nationalities drawn from all over Europe would dance and party until midnight. Dad loved it; his eyes bright with delight, on occasions doing a short jig in his chair, it being against his religion to dance. Parents, children, couples, grandparents – all (except us) would get up. My father did comment that it was strange that men had fought and died where now they partied. He found it both disconcerting and reassuring.

They were a languid few days, idling the time away, all thought of the eventful trip out fast fading. Already I was imagining meeting friends back home and entertaining them with our story – how best could I distort the truth? But we were not yet safely back, and to ensure a trouble-free homeward leg several phone calls had been made and I was repeatedly assured that there would be no problems on the return journey.

Confident that there would be no repeat of our outward leg, we were seated before four o'clock on the Monday morning, the 12th of July 2004 in the hotel foyer, awaiting the taxi transfer to the airport. Dad had insisted on taking no chances; our transport was not due until 4:30 and it was best to be a little early. By five I was getting anxious, and the duty manager had called us a cab. The saga was about to restart. Shortly after 5:10 a local taxi raced up the driveway and we hastily explained our predicament to a dishevelled driver. His hair was unkempt, his shirt hanging out, and his eyes full of sleep having just been rudely awoken from his slumber. He quickly grasped the situation and hurriedly we set off at a frantic pace, trying to make up for lost time. As we sped off into the dawn, racing along the length of Luccin island, we finished off the situation report. Several problems immediately became apparent.

Villa Punta, 2004, now rebuilt and now used as holiday flats.

Ken at the low wall he and Tansy dived behind for shelter.

Ken reflecting at Mali Lussin fishing harbour.

Ken relaxing at Mali Lussin harbour side.

Even if we had set off on time there was doubt as to whether we would have made the first ferry. It left Cres at 6:30 and our scheduled flight departure meant we had to be on the first crossing. Our driver, after finishing his shift the previous night, had failed to fill up due to a long queue at the pumps, so we were short on fuel. We were also low on funds, having run down our supply of Croatian currency, leaving only enough to tip the expected courier and purchase some duty-free tobacco, having used a prodigious amount of the substance in the past week. Undaunted, we raced on, coming up with the following solutions. There was bound to be a cashpoint at the airport, and a petrol station was situated at the end of Lussin island. The rest we left to fate.

Fate was not being good to us. We skidded to a halt in a cloud of dust outside a deserted petrol station. With the red light glaring at us we pushed on to the next source of fuel in Cres town, a few miles short of the ferry. Fortunately, the swing bridge was down, and we eventually glided into the filling station, running on fumes, only to discover a chain across the entrance and no one at home. By now we were well acquainted with our driver, Oliver, who jumped out, fruitlessly tugging at the chain and pulling his hair in frustration. It was six o'clock. Miraculously it had the desired effect: a man strolled out of a side street and started to undo the chain. A hasty conference took place, Oliver finished off removing the chain and pulled his vehicle up to the pumps, the man hurried to his office and switched on the machines, and Oliver put in some fuel and sped off with a promise to return later and pay.

We had less than half an hour to make the ferry. The terminal was on the far side of a large hill from the town, and the road ran around this, descending to the quay. We tore around a sweeping bend to be confronted by the tail end of the extensive ferry queue. There were far more vehicles than spaces available, so, ignoring the stationary line, we drove on, Oliver muttering something about coaches having priority, and as an afterthought added taxis. Pulling up outside of the ticket office we were forced to double-park as no one was willing to let us jump the queue. Oliver gave a brief impression of a headless chicken before muttering something in Croatian (Dad gave a translation of, "Oh, stuff it"), and just drove on. The man in charge of boarding had no reservations and just waved us through. Phew! Oliver was in dire need of caffeine and left us in the car. We weren't moving.

The taxi pulled up at the airport in time and I ran inside with the passports and tickets. After Pula this was the second quietest airport, I had ever been in. What staff were there were busy doing nothing. The check-in desk was easy to find and the three people manning the station eagerly dealt with me as Oliver and Dad arrived with the baggage. Our driver then went off in search of a cashpoint, leaving us to finish with the booking-in procedure.

Oliver returned with yet more unexpected bad news: there

was no 'hole in the wall' cash machine! Emptying our pockets and combining the remaining Croatian money with Dad's stash of sterling currency, we managed to settle with Oliver, who had earned every penny. There was even enough to pay a generous tip, although he had to pay for a round of coffees as we were skint. The relief was tangible. Oliver left for a well-deserved breakfast following much thanking and shaking of hands, and we cautiously began to relax. Although there was another moment of anxiety when a man raced up to us from the checking-in desk, explaining that there had been a mistake: we had only been issued with one boarding pass. He quickly resolved the mistake. I joked with Dad, saying that it was OK as luckily the one issued was mine.

I began to look around and take stock of the ominously quiet airport. The conspicuous lack of any aircraft, other than a couple of small two-seaters, was alarming. A glance at the departure board offered some degree of reassurance. The board was a wooden affair, about two feet square and hung from nails driven into the wall. Plywood slats slid into them to display the airport's total arrivals and departures for the day: about ten movements.

Time passed slowly in the largely deserted building, not helped by nervous jokes about the possible misfortunes about to befall us. The Tannoy system crackled into life, and after a brief message in Croatian (in which I recognised the word 'Stansted'), an English translation was announced: "Would all passengers on the Stansted flight please make their way through customs and security to the departure lounge?" We were the only ones in the terminal to move. Apprehensively we made our way, outnumbered by the security staff. Still no sign of any plane to board. Was someone playing a sick joke on us? Dad was having a field day with his one-liners.

The departure lounge was not much larger than my front room and we seemed a trifle isolated in there. Reassuringly, some more passengers did eventually join us, but they amounted to no more than eight and there was still no sign of any plane. A doorway ran off the lounge to a duty-free shop staffed by two ladies, and they took plastic! I, ever the optimist, loaded up on duty-free, ensuring that Dad had a good supply of tobacco but praying it wouldn't be needed for any further luggage-watching duties. I sat back down just in time as a coach pulled up outside and discharged a full complement. They proceeded to join us in the departure lounge. It was standing room only. The departure board displayed a second obscure destination somewhere in Northern Europe. "Guess where we are going to end up tonight," joked my father.

Then events started to move. Two jets noisily landed, taxiing almost up to the window. "Now that's service," said Dad. His other comment, "Just watch them put us on the wrong plane", was less comforting. Our aircraft was loaded first, and we edged our way through the throng and out into the bright sunshine for the short stroll to the jet. We were greeted, led aboard and seated.

I have so many memories of that short, eventful holiday (although I say that last word with reservations): Dad sat calmly rolling his cigarettes; his sharp, incisive one-liners; the obvious enjoyment of the music evenings; sitting around the pleasant harbour; Dad's unflappability; the Croatian taxi drivers. Above all, the picture of my father lost deep in thought, remembering the past.

The journey was partly funded by a donation from the Royal British Legion's Heroes Return fund. Thank you.

2004 Lussin Trip

THE SPECIAL AIR SERVICE REGIMENTAL ASSOCIATION

Hereby award this Certificate of Service to:

Corporal Kenneth Smith

In recognition, and grateful appreciation for your gallant wartime service to the Regiment and your Country

The Viscount Slim OBE DL
President SAS Regimental Association

The Rt Hon The Earl Jellicoe, DSO, MC, PC,
Patron SAS Regimental Association

Kens Certificate.

THE SPECIAL AIR SERVICE REGIMENTAL ASSOCIATION

Hereby award this Certificate of Service to:

Marine Ralph Bridger

In recognition, and grateful appreciation for your gallant wartime service to the Regiment and your Country

The Viscount Slim OBE DL
President SAS Regimental Association

The Rt Hon The Earl Jellicoe, DSO, MC, PC,
Patron SAS Regimental Association

Ralphs certificate.

July 2004; eighty-two-year-old Ken Smith sat on the beach in front of Villa Punta.

Every effort has been made to obtain the necessary permissions with reference to copyright material, both illustrative and quoted. I apologies for any omissions in this respect and will be pleased to make the appropriate acknowledgements in any future edition.